A JOHN CATT PUBLICATION

I defy any teacher not to find this book both instantly engaging and immensely useful.

Andy Buck

**Research & Resources
for every classroom**

Kate Jones

T0198467

First Published 2018

by John Catt Educational Ltd,
15 Riduna Park, Melton, Woodbridge, Suffolk IP12 1QT
01394 389850
enquiries@johncatt.com
www.johncatt.com

Tel: +44 (0) 1394 389850
Fax: +44 (0) 1394 386893
Email: enquiries@johncatt.com
Website: www.johncatt.com

Opinions expressed in this publication are those
of the contributors and are not necessarily those
of the publishers or the editors. We cannot accept
responsibility for any errors or omissions.

ISBN: 978 1 911382 95 9

Set and designed by John Catt Educational Limited

PRAISE FOR
LOVE TO TEACH

'Packed full of tried-and-tested ideas and activities, this practical compendium of hundreds of teaching techniques is seriously rooted in an impressive synthesis of educational theory and research. I defy any teacher not to find this book both instantly engaging and immensely useful.'

Andy Buck
CEO Leadership Matters

'This book comes at a time when education has more pressures than ever and is a timely reminder about why many of us joined the profession in the first place. Love to Teach is jam-packed full of reference, research and resources that will impact upon teachers new to the profession or those who have more years under their belt. What is superb to see is the inclusion not only in examples throughout the book but also with a section that looks specifically at technology in education. Too many educators see **edtech** as something separate to their practice. It isn't and Jones has rightly included selected teaching and learning ideas both with and without technology, just as it should be in any classroom.'

Mark Anderson @ICTEvangelist
Award-winning educator, blogger, keynote speaker, consultant and author of Perfect ICT Every Lesson

'In Love to Teach, Kate Jones draws on research from cognitive science and makes it actionable. Her strategies are evidence-based, insightful, and practical. Love to Teach is a valuable resource for all educators who are passionate about best practices in teaching based on the science of learning.'

Dr Pooja Agarwal @Poojaagarwal
Cognitive scientist and author of Powerful Teaching: Unleash the Science of Learning with Patrice M Bain, creator of retrievalpractice.org

'Kate Jones has created something unique in Love to Teach; she has drawn together a comprehensive overview of current educational research and presented it in accessible yet unpatronising way. What I admire about Kate's work is that she not only guides the reader through the current educational landscape – pointing out interesting aspects and features – she also goes the extra mile in terms of helping the reader to apply this new knowledge through suggested resources and techniques. Having been lucky enough to watch Kate teach I know that she 'walks the walk' which makes this book all the more credible.'

Michael Strachan, Deputy Headteacher at Repton School Dubai

'Written with the same passion, reflection and drive that runs through everything Kate does, Love To Teach is a real gem. Kate explores a huge range of practical pick-up-and-use strategies rooted deeply in educational research. The book is an equal balance between thought-provoking and extremely useful. Love to Teach is a great resource for all teachers who are committed to improving their practice and increasing their impact upon the futures of the young people they teach. A must read.'

Sarah Findlater, @msfindlater
Secondary Principal at Gems First Point School, Dubai. Author and series editor of the Bloomsbury CPD Library.

Dedicated to Mum and Dad
(Heather and Andre)

CONTENTS

ABOUT THE AUTHOR

Kate grew up and spent most of her life in North Wales. In 2009, she graduated from the University of Wales, Aberystwyth with a BA Honours in History and completed her PGCE in Secondary Education with History there the following year. In 2010, Kate took on her first teaching role at Elfed High School, Buckley where she remained for six years. During this time Kate progressed to Head of Department, school-wide More Able and Talented Coordinator, Connecting Classrooms Lead, working alongside the British Council, and she had responsibility for school-wide spiritual development and daily acts of collective worship. In 2015, Kate achieved the prestigious SSAT Lead Practitioner accreditation.

In 2016, Kate made the decision to relocate to Abu Dhabi. She is currently History Coordinator at the 'Outstanding' Brighton College Al Ain, which delivers a British Curriculum for children aged 3-18. Another role Kate takes great pride in is Governor on the Advisory Board of Manor Hall International School. This position gives her the opportunities to work with leaders, teachers, parents and all stakeholders involved in the development of this American Curriculum School.

Kate has presented at various educational events across the UK and Middle East. In addition to being an award-winning educational speaker, her website **lovetoteach87.com** has twice been nominated for the UK Blog Award in the Individual Education category and she is a finalist for the Middle East Education Influencer Award.

In her spare time Kate loves to read, travel, explore and spend time with her close friends and family.

ACKNOWLEDGEMENTS

I will begin thanking the teachers that have educated and influenced me. Maya Angelou famously said 'people will forget what you said, people will forget what you did, but people will never forget how you made them feel'.

At Ysgol Estyn Primary School, I can remember very clearly feeling special and cared for by all my teachers there. At Castell Alun High School, my history teachers had a profound and positive impact on my life – Mr. David Healey and Mr. Kevin Davies, or KD as he was known. KD was funny, popular and his lessons were always interesting and memorable. It wasn't until he taught me at GCSE and A-Level that I really appreciated how good a teacher he was. His subject knowledge and understanding of the examination technique have stayed with me as an adult as I have tried to support my students in the same way. Mr. Healey is well-known in my local community. I know many people would agree with me when I describe him as a local hero. He is passionate about history, especially the history of the local area. He was extremely kind, helpful and such a wise teacher. I am completely in awe of his vast and deep subject knowledge. I feel very lucky to have had such admirable teachers and am thankful for everything they taught me.

I must thank all the colleagues I have had the privilege to work with at Elfed High School, Buckley and Brighton College Al Ain, there are far too many to name. Everyone should have a close friend in the workplace. I have been fortunate to have a best friend in both the schools I have worked at. Thank you Jade Lewis-Jones and Louise Rycroft for all the professional and personal support you have given me, in addition to all the laughs. Other teachers that have particularly inspired and supported me are Rachael Bethell, Thomas Rogers, Evo Hannan and Joe Hall.

During this process many colleagues have proofread chapters and provided feedback that has been invaluable. I feel very grateful to have worked with two incredibly supportive, friendly and reassuring headteachers, Rosemary Jones OBE and Dr Kenneth Greig. Their doors have always been open and welcoming. I would not have been able to write this book without their support and encouragement throughout my career.

I have connected with teachers from around the world through social media and at educational events. I want to thank the teachers that inspire and motivate me on a daily basis and teach me so much about this profession.

A special thank you has to be dedicated to Mark Anderson, he is referenced in this book throughout which is not surprising because I have learnt so much from him about all aspects of teaching and learning. Mark gave me the courage and confidence to launch a website to share ideas and reflect on my practice, which eventually led to writing this book.

I also want to thank all of the people that have agreed to feature in this book, it is an honour to include your contributions.

A huge thank you to Alex Sharratt and Meena Ameen from John Catt Educational Ltd. Writing a book in addition to being a full-time teacher and middle leader is not easy! Alex has been patient, helpful and very understanding. I am very proud to have my book published with John Catt. In my opinion, the book *What Does This Look Like In The Classroom? Bridging the Gap Between Research and Practice* was the best educational book published in 2017. It has been well received and had a huge impact on my practice. This book was authored by Carl Hendrick and Robin Macpherson and I am absolutely delighted that Robin has written the foreword for my book. It is a real honour and privilege, thanks to Robin.

Finally, I want to thank my friends and family. I am blessed to have loving and caring friends, especially Hannah Bellis and Emma Chidlow. My sisters Emily and Jessica (who once pretended to be teachers when I hosted a TeachMeet event, because I was worried no one would attend) are my biggest champions and inspire me more than they will ever know.

Thanks also go to some more special people in my life Joanne, Ben, Ella and my Gran Hazel. The biggest thank you must go to my incredible, lovely and simply wonderful parents Heather and Andre. They have always supported me, showing me unconditional love. Thank you.

FOREWORD
ROBIN MACPHERSON

This is a courageous book.

I say this firstly because Kate Jones has opened both her professional practice, and herself as a person, so that other teachers can learn from her experience. The thing that strikes me most after reading the book is that she has compiled this after just eight years in the profession. To be so well read, so insightful, and so wise at this stage is uncommon. It goes to show that experience comes not from years of service, but from what you achieve as a teacher. Kate is a teacher, an historian, a blogger, a trainer, a keynote speaker, a school governor, and now a fully-fledged author. I can't even begin to imagine what she's going to do with the rest of her career.

You can only achieve this in under a decade if you truly love what you do, and this is why her book is so well titled. I defy you not to be enthused by what she writes, and how she writes it. If you know Kate you will probably read this with her voice in your head; she has an inimitable style that you can just imagine her pupils revelling in. Yet even if you haven't had the privilege of meeting her, you can easily tell that she lives and breathes education. Without wishing to spoil some of the plot, I'm willing to bet that this book will make you want to head to your nearest Gurdwara, such is the power of her infectious enthusiasm.

The second reason why this book can be described as courageous is that Kate covers the full spectrum of opinion. She can talk with ease about leading figures in education and the panoply of research that is out there. Yet rather than slide into one side of a debate that has polarised around traditional or progressive ideologies, she covers the full range with a refreshing objectivity. This ecumenical approach can be demonstrated in the insightful reflection that 'research is one piece of a complex puzzle when it comes to working with children in schools'.

She also has the historian's eye, in that she covers research that spans the period from 1885 to 2018 and shows not just what has been argued, but how thinking has evolved. Many books show where we are now, but Kate also shows how we got here.

This said, she doesn't pull her punches. Take this comment, on the traditional method of CPD delivery: 'One off expensive courses in a hotel conference room with a free lunch won't change your life but taking control of your professional development can.' This is one of the best books available on how to make meaningful progress in professional learning, and at a very low cost. Kate has become a powerful voice in international education through her use of media and blogs. Building a professional network is difficult to do and is often overlooked in books on leadership, but she gives a blueprint that you are advised to follow if you want to operate effectively in middle or senior leadership now, or in the future. Keeping your finger on the educational pulse is essential and the way it is done now is totally different to a decade ago. This book is written by one of the pioneers of that change.

Finally, the concluding chapter on relationships is a welcome addition to the field of educational books. The time at the start of the day in most schools is really about ticking off names to see who's in the building and who isn't. Making this time meaningful seems nigh on impossible; too many bodies in the room, too little time. Kate shows how this can be turned on its head. Her practical advice is excellent. It serves as a powerful reminder that for young people, having a positive and supportive interaction with an adult who values you is something that can and should happen every single day. The possibilities afforded by their education can be expanded enormously by this human touch.

So enjoy. Each chapter makes you want to get into a classroom and just teach. This book is a phenomenal synthesis of all the most important reading currently available on education, written by someone who is genuinely a teacher's teacher. It doesn't matter if you are new to the profession or a long-serving headteacher; you are bound to find much that is fresh and inspiring.

Robin Macpherson, Assistant Rector at Dollar Academy Scotland. Author of *What Does This Look Like In The Classroom? Bridging the Gap Between Research and Practice* **(2017) @robin_macp.**

INTRODUCTION

'To be an effective teacher involves a high level of commitment – commitment to children and young people, to their wellbeing and future lives, commitment to knowledge and the importance of being able to think independently and effectively.'
Graham Nuthall

I once read that the key difference between a primary and secondary teacher is that a primary teacher has chosen to teach children and a secondary teacher has chosen to teach their subject to children. That was my ambition, to teach history to children. It felt a natural decision for me to combine my enthusiasm for history and working in a school environment. I was once told that my eagerness as a trainee would disappear once I 'really start teaching'. I was then warned to 'give it another five years' and I would be looking for an escape route. Well, eight years later and here I am, celebrating the profession and I still love to teach. Teaching can be difficult, challenging and demanding, but it is also incredibly rewarding, enjoyable and fulfilling – it's the best job in the world.

Throughout my career, despite history being my specialism, I have taught a wide variety of subjects: RE, geography, social studies, Welsh second language, drama and politics. I have experience teaching Key Stages 2, 3, 4 and 5 – although secondary is my specialism. This variety and experience will be evident throughout my book. The majority of the resources I have created are easily adaptable across year groups and different subjects. I created many cross-curricular resources and activities to support my own workload in addition to my students learning. This book wasn't written specifically for history teachers (although I do hope readers of this book are history teachers) but instead the target audience is teachers of both primary and secondary schools.

Research

Initially, this book was intended to be sharing teaching ideas and resources with an explanation how I use them in my classroom. In recent years, however, I have become fascinated and engaged with educational research and how that can be applied in the classroom. Engaging with educational research is not always easy but it is becoming much more accessible. Teachers on Twitter and other forms of social media are regularly sharing research journals, publications and blogs about how they implement research in their practice. There are events aimed at teachers that focus on sharing educational research, most notably ResearchEd. The Chartered College of Teaching provide their members with access to a wealth of resources and research too. I have also read a wide range of literature about different aspects of research and the impact this can have in the classroom.

After each chapter I have recommended a few books in no particular order that I would highly recommend to other educators. Research can often confirm what years of teaching experience have taught us. Research can also challenge and question our views and beliefs too. I have been completely overwhelmed by the sheer volume of research, as one research journal often leads to much more reading. The research I have referenced dates back from 1885 but there are also recent research articles, blogs, books and I explore a new model linked to learning that was revealed in September 2018! I hope all of the authors and researchers I have referenced and credited in this book feel I have done so in the correct context. I should add I am not an educational researcher or cognitive scientist. I am a teacher who blends research with experience and knowledge. I am continually learning.

Leading educational researcher and author – who I will regularly reference in this book – Graham Nuthall amongst others in this field, have warned teachers that not all research can be trusted.[1] Not all research is equal or carried out in contextual conditions and settings. There has also been information and theories sold to teachers as educational research, which are now better known as debunked learning myths. All of this I will explore. I believe being research-informed supports why teachers do what we do in the classroom. We make decisions and judgments based on our experiences, in addition to being evidence-informed. Research is one piece of a complex puzzle when it comes to working with children in schools.

Resources

I hope you enjoy reading this book and find yourself filled with practical ideas, examples and resources to implement in your own classroom. I have provided links to websites where the majority of the resources

---

1. Nuthall, G. (2007) *The Hidden Lives of Learners.* Wellington, New Zealand: NZCER Press.

shared can be downloaded for free, to use in your classroom. At the back of this book there are QR codes to direct you to materials you can download. Senior leader and blogger, Amjad Ali often writes on his teaching website www.trythisteaching.com when looking at resources, teachers should try, refine or ditch! This book includes a range of strategies to try with your students.

Nuthall stresses the point that teaching is about adaptation. He writes that teaching is 'about adjusting to the here-and-now circumstances of particular students. It is about making moment-by-moment decisions as a lesson or activity progresses. Things that interest some students do not interest others. Things that work one day may not work the next day. What can be done quickly with one group has to be taken very slowly with another group.' In addition to these and other variations, he posed the question to teachers: 'what adaptations do you make?'

It is very likely you will need to refine, adapt or tweak ideas. Indeed, there may be some that you want to ditch that aren't right for you or your classroom. Author, teacher and researcher Pedro De Bruyckere pointed out that in education 'lots of things work, but not always, not for everyone, not for every purpose and not in every context'.[2] Context is key. I have worked in two very different schools, from North Wales to Abu Dhabi, so I regularly adapt my own resources for my very different classes and students.

Renowned teacher, researcher and writer Dylan Wiliam has also said that 'what works?' is rarely the right question to ask, because everything works somewhere and nothing works everywhere. Wiliam said that teachers should be asking, 'under what conditions does this work?' He also emphasises the importance of context. I think these points are very important to keep in mind when reading this and other educational books.

The structure of this book is a buffet style so that you, the reader, can dip in and out of chapters – although I would recommend reading the chapters in order to begin with. Hopefully, you will return to specific chapters again. I enjoy reading books where I revisit a chapter, and the layout of the book allows me to do so. Chapter 8 is unique as it focuses on the pastoral role teachers have; I believe our pastoral duty of care is of great importance. Chapter 8 will be of use to primary teachers, secondary form tutors and leaders with pastoral responsibility.

---

2. De Bruyckere, P. (2018) *The Ingredients for Great Teaching*. London, England: SAGE Publications.

Please feel free to contact me to provide feedback or ask any questions. Let me know if, or how, any of my ideas have worked in your classroom. I would love to hear from you. You can contact me via my website **lovetoteach87.com**, send me a Tweet **@87History**, or use the hashtag **#LoveToTeach**.

CHAPTER 1:
THE BEST WAY TO START
A LESSON

'Before you start something new, review the old.'
Paul A. Kirschner

There you have it – simple! Before starting a new unit or introducing new content, don't forget to review, revisit, retrieve older content, or make links with prior learning. Despite the simplicity of the quote above, I do believe that this is revolutionary to teaching and learning. I argue this because previously it seemed that the main aim of the starter activity was to engage learners as soon as they walked through the door with something exciting to grab their attention. I have observed lessons where the starter activity was enthralling but I struggled to see the connection between the task and the content of the lesson. I have been guilty myself of delivering a snazzy starter, with a weak link to the content that, on reflection, could have been much more effective. I have also been fortunate enough to observe many lessons where the starter activity was used to great effect and was part of a clearly embedded classroom routine.

Over time I discovered the problems that occurred when the aim of the starter activity was to hook or entice students into learning. The focus became the entertainment factor instead of considering what was really the most effective way to begin a lesson. Tasks could be engagement rich but learning focus poor – engaging but empty. Cognitive psychologist, university professor and author Daniel T. Willingham writes in his revolutionary book, *Why Don't Students Like School? A Cognitive Scientist Answers Questions About How The Mind Works And What It Means for the Classroom* that 'the transition from one subject to another is enough to buy at least a few minutes of attention from students. It is usually the middle of the lesson that needs a little drama to draw students back from whatever reverie they might be in'.[3] We don't need something too bold and attention grabbing to begin the lesson. There is a wealth of research and evidence that I will explore in this chapter that now inform and suggest that the best way to start a lesson is with a regular review.

There has been a move away in recent years from the novelty tasks that were once encouraged but can actually distract from learning. Gimmickry can have a negative impact on learning, lead to behaviour problems and detract from the actual content we teach. There are a selection of activities in this book that could be interpreted as gimmicks but I aim to explain and justify their purpose in the classroom. Teachers should not be afraid or reluctant to be creative in their classrooms. What might appear as a gimmick to one teacher, could serve a useful purpose for another.

I had the privilege of listening to Robert Coe, Professor of Education at Durham University, where he discussed engagement in the classroom. During his presentation he argued that engagement is a poor proxy for learning. In this he means that just because students are engaged, busy or lots of work is being done, it does not mean they are actually learning.[4] This appears obvious but I think that, as a profession, a lot of people – myself included – lost sight of this at times. When observing lessons, we need to be mindful of the research relating to engagement.

I have already mentioned Graham Nuthall, but I wanted to briefly discuss the work and research he and his colleagues undertook. You may or may not be familiar with work of Nuthall; if you are, please indulge me for a moment.

Nuthall had a wide and extensive career in educational research of over 40 years. His groundbreaking book *The Hidden Lives of Learners* shares some of this research and, although he died before its publication, his wife and colleagues were able to complete it as he had requested. Nuthall and his team spent a significant amount of time in classrooms, observing lessons and collecting data. Observations were recorded using various devices and equipment. His book explores the public discussions that take place within the classroom, as well as the private conversations between peers (all teachers and students involved were anonymous in the book). Nuthall clearly expressed that his book was not written to tell teachers how to teach and most research I have encountered does not tell

---

3. Willingham, D, T. (2010) *Why don't students like school? A Cognitive Scientist Answers Questions About How The Mind Works And What It Means For The Classroom.* San Francisco, CA: Jossey-Bass.

4. You can view presentations delivered by Professor Robert Coe at http://community.dur.ac.uk/r.j.coe/ Presentations.htm

teachers how to teach, but instead suggests strategies and explain why they are considered effective. Instead, Nuthall made many observations for teachers to consider and reflect upon. His research was presented to readers in a way that is clear and supported by examples from the classroom. One key observation Nuthall addressed was that being attentive and engaged is often equated with learning, but his research showed that in a lesson it can appear that students are highly motivated and actively engaged in interesting classroom activities without actually learning anything new.[5] When we think about engagement in the classroom, we need to do so with caution and consideration.

It is helpful though if our learners are engaged and interested. We know that if you don't pay attention to something you can't learn it.[6] Author, blogger and trainer Dr Debra Kidd contributes to the engagement debate writing that 'boredom is a negative state in which learning does not take place' and she further adds: 'Engagement, relevance, big questions ... these are not embellishments to learning. They are routes to learning and it is time we reclaimed that language'.[7] Kidd is not an advocate for activities that just keep children busy, instead she believes children can learn and enjoy themselves in the process. Connected to that point, people pay even more attention if they are interested.[8] One of the key reasons I chose to teach at my current school is because the school actively promotes a love of learning and a desire for students to enjoy their lessons. This includes the lesson content, activities, tasks and all aspects of wider school life. Whilst engagement is important, it should not lead our lesson planning.

I am not suggesting that recapping prior knowledge at the start of the lesson has to be dull or boring. Education consultant and author Ross Morrison McGill advises teachers to choose five starter ideas to use each half term and stick with them, delivering the starters each week and rotating them.[9] This is sound advice because it removes the pressure of constantly striving to find or create a new starter task every lesson. To help me with my teaching, I have developed a range of strategies that I regularly use in my classroom to start the lesson. The tasks continually

5. Nuthall, G. (2007) *The Hidden Lives of Learners*. Wellington, New Zealand: NZCER Press.
6. Bennett, T. (6 July 2018) 'Tom Bennett speaks to... Professor Daniel Willingham'. (ResearchEd) Available at: www.researched.org.uk/tom-bennett-speaks-to-professor-daniel-willingham-2
7. Kidd, D. (29 September 2014) 'Relevant and Engagement are not Embellishments'. (Love Learning) Available at: www.debrakidd.wordpress.com/2014/09/29/relevance-and-engagement-are-not-embellishments
8. Smith, M & Firth, J. (2018) *Psychology in the Classroom: A Teacher's Guide To What Works*. Abingdon, Oxfordshire: Routledge.
9. McGill, R, M. (2013) *100 ideas for Secondary Teachers: Outstanding Lessons*. London, England: Bloomsbury Education.

revisit and test students prior learning and knowledge. This supports the embedding of knowledge within long-term memory – which is explained and explored in more depth in the next chapter – and the ability to access and retrieve information at a later date.

Rosenshine's Principles of Instruction (2012)

I firmly believe, as do many other educators, that Barak Rosenshine's 'Principles of Instruction: Research Based Strategies That All Teachers Should Know' is an exceptional article that all teachers should read and be familiar with. It is a clear, concise and comprehensive paper that is perfect for teachers looking to engage with research linked to education and how this can be applied in the classroom. The article I refer to is an adapted version of the original more in-depth report. Rosenshine's Principles of Instruction printed in the *American Educator* can be easily accessed for free online.[10] It contains ten research-based principles of instruction that are applicable, relevant and can be used effectively in every classroom. It also includes some subject-specific examples of the different principles that can be used in a classroom setting.

It is my belief that every staffroom or CPD library should contain copies of this seminal paper. It is not wrapped in academic jargon or too time consuming to read either. It is a great place to start when engaging with educational research. Even if you are already using research-informed strategies in your practice, this is a document that can be referred to again and again.

The principles stem from three different sources that are combined. Firstly, research in cognitive science – how the brain encodes and stores information. Secondly, research on cognitive support with strategies to help students learn complex material. Thirdly, and finally, it uses evidence based on the work of 'master teachers', who Rosenshine describes as 'those teachers whose classrooms made the highest gains on achievement tests'. Fusing together these different strands of research and experience, Rosenshine has devised a set of principles that are universal in education.

Below is a brief summary of Rosenshine's ten key principles:

1. Start the lesson with a short review of previous learning; this can be achieved through various tasks. I will share examples in this chapter.

---

10. Rosenshine, B. (2012) 'Principles of Instruction: Research-Based Strategies That All Teachers Should Know'. (American Educator) Available at: www.aft.org/sites/default/files/periodicals/Rosenshine.pdf

2. Present new material and information to students in small and manageable steps. Ensure student practice after each step, before moving onto new material.

3. Ask a large number of questions, checking the response from all the learners in the classroom (a common mistake is to accept answers from some members of the class, and then assume everyone else has that same level of understanding).

4. Provide students with models and worked examples to support problem solving. A worked example is where a problem has been shown to the class, with every part of the process explicitly explained through a teacher demonstration, and the problem has been correctly solved. The students will then apply this process or concept to another problem or question. This strategy is best used with novice learners, as it is not regarded as an effective strategy to use with expert learners.[11] The worked example strategy works very well in maths and science.

5. Continue to guide student practice. Rosenshine stated that research findings tell us that 'it is not enough simply to present students with new material, because the material will be forgotten unless there is sufficient rehearsal'. This can be achieved through questioning, additional explanations, consolidation tasks and students summarising the main points of the lesson content. Nuthall suggested that students need to encounter information at least three times before they understand a concept and that students need opportunities to approach new material in different ways.[12]

6. Continually check student understanding, addressing any misconceptions and support the process needed to move new information to long-term memory.

7. Ensure students obtain a high success rate in the lesson. A success rate of 80% shows that students are learning the material, and it also shows that the students are challenged.[13] The Goldilocks principle is getting the level of challenge just right!

8. Provide scaffolding for students with difficult tasks, ensuring depth and challenge for all. Rosenshine states that 'a scaffold is a temporary

---

11. Hirsch, E, D. (2016) *Why Knowledge Matters: Rescuing Our Children from Failed Educational Theories.* Cambridge, Massachusetts: Harvard Education Press.
12. Nuthall, G. (2007) *The Hidden Lives of Learners.* Wellington, New Zealand: NZCER Press.
13. Rosenshine, B. (2012) 'Principles of Instruction: Research-Based Strategies That All Teachers Should Know'. (American Educator) Available at: www.aft.org/sites/default/files/periodicals/Rosenshine.pdf

support that is used to assist a learner' and will eventually be removed as the student progresses.

9. Require, monitor and promote independent practice. Rosenshine explains that 'in a typical teacher-led classroom, guided practice is followed by independent practice – by students working alone and practicing the new material. This independent practice is necessary because a good deal of practice (over learning) is needed in order to become fluent and automatic in a skill'.

10. Engage students in regular review, this can be weekly and/or monthly to revisit prior learning and support long-term memory. Once again this links with the resources in this chapter.

This is a brief overview and I do encourage anyone who has not read this document to do so in its entirety. Education consultant, former headteacher and successful author Tom Sherrington widely shares and praises the work of Rosenshine, through his blogs and at conferences. Sherrington does warn that it should not be turned into a checklist; it should be used as a guide for professional learning.[14] I strongly agree with this advice because when teachers feel the pressure to do something to tick a box, the purpose of that task shifts.

The first and main principle I will be exploring in-depth in this book (although I believe all of the ten principles are of equal weight and importance) focuses on how to start a lesson. Rosenshine clearly advises teachers to begin a lesson with a short review of previous learning because this will strengthen previous learning and can lead to recalling information with fluency. Rosenshine shares examples of teachers regularly starting their lessons with review and seeing a positive impact on retention and recall with their students at a later date. It is also suggested that five to eight minutes of every lesson should be spent on daily review, which I think is a useful and appropriate guidance. The focus on the review can be revisiting subject content, practising skills, concepts, checking understanding of vocabulary, or anything linked to prior learning.

It is not just Rosenshine who suggests starting lessons with daily review. I have encountered a wide range of research and reading materials that suggest the same principle. Classroom practitioners, experts in psychology and authors Jonathan Firth and Marc Smith

---

14. Sherrington, T. (10 June 2018) 'Exploring Barak Rosenshine's seminal Principles of Instruction: Why it is THE must-read for all teachers'. (Teacherhead.com) Available at: www.teacherhead.com/2018/06/10/exploring-barak-rosenshines-seminal-principles-of-instruction-why-it-is-the-must-read-for-all-teachers/

warn against starting lessons with a set of facts, but instead also suggest beginning with questions or problem solving.[15] Therefore, the activities below are all linked to this principle of daily review and should be applied in the same way. The aim of the tasks in this chapter is to revisit previous material and ensure regular review becomes an established classroom routine to strengthen learning.

Retrieval practice

I have become fascinated with memory and how our memories work – I find it really intriguing but also, at times, baffling. I was having a coffee with my dad following a trip to Copenhagen, and I described to him how I travelled to Sweden and spent a day in Malmö. In response, my dad asked if I went to Helsinki before realising that Helsinki is actually in Finland, not Sweden. He had meant to say the capital city of Sweden instead but couldn't remember the name. Even though he did actually know what the capital was, he just couldn't recall that piece of information, much to his frustration. I am sure most people have experienced something similar before, where they know that they know a piece of information, but they just can't recall it at that precise moment. This is where the well-known phrase 'it is on the tip of your tongue' derives from. I also knew the capital of Sweden but I could not remember it either. My general knowledge of capital cities around the world is generally good but I was blank, as was my dad. This was very annoying, but like the typical millennial that I am, I said 'I'll Google it' but my phone battery was flat.[16]

For about five minutes we both sat in silence, secretly trying to recall the capital of Sweden. Then, following a change in topic and midway through a new conversation, he roared 'Stockholm'. Of course it is! He was able to remember, and as soon as he said it I thought to myself, 'I knew that so how did I forget?' Later, when telling my mum about the Stockholm incident, she replied: 'Well, you either know something or you don't.' Actually, she was wrong – sorry mum. There are indeed times when we either know the answer or we don't, as Chris Tarrant used to say, 'the questions are only easy if you know the answer.' However, in this scenario, it wasn't that my dad and I didn't know the answer, if he didn't know it was Stockholm how could he recall that correct answer five minutes later? That knowledge was there in his long-term memory – it just took him a while to retrieve it.

---

15. Smith, M & Firth, J. (2018) *Psychology in the Classroom: A Teacher's Guide To What Works.* Abingdon, Oxfordshire: Routledge.
16. To find out more about the term millennial then you should watch this popular video with Simon Sinek describing millennials in the workplace: www.youtube.com/watch?v=hER0Qp6QJNU

Retrieval practice is essentially the process of bringing information to mind from memory, without that information in front of you. Recalling previously studied material is not new in education, this has been a common strategy in the classroom. Retrieving information from memory is the main method of assessment, for both internal and external examinations. Retrieval practice refers to recalling information from memory as a learning technique to strengthen the memory by doing so, not as a form of assessment that is the key difference. The act of retrieving information actually supports long-term memory; therefore, it can be used as a powerful learning strategy.

Retrieval practice is a term that I have only become familiar with in recent years, but like Rosenshine's Principles of Instruction, it has had a big impact on my teaching and my students learning. The team of researchers and authors of the popular book *Make It Stick: The Science of Successful Learning* explain that practising retrieval makes learning stick for students far better than re-exposure to the original material.[17]

The main aim of retrieval practice is to retrieve information from memory – by doing so, it makes the memories stronger each time, cementing long-term learning, and making it easier to retrieve at a later date. Recalling information from memory can be challenging for students but it also identifies gaps in their knowledge, showing what they can and cannot recall. Retrieval storage refers to how well information is embedded in long-term memory and retrieval strength refers to how easily a piece of information can be brought to mind when required.[18] There are many educators who have written about and discussed the benefits of retrieval practice. I can highly recommend the work and research of cognitive scientist and author Dr Pooja K. Agarwal. You can read a wide range of research papers and articles in addition to a range of resources linked to retrieval practice on her website www.retrievalpractice.org

Although, I will be recommending starting lessons with regular retrieval, research does not explicitly state this is the most appropriate time in the lesson to carry out retrieval practice. It is an effective strategy that can be used at any point during a lesson. It has become widely recognised as one of the most effective educational interventions to support learning.[19] Retrieval practice will also be more effective if

17. Brown, P, C, Roediger, H, L & McDaniel, M, A. (2014) *Make It Stick: The Science of Successful Learning.* Cambridge, Massachusetts: Harvard Education Press.
18. Didau, D & Rose, N. (2016) *What Every Teacher Needs To Know About Psychology.* Melton, Suffolk: John Catt Educational Ltd.
19. Smith, M & Firth, J. (2018) *Psychology in the Classroom: A Teacher's Guide To What Works.* Abingdon, Oxfordshire: Routledge.

we allow for some forgetting to take place before we try to retrieve the information, this links in with Ebbinghaus' Forgetting Curve.

Ebbinghaus' Forgetting Curve

When I first encountered the Forgetting Curve I assumed it was an example of modern research, but in fact German researcher and psychologist Hermann Ebbinghaus published his findings in the 1880s. The results of his experiment have become known as the Ebbinghaus Forgetting Curve. Ebbinghaus conducted the experiment on himself, to test his own memory and the length of time it would take for new information to be forgotten. Ebbinghaus would memorise lists of what he called 'nonsense syllables' which had no semantic associations (deep meaning). He was able to write them down in the correct order with accuracy and then test himself periodically to see how many syllables he could remember. After various time delays he would attempt to relearn the list of nonsense syllables and record the numbers of rehearsals he would require to gain accuracy.

This sounds very basic, but he was one of the first researchers to carry out experiments and studies into how the memory works. Ebbinghaus discovered that his ability to recall the information he had memorised quickly declined.

The Forgetting Curve illustrates how forgetting happens after the initial period of learning has taken place, occurring rapidly in the first instance then slowing down. It shows that once information has been encoded, then the first 20 minutes after this are prone to forgetting. Within roughly an hour the majority of that new information will be forgotten. Author of *Brain Rules: 12 Principles for Surviving and Thriving at Work, Home and School*, John Medina has commented that 'people usually forget 90% of what they learn in a class within 30 days ... and that the majority of this forgetting occurs within the first few hours after class'.[20] The curve shows that after the first day, forgetting occurs at a slower pace. Medina furthers adds that 'Ebbinghaus showed that repeated exposure to information in spaced intervals provides the most powerful way to fix memory into the brain'.[21]

Although Ebbinghaus carrying out an experiment where he is his only test subject does not appear to be highly scientific, this experiment was then replicated many times by different researchers and cognitive

---

20. Medina, J. (2009) *Brain Rules: 12 Principles for Surviving and Thriving at Work, Home, and School*. Seattle, Washington: Pear Press, p. 130.
21. Ibid. p. 149.

psychologists. The repeated studies demonstrated similar results. One experiment carried out had a subject spend 70 hours learning lists and relearning them after 20 minutes, after an hour, nine hours, a day or 31 days. The results were similar to the original conclusion Ebbinghaus came to.[22]

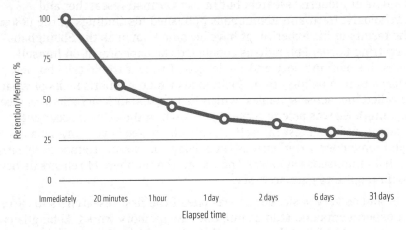

Ebbinghaus' Forgetting Curve (1885) demonstrates that new learning is subject to significant forgetting which is rapid in the initial hours or days since encountering information.

Ebbinghaus' Forgetting Curve (1885)

Ebbinghaus suggested that all individuals forget new information in a similar manner and at a similar rate, regardless of the content and complexity. De Bruyckere writes about this in his terrific book *The Ingredients for Great Teaching*, informing the reader that content that has been learnt, forgotten and then learnt again will become more quickly and firmly re-established in the memory.[23] This illustrates that forgetting is crucial and beneficial for learning when combined with regular review and retrieval. Brown et al point out that 'a little forgetting between practice sessions can be a good thing if it leads to more effort in practice, but you do not want so much forgetting that retrieval essentially involves relearning the material'.[24]

When we check understanding at the end of a lesson, the information will likely still be in a students' short-term memory. If we wait too long to check if knowledge has been retained then that information can be

22. Murre, J, M, J & Dros, J. (2015) 'Replication and Analysis of Ebbinghaus' Forgetting Curve', PLoS One, 10(7).
23. De Bruyckere, P. (2018) The Ingredients for Great Teaching. London, England: SAGE Publications.
24. Brown, P, C, Roediger, H, L & McDaniel, M, A. (2014) *Make It Stick: The Science of Successful Learning.* Cambridge, Massachusetts: Harvard Education Press.

forgotten and need to be relearned. If we wait for some forgetting to occur and then use retrieval practice, the strategy will strengthen the information to counteract the Forgetting Curve. The Forgetting Curve can have very powerful implications for learning and teachers should be aware of this information. Careful planning and factoring in retrieval into lessons can support the forgetting process.

Find out what students know and don't know

Nuthall revealed that through his extensive research 'students can be busiest and most involved with material they already know. In most of the classrooms we have studied, each student already knows about 40–50% of what the teacher is teaching'.[25] The reality is that some students will know things that their peers don't. Therefore, teachers should aim to find out what students know or don't know before progressing further. A great way to introduce a new topic is to find out two key components of information from your students:

1. What do they already know about this topic? Prior knowledge and understanding may also lead to misconceptions that need to be addressed before moving forward. Misconceptions established at an early stage can create serious barriers to new learning and need to be dealt with. It is very difficult to unlearn something that has been incorrectly learnt, but obviously not impossible.

2. How does this new information link to what students already know? Are there links and connections that can be made? I will often use the five Ws where relevant as a good starting point for questioning and discussion: what, where, when, why, and who?

Sharing an image with the class or a piece of text can be a useful starting point. This can prompt discussion with students asking and answering questions. An example of this was when I showed an image of The Sheikh Zayed Grand Mosque in Abu Dhabi to my Year 6 students. From just this image they had to annotate what they could learn about the Mosque.

It was really surprising to find out what they could infer and learn from one image, but again be mindful of any misconceptions. Students then had to share their ideas with their partner or group with the aim to further develop their ideas. Finally, all students had to feedback to the class.

If you are regularly using images from the internet – to create resources or embed in your presentations – then you should take care to consider and understand digital copyright, which our students should be aware

---

25. Nuthall, G. (2007) *The Hidden Lives of Learners*. Wellington, New Zealand: NZCER Press, pp. 24–25.

of too. Most teachers carry out a quick search in a well-known search engine and select one of the images they find to put into their PowerPoint presentation, unaware of the potential legalities and issues. Many people assume they can freely use any image they discover online – this is incorrect. Although there are some examples, if an image, text, or video, for example, is being used for educational purposes, there might be more flexible copyright rules, but not always.[26]

A way to easily avoid using images that are subject to licensing are to use websites that offer a wide range of impressive, high-quality images with the guarantee that they are all published free of copyrights under Creative Commons CC0[27] – essentially, it is acceptable to select the images and use them as you want. Websites that offer beautiful and free stock photos include Pixabay.com, Pexels.com and Unsplash.com. Another site to use, especially for younger children, is www.safesearchkids.com/safe-image-search as it provides a range of filtered and safe images, powered by Google.

Cops and Robbers

From my experience, students really enjoy this activity and it serves the purpose of retrieval well. This task provides an opportunity for daily review that can be achieved in the first eight to ten minutes of the lesson (slightly longer than Rosenshine suggested, but that is just a guide). The sheet can be generic and printed to be used with different classes or personalised, your choice. Even better, this can be completed in class books as all that is required is a ruler to divide the page. The 'Cops' column is for students to write as much as they can from memory about a specific topic, or previously covered material. They will have a time limit to do so. Once the students have had about four to five minutes to write as much as they can from memory they then have to complete the 'Robbers' section. This is where everyone in the class needs to get out of their seats and read their peers work, swapping and sharing their ideas and content. I always love watching this happen. Students will often read another students 'cop column' and see information that they forgot or didn't have time to include. When this happens they should add that extra information to the 'rob column'. It is not designed as a competition but instead focuses on recall and working with others.

26. Waters, S & Burt, R. (2017) 'The Educator's Guide to Copyright, Fair Use, and Creative Commons'. (The Edublogger) Available at: www.theedublogger.com/copyright-fair-use-and-creative-commons/

27. Anderson, M. (2017) 'I Got It Off Google Images…' (ICT Evangelist) Available at: www.ictevangelist.com/i-got-it-off-google-images/

Your own knowledge and information (Cops)	Knowledge and information you have 'stolen' from your peers (Robbers)
- The Navy work at sea - One of the many ships was the HMS Victory - The powder monkey was a child who helped deliver messages and climb riggings to do jobs. - The sailors had to be well trained - They ate biscuits and drank grog (water and alcohol)	- There were lots of decks - One of the decks was the poopdeck - The surgeon had his own room - Nelson lost the sight in his right eye - HMS Victory is now in Portsmouth - They were punished for being drunk

Low stakes multiple-choice quizzing

Who does not enjoy a good quiz? Quizzing is nothing new in the classroom. I remember regular quizzes as a student myself – either answering questions individually or within pairs or groups. I am certainly not anti-group work or working with others (as examples in this book will demonstrate), but when it comes to quizzing I believe students should be quizzed individually. This informs the student and teacher as to what that specific individual can remember, recall and understand. Students often like participating in a quiz and interestingly the terminology here is important depending upon whether we use the term testing or quizzing.

Essentially, a quiz will gauge students' subject knowledge and understanding whilst a test carries connotations of pressure and formal grade reporting, which often involves informing parents. A test can be in the form of an examination paper or assignment amongst other types of assessment.

The aim of low stakes quizzing is to reduce the stress, panic and fear associated with testing by removing any formal grading or reporting. No stakes quizzing is where the results aren't always shared with the teacher or shared with anyone apart from the student taking the quiz. This is because the quiz is being used as a learning tool to improve memory, not as a formal assessment tool to record data.

Another way to reduce the anxiety associated with quizzes and testing is to avoid a surprise 'pop quiz'. If quizzing takes place in your classroom regularly, then it becomes a normal part of your lesson routine and students will get used to this. Taking away the stress can benefit learners because, in addition to the negative impact on student wellbeing, anxiety can also hamper and hinder the ability to learn.[28] Therefore, we need to create a culture where quizzing becomes part of a regular classroom routine without the perceived negative connotations and worries associated with testing.

The term 'testing effect' links to retrieval practice as it refers to any process that makes you recall information from memory and, by doing so, strengthens retention and recall. Students need to understand that quizzing and testing are tools to support learning, not just measure it. An enlightening article entitled *Ten Benefits of Testing And Their Applications to Educational Practice* revealed that 'quizzes and tests are given frequently in elementary schools, often at the rate of several or more a week, but testing decreases in frequency the higher a student rises in the educational system. By the time students are in college, they may be given only a mid-term exam and final exam'.[29] Certainly, as students progress throughout school the pressure and stakes increase with SATs, GCSEs and A-Level examinations, in addition to other assessments that can be used to place students in the appropriate class setting in some subjects.

The article also acknowledges how testing can be used to improve performance. It describes several experiments that were carried out under different conditions to demonstrate the various benefits of testing on learning. It challenges the notion of testing as a form of 'kill and drill' and instead highlights that 'proponents of testing argue that retrieval practice induces readily accessible information that can be flexibly used to solve new problems' and 'retrieval practice also improves the transfer of knowledge to new contexts'. The examples of quizzing and testing I

28. De Bruyckere, P. (2018) *The Ingredients for Great Teaching*. London, England: SAGE Publications.
29. Roediger, H, L, Putnam, A, L & Smith, M, A. (2011) 'Ten Benefits of Testing And Their Applications to Educational Practice', *Psychology of Learning and Motivation*, 55, pp. 1-36.

share in this chapter and throughout this book haven't been perceived by students or parents as 'kill and drill', far from it. Referring back to Rosenshine's Principles of Instruction, the research in the article found that classes that had completed weekly quizzes, in comparison to classes that only completed one or two quizzes per term, scored better on final exams. This is clear evidence showing the benefits and impact quizzing can have on academic progress and achievement. We need to educate all stakeholders of the plentiful benefits of the 'testing effect'.

Quizzes are not only an enjoyable way of starting and ending a lesson but also a very useful strategy to revise and review subject knowledge. Quizzing is a reliable method of illustrating what a student has learned, showing what information has or hasn't been transferred to long-term memory. The gaps in knowledge addressed by a quiz can motivate students to study and improve that specific area as the article notes 'if students are quizzed every week, they would probably study more (and more regularly) during a semester than if they were tested only on a mid-term and a final exam', illustrating the indirect effect of testing on study habits as students become more aware of their areas for improvement.

Mini-whiteboards can be used as a good method of assessment. Even a simple quiz, writing the answers in the back of their class book can work well. If your students do have access to technology, they can easily complete a quiz using an app or website. The benefits of using technology for quizzing are that the apps and sites often record results, tracking data and individual progress for the teacher, which can be very supportive in terms of workload. There are now many quizzes that have pre-prepared questions, once again saving time for the busy teacher (although that might not always be appropriate as I discuss later).

Below are four of my favourite interactive quizzes to use in the classroom. All of the suggested online quiz tools are free to access, but require registration and login using an email address. Online quizzes document and record learning instantaneously, in addition to making it easy to revisit the learning or repeat the quiz with students at a later date.

1. **Plickers** is a great quizzing tool, especially if your school and students don't have access to technology as only one device is required. The single device required is for the teacher, who will scan the class answers. You could use your own smartphone or tablet to do this. A teacher will need to set up an account on the website Plickers.com. Then class lists need to be uploaded, this is much easier for teachers with one class or smaller class sizes. Although inputting the class lists can be slightly time-consuming,

once all the names are saved on the account, they can be used for the rest of the academic year. The teacher can easily create their own multiple-choice quizzes on the website with a possibility of up to four multiple-choice answers or true/false. The quizzes are then saved to use in the lesson. Students will each have their own card known as a paper clicker that can be downloaded for free at Plickers.com.

The cards are used by the students to answer questions. A question with a choice of answers will be projected onto the board and each student will hold their paper clicker card up (see image below) to represent their answer. Everyone has a different card with a unique code so students cannot copy one another or see how others have answered because he or she must rotate the card to illustrate their answer.

Plickers is such a simple website to navigate. If you need any extra guidance there are plenty of YouTube tutorial videos posted by teachers and, in fact, there are lots of useful online tutorials for each of the quizzes suggested below. I find it helpful that Plickers records all the data from the quizzes so you could repeat the quiz again at the end of the lesson or the following lesson and be able to quickly view the progress made. I have created quizzes and used them for three years in a row with different classes as they can be easily edited too.

If you have a large class, it can be difficult to check all the answers when using mini-whiteboards, but with Plickers the device scans and stores every individual answer and result for the teacher. Plickers has been around for a few years and due to its simplicity, I'm sure it will continue to be used by many teachers around the world as a useful and interactive approach to recall and revisit prior learning.

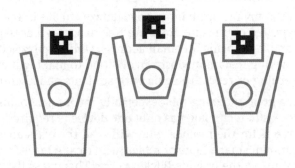

2. **Quizizz** is another excellent website and app, which currently boasts over ten million users including students and teachers. This is my

personal favourite online tool for quizzing in the classroom. Similar to Plickers, the teacher must set up an account so they can record quizzes and results. Users can create their own quizzes, but unlike Plickers there is no need to input student names and class lists, as students do this themselves when they take part in a Quizizz quiz.

The best feature of Quizizz, in my opinion, is the teleport function. The teleport feature allows teachers to view other quizzes created by other teachers – you simply search the topic of your quiz and related quizzes will appear. You can then select specific questions from other quizzes – as well as creating your own questions if you want – in order to create a personalised quiz for your classes. Students join the game and answer the questions on their screens. Devices are required for Quizizz, which can be a smartphone, tablet or computer/laptop. Quizizz is proving to be very popular with both teachers and students so if you're not using Quizziz I can highly recommend it.

3. **Kahoot** is another well-known assessment tool where students answer from a series of multiple-choice questions. Kahoot is also very easy to use, which has added to its popularity since it is straightforward for teachers to create their quizzes and students can grasp it instantly. Results are recorded and how fast students answered. I don't like that a student will get more points for answering correctly quickly. I would rather students take time to consider the question, as students know they get points for speed there is the temptation to rush, not read the question properly and make silly mistakes. There is the option for teachers to use quizzes created by other teachers.

Unlike the teleport feature with Quizizz, if you want to use a quiz created by another teacher on Kahoot you cannot pick and choose individual questions, you have to use the whole quiz and perhaps not all of the questions are relevant or provide the appropriate level of challenge. Despite the negative points I have highlighted it is still a good quizzing tool.

4. **Google Forms** is unlike the other types of quizzes above and perhaps might seem an odd choice as it is often used as a surveying tool. Google Forms already provide users with a wide range of quiz templates specifically designed for use in the classroom. It is another platform that is very easy-to-use to create a quiz and share with your students. As well as the ability to ask multiple-choice questions, Google Forms also allows students to input written and extended answers, unlike the quizzes above. This does not allow for any guess work or randomly picking one of

the four options, instead students have the opportunity to submit their answers writing keywords, full sentences and if required a paragraph or more.

Other interactive and online tools for assessment and regular quizzing include Quizlet, Nearpod, Socrative, Edmodo and Quizalize. I like to use a variety of online tools as different students have their own personal favourites and there are advantages and disadvantages to each of the quizzes discussed above. I'm not implying that you should use all of the quizzing tools but find one or two that suit you, support your workload and most importantly supports your students learning with regular review and recall. It may take yourself and your students more than one attempt to become confident using the online assessment tools but if used regularly then using the technology will become automatic, as the focus must always be on the learning rather than the technology itself.

Science teacher and blogger, Adam Boxer raises a valid point about quizzing in the classroom. He writes that, 'when students are involved in competition, the thing they are focused on is the competition. Their mental energies are dedicated to finding the quickest, easiest and most effortless way of winning the competition. Thinking hard or learning plays second fiddle'.[30] Encouraging students to focus on improving their previous score and achieving their personal best would be a better approach for learners to adopt, instead of focusing on competing against other members of the class.

Another issue that can arise with quizzes like Kahoot is that the same students win again and again and this is visible for all to see with the leaderboard feature. Quizizz allows the teacher to remove the leaderboard option in the game settings so students do not know how they compare against others and thus removing that element of the competition. We can shift the focus from a class competition to individuals striving to improve their knowledge, understanding and recall with every quiz.

Another useful strategy is to ask students to predict their score or how well they will do in the quiz, this can be done before the quiz and once the quiz has been completed, depending on the type of activity. They can then compare and evaluate their performance. This is an important aspect of reflection – perhaps students overestimated their knowledge, understanding and ability to recall a specific topic or perhaps they lacked

---

30. Boxer, A. (13 August 2018) 'Disengaged boys: just make it a competition, right?' (A Chemical Orthodoxy: Schools, Science and Education.) Available at: www.achemicalorthodoxy.wordpress.com/2018/08/13/disengaged-boys-just-make-it-a-competition-right/

in confidence in their own ability and did much better than they initially predicted.

Recognition vs. recall

Although I use regular multiple-choice quizzing there is a lot of research I have encountered that tells us students benefit more from answering questions that don't provide any cues, clues, or ask students to select the correct answer. The fantastic work of Professor John Dunlosky, *Strengthening the Student Toolbox. Study Strategies to Boost Learning* illustrates that tests or quizzes that require recall from memory will be more effective for developing long-term memory. This is not to dismiss multiple-choice quizzing as it can be a useful form of daily review.

Multiple-choice quizzes involve the process of recognition as students have to simply identify the correct answer. This is easier than recalling it without any support. Quiz questions that require short answers will need the teacher to check answers unlike the majority of the quizzing apps suggested above that do that automatically. These types of quizzes will be more time consuming for the teacher to assess but the reason short answers are more beneficial than answering a multiple-choice question is that it simply requires more effort from the student.

The Generation Effect refers to the long-term benefits of generating an answer compared to being presented with an answer or information. University Professors of Psychology and well-respected educational researchers, Elizabeth L. Bjork and Robert Bjork regularly share and discuss the generation effect. Robert Bjork writes that 'basically, any time that you, as a learner, look up an answer or have somebody tell or show you something that you could, drawing on current cues and your past knowledge, generate instead, you rob yourself of a powerful learning opportunity'.[31] Through quizzing and retrieval practice we can provide our students with lots of powerful learning opportunities.

Teacher and author Peps Mccrea explains in his must-read book *Memorable Teaching: Leveraging memory to build deep and durable learning in the classroom* that the less assistance we provide students during retrieval the greater the strengthening effect will be.[32] It is important that if we use multiple-choice quizzing that we also provide opportunities for quizzing and testing that does not involve multiple-choice too. Research has suggested teachers should combine the two

---

31. Bjork, R, A. (1975) 'Retrieval as a memory modifier: An interpretation of negative recency and related phenomena', *Information Processing and Cognition: The Loyola Symposium*, pp. 123-144.
32. Mccrea, P. (2017) *Memorable Teaching: Leveraging memory to build deep and durable learning in the classroom*. Scotts Valley, California: CreateSpace.

---

methods of multiple-choice and short answer. This is because multiple-choice quizzing often leads to greater retrieval success than short answer questions. The benefits of retrieval practice can depend on both the retrieval difficulty and retrieval success, so combining the harder questions with opportunities for success would be optimal.[33]

Challenge Grid

Bjork and Bjork have written about the term they coined 'desirable difficulties'. Desirable difficulties refer to challenge that requires encoding and retrieval to support learning, comprehension and remembering. This is desirable in the classroom. If a student does not have the relevant background knowledge, understanding or skills to respond to a task or question successfully, this is an undesirable difficulty.[34] As teachers we need to ensure that the difficulties we present our students are accessible and desirable. Brown et al state that for a task to be desirable the level of difficulty must be something that learners can overcome through increased effort.[35] If they feel that achieving a goal is unlikely or unrealistic, then they will give up and this is undesirable.

A Challenge Grid is a grid with a range of questions for students to answer, no support, clues or multiple-choice answers. The aim of the Challenge Grid is to provide different questions that vary in the level of difficulty and depth. This works well if you have a mixed ability class as there are questions that everyone should be able to access. The Challenge Grid provides the opportunity for every member of the class to access challenging questions. Teachers and authors Shaun Allison and Andy Tharby highlight in their superb book, *Making Every Lesson Count: Six Principles to support great teaching and learning*, 'it is unfortunate that all too often challenge is presented in the context of challenging the most able'.[36]

33. Smith, M, A & Karpicke, J, D. (2013) 'Retrieval practice with short-answer, multiple-choice and hybrid tests', *Memory*, 22(7), pp. 784–802.
34. Bjork, E & Bjork, R. (2011) 'Making things hard on yourself, but in a good way: Creating desirable difficulties to enhance learning', *Psychology and the Real World: Essays Illustrating Fundamental Contributions to Society*, pp. 56–64.
35. Brown, P, C, Roediger, H, L & McDaniel, M, A. (2014) *Make It Stick: The Science of Successful Learning*. Cambridge, Massachusetts: Harvard Education Press, p. 99.
36. Allison, S & Tharby, A. (2015) *Making Every Lesson Count: Six principles to support great teaching and learning*. Carmarthen, Wales: Crown House Publishing, p. 14.

The Challenge Grids are designed to challenge every individual in the classroom. Allison and Tharby also add that challenges should be firmly rooted in subject content' ,[37] so we should ensure the challenge is with the content not the actual completion of the task or activity itself. Each question is worth a certain amount of points and the points increase as the level of difficulty increases. I usually allow students about eight minutes to answer as many questions as they can using the retrieval practice strategy from memory, not using any notes or their books and they can select which questions they want to answer.

It is interesting to see that some learners tackle the hardest questions first whereas other students will answer as many of the easier questions as quickly as possible. This can be linked to their confidence and grasp of the content. I have used this resource with Year 5 and A-Level classes and all the year groups in-between. It can be used at the start or end of a lesson although my preference is at the beginning of a lesson. I always put careful thought and consideration into creating the questions and varying the level of challenge.

As previously mentioned, when it comes to challenge we need to apply the Goldilocks principle – not too easy, not too difficult, but pitching it just right. This is where teachers can use their expertise, experience and knowledge of their subject and students. Dylan Wiliam wrote that 'if you make learning too easy, students don't have to work hard to make sense of what they are learning, and as a result will forget it quickly' ,[38] but if we make learning too difficult students can become frustrated and stop working.[39] This again links directly to 'desirable difficulties'.

The Challenge Grid is another example of how a starter activity can be engaging and enjoyable without losing focusing on subject content and reviewing knowledge.

37. Ibid. p. 25.
38. Wiliam, D. (2016) 'The 9 things every teacher should know'. (TES) Available at: www.tes.com/news/9-things-every-teacher-should-know.
39. Smith, M & Firth, J. (2018) Psychology in the Classroom: A Teacher's Guide To What Works. Abingdon, Oxfordshire: Routledge, p. 68.

Challenge Grid

Define the term militarism	Describe the two main alliances pre 1914.	Why was Alsace-Lorraine a cause of tension?	Describe the First Moroccan Crisis.
Define the term imperialism.	What is a dreadnought?	Describe Kaiser Wilhelm II.	Describe the second Moroccan Crisis
Define the term nationalism	Explain why Britain was so powerful at the start of the 20th century.	What was the policy of 'splendid isolation'?	When and why did Germany start building dreadnoughts?
1 point	2 point	3 points	4 points

Students can also create their own Challenge Grids outside of the lesson for their peers to answer and complete. This has proven to be a great homework task as students have to think carefully to create a range of questions linked to the content and create questions that vary in level of challenge and difficulty. A Challenge Grid can be self-assessed and corrected. As Wiliam has recommended 'the best person to mark a test is the person who has just took it'.[40]

Retrieval Practice Challenge Grid

Mccrea advises that as teachers we should begin with the assumption that our students will forget what they have learned unless we take deliberate steps to help them remember that information.[41] I designed the Retrieval Practice Challenge Grid (which have become known online as Retrieval Grids) to purposefully revisit subject knowledge and content previously studied. It is an adaptation of the Challenge Grid. The questions differ based upon **when** the subject content was taught. It is another simple concept, the further back the subject content was covered, the higher the points.

40. Hendrick, C & Macpherson, R. (2017) *What does this look like in the classroom? Bridging the Gap Between Research and Practice*. Melton, Suffolk: John Catt Educational Ltd, p. 35.
41. Mccrea, P. (2017) *Memorable Teaching: Leveraging memory to build deep and durable learning in the classroom*. Scotts Valley, California: CreateSpace, p. 80.

Retrieval Practice Challenge Grid: What's your score?

Who was Head of the Cheka in 1917	Explain the term bourgeoisie.	Who was Anatoly Lunacharsky?	List four different enemies of the Cheka.
Describe Khrushchev's attitude towards religion.	Explain the term 'Proletkult'.	List three aims of the NEP.	What was the October 1917 Decree on Land?
Explain the term 'show trial'.	Who was Patriarch Tikhon?	What were the aims of agitprop?	Describe one strength and one weakness of War Communism
Last lesson (1)	Last week (2)	Two weeks ago (3)	Further back! (4)

Educator and podcast host, Jennifer Gonzalez, has referred to retrieval practice as the 'most powerful learning strategy you're not using'.[42] For the first five years during my teaching career I didn't realise regular retrieval practice was such an effective form of learning. Although quizzing has always been part of my teaching practice, I mainly used testing as a form of assessment. I also tended to rush through content at a fast pace, which can result in a lack of depth and missed opportunities for retrieval. This is where curriculum design can be important. Adopting a 'less is more approach' whilst still ensuring breadth – although this is not possible with examination classes and specifications – is beneficial to learning.

I focused on delivering new content and return to recall knowledge and understanding at a much later date, before an upcoming internal or external examination.

On reflection, it seems obvious that revisiting a topic months later in the classroom, or just before the examination, won't be as effective as regular recall and retrieval. I use the Retrieval Practice Challenge Grid at the start of the lesson as it includes a wide range of questions that require students to recall information from last lesson, last week and even further. This works well with senior classes as a useful revision strategy to revisit subject content, but I use it with all of my classes. It is a simple but efficient and effective way to start the lesson.

---

42. Gonzalez, J. (2017) 'Retrieval Practice: The Most Powerful Learning Strategy You're Not Using'. (Cult of Pedagogy) Available at: www.cultofpedagogy.com/retrieval-practice

You can download a free template of the Retrieval Practice Challenge Grid on the website ICTEvangelist.com. Mark Anderson has generously created different versions that can be downloaded ready to use in your classroom. To view more examples of the Retrieval Practice Challenge Grid, that have been created by other teachers, visit my website lovetoteach87.com. There are currently examples from the following subjects: maths, science, English literature, MFL, PE, business, geography, history and ICT. I am absolutely delighted to see so many educators use this resource in their classroom with their students.

Retrieval Practice Summary Grid

This is a similar idea to begin the lesson with daily review. The resource itself can involve very little preparation from the teacher but is useful for revisiting previous topics and material. I have dedicated hours in the past to creating, cutting, sticking and laminating starter activities. These tasks have been completed in a matter of minutes and haven't challenged students or provided an opportunity for review. This idea has far more of an impact. The idea with a summary grid is to provide students with a grid that contains titles, headings, events, concepts, questions or keywords from previous learning and students write down from memory what they remember. Each box acts as a prompt but this is more challenging than multiple-choice quizzing.

Five a day

We are all familiar with the five a day message, we should have five portions of fruit and/or vegetables as part of our daily routine to stay healthy. This concept can be applied to the classroom with a twist, focusing on daily review of five a day to promote healthy retrieval! Five a day can simply be five quiz questions to start the lesson with peer or self-assessment or discussion of the answers collectively as a class. I have done this with classes several times where five questions are on the board and extension questions can be included. Students are quick to focus and attempt the questions.

Another idea is to have five keywords on the board and for students to define each word or write a paragraph to summarise previous learning including the five keywords or alternatively create five questions where each keyword is the answer. There could also be five keywords and definitions to match.

In my history lessons I have provided students with five historical events that they need to put in the correct chronological order. Another idea is to spend five minutes simply writing down from memory as much as students can about a specific topic or a previous concept studied. Any opportunity for daily review that requires minimal preparation but high impact is great to help learners and help you save time.

Retrieval Practice Summary Grid
A divided union: Civil Rights in the USA 1945-74

Segregation	Jim Crow Laws	Bus Boycott
Brown v Topeka	Little Rock	MLK Approach
Washington March	Sit-ins	Freedom riders

This idea was inspired by Doug Lemov's *Teach Like a Champion* strategy the 'Do Now', explained below by Lemov:

'The first step in a great lesson is a 'Do Now'– a short activity that you have written on the board or that is waiting for students as they enter. It often starts working before you do. While you are greeting students at the door, or finding that stack of copies, or erasing the mark-ups you made to your overhead from the last lesson, students should already be busy, via the Do Now with scholarly work that prepares them to succeed. In fact, students entering your room should never have to ask themselves, 'What am I supposed to be doing?' That much should go without saying. The habits of a good classroom should answer, 'You should be doing the Do Now, because we always start with the Do Now'.'[43]

The 'Do Now' activity should be carried out regularly so that it becomes a classroom routine and requires minimal instruction, something students can begin without support from the teacher.

Lemov suggests the activity should take about five minutes and the focus should be on previewing the lesson or reviewing previous lesson material.

---

43. No author. (2014) 'The Do Now: A Primer.' (Teach Like a Champion) Available at: www.teachlikeachampion.com/blog/now-primer/

The three-part lesson idea where you have a starter, main and plenary has come under some scrutiny and challenge in recent years. Many schools have abandoned this concept, but others continue to promote it. Structure and routines are important, can support behaviour management and lead to automacy which reduces cognitive load; all of which can enhance learning. I was instructed to use a three-part lesson at the start of my career and I did find this helpful at the time. There are critics of the three-part lesson and I understand the arguments against this. There may be times where students have to complete an extended piece of writing and the teacher believes that the most valuable use of lesson time would be to focus on that throughout the whole lesson, removing a starter and plenary task.

A lot of lessons are more complex than starter, main and dessert – as I have seen this lesson structure described! Professional judgment here is key.

Authors Jonathan Firth and Marc Smith inform that the messages we give to students at the start and end of a lesson are the most important ones.[44] Based upon the research and evidence I have presented so far about long-term memory, we can deduce that at the end of a lesson, not enough time has passed for the content to be forgotten. We will be unable to check if the information from that lesson has been transferred to long-term memory and has therefore been learned and can be retrieved. A plenary won't inform teachers if information has been stored in long-term memory. Regular retrieval and review will do that.

Plenaries have moved away from checking if progress has been made every 20 minutes. We know that the learning process takes much longer than that. We need to reflect and reconsider how we deliver a plenary. Teacher and blogger Mark Enser has criticised the standard type of plenary tasks expected where he contends, 'the problem is, the end of the lesson is the worst possible time to find out what pupils have learnt. Having just completed the work, with their notes in front of them and possibly on the board as well, what you are going to get is mimicry.'[45] I think Enser raises a very valid argument. I do believe the plenary can still be powerful, so long as the purpose is clear.

We can check for misconceptions at the start of a lesson, during a lesson and at the end of a lesson. It would be ideal to identify misconceptions before the end of a lesson, so students don't leave the classroom with a

44. Smith, M & Firth, J. (2018) *Psychology in the Classroom: A Teacher's Guide To What Works.* Abingdon, Oxfordshire: Routledge.
45. Enser, M. (2018) 'Plenary vs Pedagogy'. (Teach Real) Available at: www.teachreal.wordpress. com/2018/01/07/plenary-vs-pedagogy/

misunderstanding. When it comes to the plenary we need to think short-term. When it comes to learning we need to think long-term. There is a difference between learning and performance.

Bjork and Bjork are well-known for their work related to 'Learning versus Performance'. Bjork and Bjork clarify the difference, 'Performance is what we can observe and measure during instruction or training. Learning – that is, the more or less permanent change in knowledge or understanding that is the target of instruction – is something we must try to infer, and current performance can be a highly unreliable index of whether learning has occurred.'[46] This is very important for teachers to consider, especially with plenary tasks.

The end of the lesson can be used to summarise the main points, content, debate or discussion from the lesson. It can be used to check understanding and many teachers do this with quizzes and exit tickets. Whilst this is a good idea, it is important we do not assume the material has been learned. Instead we could now use what we previously used as plenaries to start our lessons. The Key Reflection example below was originally used as plenary, but I now use it as an opportunity to review previous learning at the start of the following lesson.

A report on Effective Teaching, by James Ko et al, advises teachers to give students sufficient time for reflection.[47] A prime time to do this can be the start or end of a lesson. The aim of my Key Reflection task, which can be easily adapted and tweaked for other subjects, is to focus on the key content, vocabulary and other important aspects previously studied. The template provides a summary of the previous lesson or learning content and the students recall the important facts, dates, terms, individuals, quotes or statistics. As mentioned, this can be used as a plenary, but I now tend to use it at the start of the lesson as a form of recall and to discuss prior learning. This activity can be used without the key template, I included that to emphasise the importance of selecting what information was 'key'.

46. Bjork, E & Bjork, R. (2011) 'Making things hard on yourself, but in a good way: Creating desirable difficulties to enhance learning' , *Psychology and the Real World: Essays Illustrating Fundamental Contributions to Society.* New York, NY: Worth Publishers, pp. 56–64.
47. James, K & Sammons, P. (2013) *Effective Teaching: A Review of Research and Evidence.* Oxford, Oxfordshire: Oxford University Department.

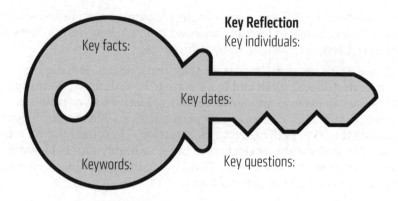

Key Reflection

Key facts:

Key individuals:

Key dates:

Keywords:

Key questions:

Summary

- Start each lesson reviewing and recapping previous lesson content. Retrieval practice is a very powerful and effective strategy to support learning and long-term memory.

- Barak Rosenshine's 'Principles of Instruction Research-Based Strategies That All Teachers Should Know' is a useful research-informed and evidence-based document that can support teachers and therefore students learning.

- The focus of the starter should not be engagement although we do want our learners interested and engaged in the lesson content and tasks.

- We should provide students with the opportunities to recognise answers with multiple-choice questions and also free call, answering questions without any clues, cues or support.

- Technology can support our planning, recording of data and workload when used for quizzing and retrieval.

- A plenary is not an appropriate time to check if learning has occurred in the lesson because not enough time has passed for information to be forgotten or transferred to long-term memory. The plenary task can be used to summarise, check understanding and provide students the opportunity for reflection.

Recommended reading

The Hidden Lives of Learners by Graham Nuthall (2007)

Brain Rules: 12 Principles for Surviving and Thriving at Work, Home and School by John Medina (2008)

Why Don't Students Like School? A Cognitive Scientist Answers Questions About How The Mind Works And What It Means For The Classroom by Daniel T. Willingham (2009)

Making Every Lesson Count: Six Principles to Support Great Teaching and Learning by Andy Tharby and Shaun Allison (2015)

Teach Like a Champion 2.0: 62 Techniques that Put Students on the Path to College by Doug Lemov (2010)

CHAPTER 2:
HOW TO MAKE
LEARNING STICK

'If you want to understand teaching, you need to understand how children learn.'
Graham Nuthall

The title of this chapter is in homage to two of my favourite books linked to education. Firstly, *Make it Stick: The Science of Successful Learning* by Peter Brown, Henry Roediger III and Mark McDaniel and, secondly, *Made To Stick: Why Some Ideas Die And Others Survive* by brothers Chip and Dan Heath.

All teachers can benefit from reading *Make it Stick: The Science of Successful Learning* as it is a book filled with useful and comprehensive educational research and practical examples for the classroom. The Heath brothers' writing is not just for teachers (although there are specific chapters and resources on their website for teachers) and their books are always informative and entertaining. The Heath brothers are very funny, intelligent and insightful. The idea of making learning, skills and experiences stick with students is very important but it is not always easy to put into practice.

Paul A. Kirschner, John Sweller and Richard E. Clark in their seminal paper *Why Minimal Guidance During Instruction Does Not Work: An Analysis of the Failure of Constructivist, Discovery, Problem-Based, Experiential, and Inquiry-Based Teaching* (2006) define learning as a change in long-term memory.[48] This is not a definition of education or schooling as clearly there are broader values included. In order for anyone to learn something it will need to be encoded (changing information into a form that can be

---

48. Kirschner, P, A, Sweller, J & Clark, R, E. (2006) 'Why Minimal Guidance During Instruction Does Not Work: An Analysis of the Failure of Constructivist, Discovery, Problem-Based, Experiential, and Inquiry-Based Teaching', *Educational Psychologist*, 41(2), pp. 75-86.

stored in the brain), stored in short-term memory, then transferred to long-term memory and later retrieved from long-term memory.

This is very powerful for teachers and students. If information has not been changed so that it can be transferred to long-term memory then no information has been learned. When we are planning lessons we not only need to combine our subject knowledge with our pedagogical knowledge, we now also need to be considering cognitive psychology. This involves the study of memory and process of information, which is highly relevant to education. If the subject that you teach is psychology you have a clear advantage in this area but what about the rest of us? You may or may not have some background in cognitive science and psychology. I have tried to cover applicable areas as clearly and simply as I can, followed by some practical examples for use in the classroom.

Models of Memory

The Multi Store Model of Memory by Atkinson and Shiffrin (1968) proposed that memory consisted of three stores. The first store is the sensory register, where information is encoded and passed on to the second store, the short-term memory. Medina describes the initial moment of learning, the encoding, as incredibly mysterious and complex.[49] When we encounter new material, the information is stored for a very brief time in our short-term memory, according to Miller (1956). The reason it is brief is because the capacity (how much information) and duration (how long we can store it) of our short-term memory is limited. The length of time information can be stored in our short-term memory can vary between different individuals ranging from a few seconds to a few minutes.[50]

Peterson and Peterson (1959) investigated the duration of short-term memory and the factors that cause short-term memory to decay. They concluded that almost all information stored in short-term memory and not rehearsed is lost within 18 to 30 seconds. Finally, if information is rehearsed and retained beyond short-term memory it is then stored in what is known as our long-term memory.

Daniel T. Willingham's well-known definition of memory as 'the residue of thought' is very useful for teachers. It implies that to really ensure information sticks in memory it must be something that students have really had to think about. Peps Mccrea summarises this by highlighting

49. Medina, J. (2009) *Brain Rules: 12 Principles for Surviving and Thriving at Work, Home, and School.* Seattle, Washington: Pear Press, p. 131.
50. De Bruyckere, P. (2018) *The Ingredients for Great Teaching.* London, England: SAGE Publications, p. 17.

that memory essentially underpins learning[51] and he adds that our duty, as educators, is to help students develop more powerful long-term memory.[52] Unlike short-term memory, long-term memory has an unlimited capacity.

Atkinson and Shiffrin (1968)   Multi Store Model of Memory

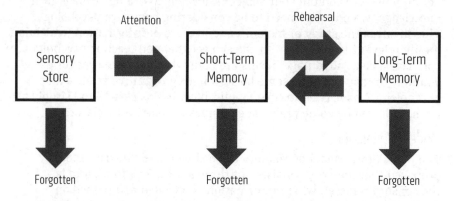

The Multi Store Model of Memory generated a lot of interest and further research into the study of how memory works. Whilst this is a useful model for approaching and understanding memory, researchers Baddeley and Hitch believed that the concept of short-term memory with the Multi Store Model was too simplistic. According to Baddeley and Hitch, short-term memory is much more complex and not a single system. They proposed a Model of Working Memory (1974) that focuses on how we can do more than one thing in our short-term memory, if we are using the appropriate slave systems. There are different systems for different types of information as shown in the diagram below.

Information can be transferred via the visuospatial sketchpad (dealing with visual and spatial information), the phonological loop (which deal with both spoken and written information) and the episodic buffer was added to the model in 2000, that acts as a backup between working memory and long-term memory. All of these systems are driven by the central executive, described as the 'boss' of working memory. The terms short-term memory and working memory are interchangeable although working memory refers to the more complex model of short-term memory.

---

51. Mccrea, P. (2017) *Memorable Teaching: Leveraging memory to build deep and durable learning in the classroom.* Scotts Valley, California: CreateSpace, p. 5.
52. Ibid. p. 13.

For teachers and students this means we need to be practising and reviewing information regularly to ensure it does not disappear completely. The Working Memory Model (1974) proposes that we can deal with different types of information including both images and text or images and spoken word at the same time.[53] Simply repeating material does not guarantee that it will transfer from working memory to long-term memory.[54] This is where retrieval practice and other strategies can support the process to transfer information to make it stick.

Baddeley and Hitch (1974)   Working Memory Model

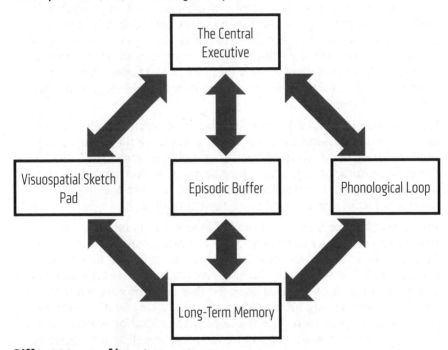

Different types of long-term memory

Episodic Memory. If we think back to our own school days we have distinct personal memories, these can include our first day at school, performing in concerts, participating in sports days, attending school discos or receiving examination results. We can remember who we were with, what happened and how we were feeling at the time. These are episodic memories. Episodic memories can be positive or negative and

53. Smith, M & Firth, J. (2018) *Psychology in the Classroom: A Teacher's Guide To What Works*. Abingdon, Oxfordshire: Routledge, p. 44.
54. Ibid. p. 9.

some return to us with certain cues. That can happen when we go to a certain place, hear a song, smell a scent or an individual can remind us of a time and place we thought we had forgot. All of these factors act as cues. Episodic memories play an important role during school years and we want our students to gain very positive episodic memories. However, these memories aren't always linked to learning, although they can be when combined with semantic memories.

Semantic Memory. Headteacher and blogger, Clare Sealy has argued that 'the key purpose of education is to build strong semantic memory, to pass on knowledge built up over centuries to the next generation'.[55] Sealy is also quick to point out that she does not think this is the sole purpose of education because she recognises the importance of episodic memories, 'if we treat our children with kindness and respect they will have episodic memories of what it was like to be treated kindly and respectfully, which makes it more likely they too will treat others with kindness and respect'.

Semantic memory is our knowledge base or our own encyclopedia of facts, information, words and concepts. Knowledge that Rome is the capital of Italy is semantic. Memories of eating gelato at the Trevi Fountain in Rome are episodic. Episodic and semantic memories can be grouped together as declarative memories because they require conscious recall, also referred to as explicit memory.

Procedural Memory. The final type of long-term memory is one that we use on a daily basis, without consciously realising that we do (the opposite of conscious recall). This involves knowing how to do something. When we tie our shoelaces we don't stop to think about each step of the process as we have repeated that same process many times, until it has become automatic. When we drive a car, we don't stop to think what happens next once the key is in the ignition, we just drive. Procedural memory does not require conscious recall so it is, therefore, classified as non-declarative memory.

Procedural memory is important in a school setting too. In the previous chapter I discussed using a range of apps for quizzing. Once students are familiar with Quizizz or Kahoot, knowing how these apps work become automatic so that working memory is freed up and can focus on the content or questions instead of how to use the technology.

---

55. Sealy, C. (16 September 2017) 'Memory not Memories – Teaching for Long Term Learning'. (Primarytimerydotcom) Available at: www.primarytimery.com/2017/09/16/memory-not-memories-teaching-for-long-term-learning/

John Sweller explains that 'automation has a significant effect on working memory. It permits working memory to be bypassed. Processing that occurs automatically requires less working memory space and as a consequence, capacity is freed for other functions'.[56]

These types of long-term memories are not isolated and can be combined. Learning to ride a bike is linked to procedural memory because eventually it becomes something we know how to do and don't have to think about doing it each time. Learning to ride a bike as a child with a sibling or parent can also be a special and personal memory, an episodic memory. A good example of how episodic and semantic memories can be combined are with school trips. I have been fortunate to experience many school field trips. A school visit involved travelling to Germany with A-Level historians.

During this trip we went to several museums and buildings and Sachsenhausen Concentration Camp. Anyone who has been to visit a former concentration camp will be aware of how intense and emotional this experience can be. There was a lot of information presented to students at Sachsenhausen, which we later discussed on our return. Students already had strong prior subject knowledge of this topic but were able to build on this by learning new information, for example hearing the harrowing stories of individuals that were sent there. The stories were sad, distressing and shocking. There is no doubt that the experience will remain with students, what they learnt will be embedded in their semantic memory and how they felt will become an episodic memory.

On another occasion, I was unable to take my Year 7 class on a school trip due to various constraints. The class were studying places of worship as part of the RE curriculum. I was preparing a lesson about the Sikh place of worship, the Gurdwara, but I was concerned that my subject knowledge about this religion and place of worship was very weak in comparison to other places of worship that had been taught. I remember learning a lot about Buddhism when I spent a month travelling around Thailand visiting many beautiful temples.

I also had knowledge of Synagogues, Mosques and Churches that had been enhanced by visiting these buildings. I am very aware of my own semantic and episodic memories that have supported my subject knowledge as a teacher.

---

56. Sweller, J. (1994) 'Cognitive load theory, learning difficulty and instructional design' , *Learning and Instruction*, 4(4), pp. 295-312. New South Wales, Australia: University of NSW.

I decided to visit a Gurdwara and after a quick internet search found that the nearest Gurdwara was located 45 minutes away in Manchester. At such short notice I was unable to arrange for my class to visit but I was able to do so in my spare time. I am not advocating or encouraging teachers to give up their weekends and personal time to plan lessons, but this was something that I really enjoyed and benefitted a lot from. After contacting the Gurdwara in Manchester I was invited to attend the Langar on a Saturday night. Langar is a community kitchen where a meal is provided for free to anyone – regardless of gender, ethnicity or religion – and all the food served is vegetarian so as to not offend anyone's religious beliefs. During this meal everybody sits on the floor as a sign of equality. This experience was very memorable and I learned a lot, which then inspired a lesson with my Year 7 class.

As I could not take the class to the Gurdwara I wanted them to gain an insight into the special experience that I had. Prior to the lesson, all of the class – both boys and girls – were instructed to bring something to cover their head, as is the protocol at any Gurdwara. At the beginning of the lesson all students removed their shoes and I explained to the class why they were removing their shoes and covering their head, as it would be respectful to do so at this place of worship.

I began the lesson finding out what students already knew about Sikhism and the Gurdwara. As I had expected, there were some misconceptions and confusion with other religions, but some students had stronger knowledge than I expected. It was a good starting point to find out this information, especially when we refer back to Nuthall's research about what students already know. We then watched an informative short video that provided a tour around a Gurdwara, exploring different rooms and features in addition to their purpose. No one in the class had ever been to a Gurdwarda so the video provided an opportunity to help students visualise one.

Together we all sat on the floor as I described my experience, followed by a break for students to ask questions. The class had the opportunity to eat some food I had prepared that was similar to the meal I ate at the Gurdwara. This wasn't an observation lesson despite sounding like an all 'singing and all dancing' lesson, but it was unique. At the end of the lesson students were then asked to write down questions they still had about a Gurdwara and – if I was unable to answer – my friend Bobbi, who worked as part of the educational support team at the Gurdwara I visited, had already agreed she would happily answer any questions. Students really relished the opportunity to ask the expert – this is not to undermine the teacher or suggest that the teacher is not an expert in their field, but instead it encourages students to think more carefully about the questions they pose and engage with others outside of the school environment. I also spent many lessons, after this particular lesson, revisiting and quizzing students on the Gurdwara and Langar.

I was concerned that students would remember this as 'the onion bhaji lesson' because there is potential for that with the activities we do. If that was the case, students would have developed an episodic memory of this lesson because it was fun, enjoyable and memorable. It was vital that students took meaning from this and retained the information about the place of worship. Teacher and host of the Mr Barton Maths Podcast, Craig Barton, shares a story in his book *How I Wish I'd Taught Maths: Lesson learned from research, conversations with experts and 12 years of mistakes* about how he attempted to make a lesson about fractions memorable for his students, by using Swiss rolls. Students were cutting up Swiss rolls to ensure 12 people had equal slices and whilst this created chaos and mess, the class loved it.

Many years later, Barton spoke to one of the students from that lesson who remembered the Swiss rolls fondly but could not remember what the content of the lesson was about. This is an example of trying to create a powerful and lasting memory, but the memory was more focused on the Swiss roll rather than fractions, which Barton realised upon reflection.[57]

I taught the same class the following year and they were able to recall the experience from the Gurdwara and Langar lesson. They recalled taking off their shoes, covering their head and sitting on the floor. More importantly, when asked, they were able to explain exactly why they did this. They could recall key information, instead of just remembering the onion bhajis! Nuthall has warned that there is 'no guarantee that engaging in classroom activities the ways in which the teacher intends will result in learning',[58] which makes our job challenging. Despite this no guarantee, Nuthall suggests that the activities we do need to be memorable.[59] I wouldn't travel miles, give up a Saturday night and cook onion bhajis for all my lessons. There are, however, opportunities we can create for students that can combine semantic and episodic memories and when we do, the learning and experience can stick with our students for a very long time.

57. Barton, C. (2017) *How I Wish I'd Taught Maths: Lessons learned from research, conversations with experts and 12 years of mistakes*. Melton, Suffolk: John Catt Educational Ltd.
58. Nuthall, G. (2007) *The Hidden Lives of Learners*. Wellington, New Zealand: NZCER Press, p. 103.
59. Ibid. p. 169.

Cognitive Load Theory

Wiliam tweeted in 2017 that Cognitive Load Theory (CLT) by educational psychologist John Sweller and colleagues is 'the single most important thing for teachers to know'. To put CLT in its simplest form, if we present our students with too much new information, all at once, this will lead to information overload (in working memory). The result will be that it becomes difficult to retain any new information, therefore hindering learning, which is known as cognitive overload.

Teaching methods should avoid overloading students working memory in order to maximise learning. Authors David Didau and Nick Rose explore CLT in their book *What Every Teacher Needs To Know About Psychology*, where they clarify that essentially CLT proposes that we want our students to think hard about the material we teach but to do so without overloading their working memory capacity.[60] To understand CLT requires a background understanding of short-term and long-term memory. Recent research suggests that 'an average person can only hold about four chunks of information in their working memory at one time'[61] and we know that long-term memory is very different in regard to duration and capacity of storage.

Students will learn better if their limited cognitive capacity (their working memory) is not overloaded in a lesson. The Centre for Education Statistics and Evaluation published a very useful document that provides a clear and thorough overview of CLT entitled 'Cognitive Load Theory: Research that teachers really need to understand'. This document highlights that anything beyond the simplest cognitive activities appear to overwhelm working memory. This can have serious implications for the classroom and has led me to reflect on my lessons and the activities I use.

CLT is something that I have become very aware of. As you will recognise from reading this book I haven't fully applied this theory to all aspects of my teaching (I write about displays in Chapter 8 and cognitive load theorists warn that displays and even clocks in classrooms can be distracting).[62] Although I do ensure I factor this into my planning, especially when introducing students to new material (more so than consolidating or revisiting material).

60. Didau, D & Rose, N. (2016) *What Every Teacher Should Know About Psychology*. Melton, Suffolk: John Catt Educational Ltd, p. 43.
61. Centre for Education Statistics & Evaluation. (2017) Cognitive Load Theory: Research that teachers really need to understand. New South Wales, Australia: Centre for Education Statistics & Evaluation.
62. Mccrea, P. (2017) *Memorable Teaching: Leveraging memory to build deep and durable learning in the classroom*. Scotts Valley, California: CreateSpace, p. 25.

There are three different types cognitive load according to Sweller. The first is intrinsic load, the mental effort required to understand subject content – this is viewed as necessary. The second refers to germane load, the process where information becomes stored in long-term memory through tasks designed by the teacher to rehearse and repeat exposure to material. This is viewed as good or positive load. Finally, extraneous load occurs when students are exposed to irrelevant information that requires extra mental processing, this is clearly negative – this links to the 'redundancy effect'.

The 'redundancy effect' by Paul Chandler and Sweller occurs when students are presented with extra information that is not relevant to their learning or when they are exposed to the same information in different formats and this can overload their working memory.[63] A PowerPoint presentation that contains beautiful clip art images but aren't directly linked to the subject content (as the main purpose of the graphics are to improve presentation) can have a negative impact on learning. I have been guilty of adding irrelevant clip art and images to my presentation that are unnecessary. If a teacher is speaking to the class whilst students are viewing text on paper or screen this can also have a negative impact, overloading their working memory. Sweller states that 'most people assume that providing learners with additional information is at worst, harmless and might be beneficial. Providing unnecessary information can be a major reason for instructional failure'.[64]

The Heath brothers explain that in order to make new information 'sticky' as they say, 'our messages have to be compact because we can learn and remember only so much information at once'.[65] This does seem obvious and we know from our own personal experiences that too much information can be overwhelming, leading to forgotten information and confusion. Yet, in many lessons, students are given a lot of information and then instructed on what to do with that information without considering whether this is compact or not. Nuthall describes a student's working memory as an 'extraordinarily busy place'.[66] I find that a useful description to keep in mind. The Heath brothers recognise that a lesson plan may actually contain a large number of concepts to share with students but in order to be effective the teacher needs to devote most of

63. Centre for Education Statistics & Evaluation. (2017) Cognitive Load Theory: Research that teachers really need to understand. New South Wales, Australia: Centre for Education Statistics & Evaluation.
64. Sweller, J. (2016) 'Story of a Research Program', In S. Tobias, J. D. Fletcher, & D. C. Berliner (Series eds.), Acquired Wisdom Series. Education Review, 23.
65. Heath, D & Heath, C. (2008) Made To Stick. London, England: Arrow, p. 51.
66. Nuthall, G. (2007) The Hidden Lives of Learners. Wellington, New Zealand: NZCER Press, p. 79.

their efforts to making the most critical two or three stick. The Heath brothers add that the difficulty teachers encounter is that there are often more things to teach than students can remember.[67] This is where careful curriculum planning is important, considering what information and skills we want to stick with our students.

Mccrea warns that the risk of working memory overload is persistently present in our practice.[68] A classroom can be filled with distractions for students, including the behaviour of others in the class, the classroom activities we design and even the learning environment. Firth and Smith explain 'it is very easy to be distracted by something with more immediate significance, stealing attention away from learning tasks, it is therefore important for teachers to limit distractions where possible'.[69] As teachers we need to consider how we can reduce or prevent cognitive overload.

Educators have commented that it is a theory so therefore we should take care as with all theories and ideas before we fully adopt this in our classrooms. There are critics of CLT despite the fact that it is currently influential in education. A criticism or issue that has been addressed about the theory is that the 'majority of studies on CLT do not consider how individual differences between learners might impact upon cognitive load'.[70] Sweller recognises there has become much more international acceptance of CLT but that it continues to be ignored by those in education. Sweller also adds that 'CLT only applies to complex information that is high in element interactivity. It is not a theory of everything and CL effects should not be expected using low element interactivity information'. It is clear there is more development, discussion and debate to be had as to how CLT can best be applied to schools and classrooms. The work of Sweller throughout his extensive career is clearly of great value and importance in education.

The curiosity gap

The Heath brothers clarify that in order 'for an idea to endure, we must generate interest and curiosity'.[71] We can do this as teachers although it can be problematic. Curiosity is similar to creativity in the sense

---

67. Heath, D & Heath, C. (2008) *Made To Stick*. London, England: Arrow, p. 224.
68. Mccrea, P. (2017) Memorable Teaching: Leveraging memory to build deep and durable learning in the classroom. Scotts Valley, California: CreateSpace, p. 48.
69. Smith, M & Firth, J. (2018) *Psychology in the Classroom: A Teacher's Guide To What Works*. Abingdon, Oxfordshire: Routledge, p. 49.
70. Centre for Education Statistics & Evaluation. (2017) Cognitive Load Theory: Research that teachers really need to understand. New South Wales, Australia: Centre for Education Statistics & Evaluation.
71. Heath, D & Heath, C. (2008) *Made To Stick*. London, England: Arrow, p. 16.

that it is often discussed and linked to education, but we can't teach students to be creative or force them to be curious. Instead we can provide opportunities to promote this in the classroom. Authors Firth and Smith write that learning activities that combine novelty, curiosity and problem solving will stand a very good chance of being retained in memory.[72] We need to combine these types of tasks with specific and in-depth subject content. We need to plan lessons to ensure the correct or intended material sticks.

Ironically, I am very curious about curiosity! Why are some people more curious than others? Why am I so curious about events of the past but not as curious about physics? These questions and many similar questions can be applied to the classroom and our students. After carrying out some reading regarding the research linked to curiosity, I found out how difficult it is to measure curiosity and explain why some people are simply more curious than others. Research does show a positive relationship between curiosity, creativity and intelligence.[73] This is not that surprising as curious people are often very highly motivated.

Willingham points out that 'people are naturally curious, curiosity prompts people to explore new ideas and problems, but when we do, we quickly evaluate how much mental work it will take to solve the problem. If it is too much or too little, we stop working on the problem if we can'.[74] The conditions and level of challenge also have to be appropriate.

Curiosity alone is not enough to motivate students to learn but it can be used as a powerful strategy in the classroom. The curiosity scale showed no pattern linked to demographic, age, gender or IQ,[75] although many tend to believe that younger children are more curious because of the questions they ask and frequency. There is debate as to how true this actually is.

American educator and economist, George Lowenstein wrote that 'curiosity has been consistently recognised as a critical motive that influences human behaviour in both positive and negative ways at all stages of the life cycle', therefore implying that students will be curious throughout all stages of their education. Researcher and author Susan

72. Smith, M & Firth, J. (2018) *Psychology in the Classroom: A Teacher's Guide To What Works*. Abingdon, Oxfordshire: Routledge, p. 16.
73. Lowenstein, G. (1994) 'The Psychology of Curiosity: A review of reinterpretation', *Psychological Bulletin*, 116(1), pp. 75–98.
74. Willingham, D, T. (2010) *Why don't students like school? A Cognitive Scientist Answers Questions About How The Mind Works And What It Means For The Classroom*. San Francisco, CA: Jossey-Bass, p. 13.
75. Lowenstein, G. (1994) 'The Psychology of Curiosity: A review of reinterpretation', *Psychological Bulletin*, 116(1), pp. 75–98.

Engel argues that the longer students stay in school the less curiosity they demonstrate and she believes 'curiosity was squelched in schools'.[76]

It is very likely we have come across students who constantly ask questions, want to find out more and are viewed as being generally curious learners. We also encounter students who are disengaged and seem to lack any interest in our subject or the content we teach. Engel identifies that 'most people, including teachers, implicitly believe that some children are curious and others are not. They don't think of curiosity as something they can actively nurture or instil in their students'.[77] I think Engel is accurate in this observation. Epistemic curiosity is a desire for knowledge that motivates individuals to learn new ideas, eliminate gaps in their knowledge and solve intellectual problems.[78] We want our students to have this epistemic curiosity and even Sigmund Freud referred to curiosity as 'a thirst for knowledge'.[79] An information gap is when an individual feels the need to fill a gap or blank in their knowledge and seek out the missing information.

This desire to close the information gap is curiosity. I am sure you can think of a situation where you asked a question or wanted to find something out and didn't stop until you found the answer you were searching for. It can be frustrating having a gap in our knowledge and once the missing information has been found we are instantly satisfied. According to the Heath brothers we can engage people's curiosity over a long period of time by carefully 'opening gaps' in their knowledge and then filling those gaps.[80]

Curiosity can also lead to some negative behaviours in the classroom, just like Adam and Eve – they weren't meant to eat the forbidden fruit, but curiosity got the better of them! Curiosity is what can distract our students too. A classroom with windows can be lovely until something happens outside and suddenly the whole class becomes intrigued and completely off task. Gossip that spreads around the school (or staffroom) happens because people are curious to find out information that other people know; they want to be in the know too.

I remember as a child finding my younger sisters diary and it was clearly labelled 'Private: Do not read Kate' – yes, it even included my name.

76. Engel, S. (2015) *The Hungry Mind: The Origins of Curiosity*. Cambridge, Massachusetts: Harvard University Press, p. 2.
77. Ibid.
78. Berlyne, D, E. (1954) 'A Theory of Human Curiosity', *British Journal of Psychology*, 45(3), pp. 180–191.
79. Lowenstein, G. (1994) 'The Psychology of Curiosity: A review of reinterpretation', *Psychological Bulletin*, 116(1).
80. Heath, D & Heath, C. (2008) *Made To Stick*. London, England: Arrow, p. 16.

Curiosity got the better of me and I am sorry Emily; I just had to read her diary. Despite these examples, teachers can harness and steer curiosity to our advantage in the classroom.

The cliffhanger strategy is a technique that teachers have been using for many years. Inspired by the soap opera dramas like EastEnders and Coronation Street, which end the episode on a dramatic cliffhanger to keep the audience in suspense and desperate to find out what happens next, I have used the cliffhanger strategy many times in my lessons. When teaching the Battle of Hastings it is important to explain the historical context of 1066 and explain why there were various contenders to the throne. At the end of the lesson students understand that Edward the Confessor died and there were complications as to who would inherit the throne. When they asked me who became King after Edward died, I refused to answer. My class couldn't believe that I wouldn't answer – some were even outraged. Our next lesson wasn't until the following week and I said I would tell them next lesson, leaving the lesson hanging on a historical cliffhanger.

The following week many of the class smugly told me that they knew what happened in 1066. Some of the class had asked their parents, others researched and read about it online and another student watched a Dan Snow three-part documentary, so was now apparently a leading expert on this topic! Not everyone in the class had found out what happened next, but the majority of the class had. Those students had to find out the answer because there was a gap in their knowledge; their thirst for knowledge needed to be quenched. I should clarify – this task wasn't designed as a homework task, not everyone found out the answer because they weren't told to do so.

Despite some students carrying out their own independent research, it was still important that the content was covered in depth in the lesson to ensure everyone had accurate knowledge of events and once again to check for any mistakes or misconceptions. Some students found out that William the Conqueror became King in 1066, but they hadn't found out that Harold Godwinson had also taken the throne of England in that same year.

Much to my delight, I have been in contact with the Heath brothers and I told them about how I created a knowledge gap with a historical cliffhanger. Dan Heath commented: 'What a brilliant curiosity gap! You know you're teaching well when your students are incensed when you won't teach them more!'

After a cliffhanger, I always look forward to the next lesson and finding out who the curious students are. I know teachers in other subjects that have used the cliffhanger strategy. During an English lesson, the students were reading a piece of text and the teacher planned carefully at which point to stop reading. It was at a gripping and pivotal point in the text, a literature cliffhanger. The cliffhangers inspire your students to find out what happens next and to continue their learning outside of the classroom. Ending any lesson with a question and gap in their knowledge can be enough to ignite their curiosity.

There are other ways we can spark curiosity, with an intriguing image or mysterious object relevant to the lesson content. Founder of Independent Thinking and author, Ian Gilbert has also written about the power of curiosity. Gilbert reveals that curiosity is a survival drive within us all and if teachers can tap into our students' curiosity this can greatly support motivation in the classroom. He also posed this question to teachers: 'To what extent are you using emotions such as curiosity to get children thinking and learning in your classroom and not as an optional extra?'[81]

Developing empathy: In their shoes

Willingham has written that emotion is not necessary for learning to occur.[82] This makes sense because how do we attach emotion to a math equation or learning how to write using different tenses? We also know that students will tend to pay more attention to things that attract them on an emotional level, which can range from feelings of shock and surprise to disgust or amusement.[83] I regularly hear students talking about practical experiments carried out in science, from animal dissections to bright flames of fire that leave them in awe and amazement. This links in with episodic memory combined with semantic memories.

We work in an environment with young people who experience a wide range of emotions and empathy is a trait we would like our students to possess. To be empathetic can at times be challenging, but it is a lovely quality to demonstrate. As teachers we often feel and show empathy towards colleagues and students, it is an unwritten aspect of our job to be caring and understanding towards others, which we demonstrate on a daily basis. Many educators have written about the importance of

81. Gilbert, I. (2010) *Why Do I Need a Teacher When I've got Google? The Essential Guide to the Big Issues for Every 21st Century Teacher*. Abingdon, Oxfordshire: Routledge, p. 105.
82. Willingham, D, T. (2010) *Why don't students like school? A Cognitive Scientist Answers Questions About How The Mind Works And What It Means For The Classroom*. San Francisco, CA: Jossey-Bass, p. 58.
83. Smith, M & Firth, J. (2018) *Psychology in the Classroom: A Teacher's Guide To What Works*. Abingdon, Oxfordshire: Routledge, p. 13.

empathy as a teacher and a leader. Empathy, like creativity and curiosity, is very important, but how do we teach this? Modelling empathy in front of students can be very powerful. I also think we can promote, encourage and create opportunities for students to build, consider or think about empathy. The resource 'in their shoes' was designed to demonstrate factual knowledge of events, individuals or characters in addition to building a strong sense of empathy.

Hattie and Yates discuss the 'empathy gap'. They explain that an 'empathy gap occurs when people are relatively unable to put themselves in the place of another person. When warm and secure, it is difficult to conceive of another person's pain and insecurities. If you have never been bullied it is hard to imagine the pain. People who have been bullied, or socially rejected, rate these experiences as severely painful. Others, who have not had such experiences, underestimate the level of hurt. It is not easy to empathise with someone whose shoes you have never walked in'.[84] The empathy gap can be applied to teachers and students. It can be difficult for teachers to grasp the experiences and emotions some of our students will experience and it can be challenging for students to demonstrate empathy towards others.

The template for this resource is very simple. It is linked to the well-known phrase 'put yourself in their shoes'. This task requires students to use their subject knowledge and develop their literacy skills, as well as focusing on empathy. Students have to write using the first-person narrative, writing as the individual connected to the topic. The students also have to fill in the toes with various adjectives to describe how they think that person would have felt at that moment in time.

A Year 9 student, studying the Civil Rights Movement in the USA, completed the in their shoes activity below. Students in the class tried to put themselves in the shoes of Rosa Parks after her famous arrest that sparked the Montgomery Bus Boycott.

---

84. Hattie, J & Yates, G, C, R. (2013) *Visible Learning and the Science of How We Learn*. Abingdon, Oxfordshire: Routledge, p. 16.

In their shoes

Imagine you are: __Rosa Parks__

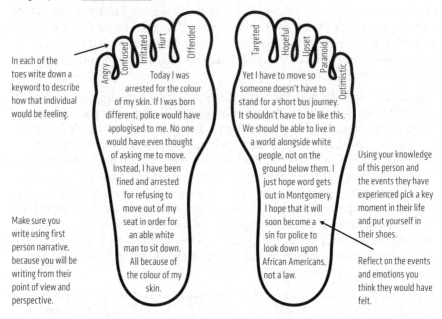

In each of the toes write down a keyword to describe how that individual would be feeling.

Make sure you write using first person narrative, because you will be writing from their point of view and perspective.

Angry · Confused · Irritated · Hurt · Offended

Today I was arrested for the colour of my skin. If I was born different, police would have apologised to me. No one would have even thought of asking me to move. Instead, I have been fined and arrested for refusing to move out of my seat in order for an able white man to sit down. All because of the colour of my skin.

Targeted · Hopeful · Upset · Paranoid · Optimistic

Yet I have to move so someone doesn't have to stand for a short bus journey. It shouldn't have to be like this. We should be able to live in a world alongside white people, not on the ground below them. I just hope word gets out in Montgomery. I hope that it will soon become a sin for police to look down upon African Americans, not a law.

Using your knowledge of this person and the events they have experienced pick a key moment in their life and put yourself in their shoes.

Reflect on the events and emotions you think they would have felt.

It was essential that students had an understanding and overview of the events to be able to explore empathy in the correct historical context. The historical content and subject knowledge is key. This activity wouldn't be suitable for novice learners. This is a good way to check for understanding and ability to recall key events and information. In the toes, the student described different emotions they believed Rosa Parks would be feeling, including 'hurt, angry, confused, or upset'. The rest of the template provided space for students to include knowledge of the event, by describing the arrest in the first person.

The example above shows how the student has also used a range of literary devices such as rhetorical question and repetition. This activity lends itself well to history, studying significant events and individuals. The activity can also highlight how students have interpreted the events and individual, with many students offering very different responses. This specific example led to a discussion about racism and discrimination in the present day, highlighting how this resource can be easily adapted and used with PSHE topics.

There are some issues using this resource in a historical context. Firstly, there are circumstances when it is advisable that children do not try to put themselves in the shoes of someone else, for example a Holocaust victim, for obvious reasons. History teacher and blogger, Ben Newmark has argued that he does not think building empathy is a legitimate aim for history in schools.[85] I found this blog really interesting, it challenged some of my views and beliefs and also made me reflect on this activity. Newmark does correctly point out that 'it is simply impossible to really know what people felt' so when a student puts themselves in the metaphorical shoes of an individual from the past, there is of course an element of fiction.

Newmark further adds that the 'best we can ever achieve is to gain something of an understanding of what their motivations, fears and beliefs were through their words and actions'. I think this argument would lead to a great discussion in the classroom with students and this post inspired other teachers and bloggers to share their views on empathy. I offer Newmark's argument so that you the reader, if you are a history teacher or not, can reflect on your views of developing empathy through activities, whether it is best placed in other subjects or just through our own actions everyday as role models. Newmark is a great writer and I can recommend reading his blogs about education at www.bennewmark.wordpress.com

Dr Debra Kidd regularly advocates promoting and developing empathy with children and I can highly recommend visiting her blog too. Her writing is compassionate, intelligent and thought provoking. Kidd argues we need to 'move beyond a knowledge rich curriculum to one that places moral, social and global issues at its heart, with a pedagogy that encourages deep thinking, empathy, autonomy and problem solving. Knowledge has a role to play in such a curriculum, but it is not the end point: it is a part of the journey'.[86] I too recognise the importance of a knowledge-rich curriculum, but can also appreciate the need to address a wide range of values within a school community.

The 'in their shoes' resource has been used across many other subjects. After sharing this resource online, other educators around the world have used it or adapted it for their classes. English and drama teachers

---

85. Newmark, B. (18 May 2017) 'Never live like common people; the problems with trying to empathise with those who lived in the past'. (Bennewmark) Available at: https://bennewmark.wordpress.com/2017/05/18/never-live-like-common-people-the-problems-with-trying-to-empathise-with-those-who-lived-in-the-past/

86. Kidd, D. (7 March 2016) 'A Compassionate Education'. (Love Learning) Available at: https://debrakidd.wordpress.com/2016/03/07/a-compassionate-education/

have contacted me to provide feedback explaining that it worked well with character exploration and analysis when studying text. Another teacher used the template with students that were learning about the global refugee crisis to help their students attempt to comprehend the difficulties that people have been experiencing and how that could possibly feel. I have seen another example of this resource adapted for MFL to practice sentence structure, past tense and using various adjectives. Empathy is not regarded as a key priority by everyone in education, but I think all educators want their students to become more tolerant, considerate and understanding. The template for this resource can be downloaded for free from my TES page.[87]

Thinking and Linking grids

Learning grids, also known as 6x6 grids, are very easy and straightforward to use in the classroom. The original idea is credited to Steve Bowkett and I first discovered learning grids in the tremendous book *Outstanding Teaching: Engaging Learners* by Andy Griffith and Mark Burns.

I have since adapted this idea in many ways, as shown throughout this book. The learning grid consists of 36 boxes, six numbers across and six numbers down. A class set of dice are required to use the learning grids. Students roll the dice twice (or a set of dice once) as they will need a number to use both vertically and horizontally. I adapted the grid to create a Thinking and Linking grid. This is more complex and challenging than the other examples provided in this book. As Willingham and other researchers and educators have specified, in order for students to truly remember information it must be something that they think about.

Coe has a simple formulation for learning – learning happens when people have to think hard. He states that he realises this is over-simplistic and vague, but he hopes teachers will ask questions during their planning like, 'Where in the lesson will students have to think hard?'[88]

---

87. K8SUE. (15 July 2016) 'In their shoes... empathy task'. (TES) Available at: https://www.tes.com/teaching-resource/in-their-shoes-empathy-task-11323911

88. Centre for Evaluation & Monitoring. (2013) 'Improving Education A triumph of hope over experience. Inaugural Lecture of Professor Robert Coe'. Durham, England: Durham University. Available at: http://www.cem.org/attachments/publications/ImprovingEducation2013.pdf

Thinking and Linking Grid: Causes of WW1. Roll the dice twice, explain how the keyword links to WW1 & can you make links between other words?

	1	2	3	4	5	6
1	Kaiser Wilhelm	Balkans	Schlieffen Plan	Alsace-Lorraince	Arms Race	Blackhand Gang
2	Triple Entente	Britain	Militarism	Gavrilo Princip	Franz Ferdinand	Aggression
3	France	Assassination	Italy	Belgium	Nationalism	King George
4	Empire	Serbia	Austria-Hungary	Morocco	Africa	Splendid Isolation
5	Russia	Tsar Nicholas	Imperialism	Treaty	Von Moltke	Germany
6	Navy	WeltPolitik	Dreadnought	Rivalry	Triple Alliance	Allies

A Thinking and Linking grid requires students to have a very good overview of a topic. I have found it be a good activity for consolidating and revising prior subject knowledge as well as checking understanding of subject-specific vocabulary.

The example above is a Thinking and Linking grid I made for a Year 9 lesson, with 36 boxes all connected to what students had been studying and learning about WW1. In pairs or small groups, students roll the dice twice to land on a box. The student then explains the connection between that keyword to WW1, for example how does the Kaiser link to WW1? Roll again to land on another box, students then have to try and link the second keyword with the previous word.

For example, if the first box they were required to discuss was Kaiser Wilhelm, a student would explain he was the leader of Germany in 1914 when war broke out (building on that answer further). Then after rolling the dice twice and having an additional keyword they would link that word back to the Kaiser, if they can. Some links are obvious, but others can be more of a challenge. So if the second box the student landed on happened to be 'Militarism', that would link to Kaiser Wilhelm because he was involved in an arms race that eventually led to WW1.

It can be complicated to explain to students but I modelled the game with a demonstration and they quickly grasped it. They made some excellent connections and links between factors.

I then adapted the Thinking and Linking grid as a revision activity for my GCSE students, but instead of using keywords I included images that represented different factors. The grid encourages students to make explicit links between connecting factors, which can be a requirement with extended examination answers and essays. This links with various examples of research I have discussed that encourage repeated exposure and rehearsal of materials and content to support long-term memory. You can download an example/template for the Thinking and Linking Grid for free from my TES page.[89]

The Civil Right Movement Learning Grid. Roll the dice twice. Explain the connection between the image and Civil Rights. Roll the dice again, can you make a link between the two images?

Secret mission cards

Your mission should you choose to accept it...

The secret mission cards are a resource that I created with specific students in mind. Students are often the inspiration behind my creative resources! This task is not explicitly linked to research I have read but not all tasks have to be. All students have their own unique strengths, areas for improvements and targets. These targets could be related to

89. K8SUE. (28 November 2016) 'Civil Rights Learning Grid revision game'. (TES) Available at: https://www.tes.com/teaching-resource/civil-rights-learning-grid-revision-game-11441918

behaviour, effort, literacy and so on. A way to help individuals focus on their specific targets and make progress in the lesson is through the personalised secret mission cards.

Examples include the following:

- Your secret mission this lesson is to answer three questions during class discussions. You must try to answer clearly and confidently when you think you know the answer.

- Your secret mission this lesson is to make sure all written work is completed. To do this you must stay focused in class.

- Your secret mission this lesson is to think of three questions to ask that you would like answered and that links with the lesson.

- Your secret mission this lesson is to spell all keywords correctly. To help you in this mission you can use a dictionary. Check your spellings with a peer or your teacher.

- Your secret mission this lesson is to ensure that you have used capital letters correctly throughout your written work.

- Your secret mission is to find out extra information about this topic and report back to the class next lesson with your findings.

The tasks can vary with each student, ranging in difficulty to suit the ability and needs of the individual, but this is an engaging method to help students achieve their target. The card acts as a reminder throughout the lesson about what they need to do. I have also connected the reward system with this task, to reward students who achieve or have tried their very best to complete their secret mission.

Not everyone in the class will receive a secret mission card, just the students that I had been working with to provide further support or challenge. This can be given to learners prior to the lesson or in a subtle way during the lesson.

The students responded really well to this, as there is a secretive and exciting element to the task. I have used this with younger classes and I know other teachers who have used this strategy in primary schools. After using the cards, I then asked for students to provide feedback and reflect on their mission to find out if they think the task helped them to progress. With lots of students their mission was accomplished! Again, I would not give this to students when they are receiving new material or information as I am aware this can be a distraction.

When consolidating or rehearsing material, the Secret Mission cards are designed to be a reminder for students to remain focused and aware of their target. The idea here is to make the targets stick so they can act on them, achieve and progress as a result.

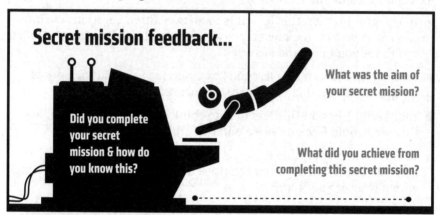

My Secret Mission cards were created easily and quickly using the free Typorama app available on iOS. To create secret mission cards using a browser I recommend Adobe Spark Post: https://spark.adobe.com/about/post

The learning styles debunked debate

I was introduced to the concept of learning styles during my Initial Teacher Training Year (ITT), although the existence of this theory in education has been around much longer. The theory focuses on how students will have a preference to learn visually, via auditory information, through reading or writing, or kinaesthetically. These are the most well recognised learning styles, but Frank Coffield and colleagues identified 71 different theories of learning styles.[90] This clearly demonstrates that the concept of tailoring lessons and experiences to suit an individual style is simply unrealistic and has very serious implications for teacher workload.

There was also a belief that students would learn better if instruction and activities were provided in a way that suited their preferred style. Teachers were encouraged to plan lessons that catered for the different needs and preferences of those in their classes, e.g. a kinaesthetic task that was designed to be more practical or information being communicated through audio for auditory learners.

90. Learning & Skills Research Centre. (2004) 'Learning styles and pedagogy in post-16 learning: A systematic and critical review.' Available at: http://www.leerbeleving.nl/wp-content/uploads/2011/09/learning-styles.pdf

I understand that learning styles encouraged different approaches to learning and that this also promotes variety in the classroom, which is important. I personally never liked the idea of learning styles simply because, from my experience, it added so much to my planning and workload by requiring the creation of different tasks to cater for the visual, auditory and kinaesthetic learners and their preferred style.

I was told that learning had to be personalised for every child in my class. I tried my best to do so by focusing on preferred learning styles. I still regularly see references to learning styles in school policies and literature, especially as an expectation with lesson observations. As a trainee teacher I would have never dared criticise this or any theory that I was introduced to. In recent years many other people in education have challenged and questioned learning styles.

In 2014 Professor Paul A. Howard-Jones asked over 900 teachers from different countries whether they agreed or disagreed (there was also an 'I don't know' option) with the following statement: 'Individuals learn better when they receive information in their preferred learning style (for example, visual, auditory or kinaesthetic).'[91]

The percentages below show how many teachers of those asked, selected that they agree with the statement:

United Kingdom – 93%

Netherlands – 96%

Turkey – 97%

Greece – 96 %

China – 97 %

This demonstrates how influential learning styles have become across different countries around the world. The results highlight that many classroom teachers are familiar with learning styles and are likely to use it in their classroom if they believe individuals learn better as a result of doing so. Howard-Jones refers to learning styles as a 'neuromyth'. Alan Crockard coined this term in the 1980s to refer to unscientific ideas about the brain in a medical capacity.[92] This term was redefined in an OECD report (2002) as 'a misconception generated by a misunderstanding, a misreading or misquoting of facts scientifically established to make a

---

91. Howard-Jones, P, A. (2014) 'Neuroscience and education: myths and messages', *Nature Reviews Neuroscience*, 15, pp. 817-824.
92. Ibid.

case for use of brain research in education and other contexts'.[93]

This same report stated that 'many myths and misconceptions have arisen around the mind and brain outside of the scientific community' and further added that 'the decade 1990-2000 was declared the 'Decade of the Brain' in the United States. Although much of this research has been of very high quality, some of its findings have been over-interpreted in terms of their implications for learning'.

Willingham has provided research to dispel and challenge the learning styles theory for many years now. He argues that using learning style theories in the classroom does not bring an advantage to students.[94] You can listen to his explanation on YouTube, with his video 'Learning Styles Don't Exist' that presently has over 329K views! Hirsch drawing on the work of Willingham noted that 'the evidence for individual learning styles is weak to non-existent'.[95] Nuthall also stated that there was no valid research evidence to support the claims that adapting classroom teaching to students' learning styles makes any difference to their learning.[96] Hattie's well-known survey of 150 factors that affect students' learning, highlighted that matching teaching to the learning styles of students was found to have an insignificant effect of little above zero.

In addition to the 'big' names in education such as Willingham, Hirsch and Hattie there are others that have addressed the problem with learning styles. Authors of *Make It Stick: The Science of Successful Learning discuss learning* styles explaining that they found very few studies designed to be capable of testing the validity of learning styles theory in education. The studies that they did found that virtually none validate it and others even contradict it.[97] Mccrea wrote that learners are more similar than different in how they learn and teachers labelling of students in this way (learning styles) can be limiting.[98]

93. OECD. (2002) 'Neuromythologies', *Understanding the Brain: Towards a New Learning Science*, pp. 69-77. Available at: http://www.oecd.org/education/ceri/31706603.pdf
94. Willingham, D, T. (2005) 'Ask the Cognitive Scientist: Do Visual, Auditory, and Kinesthetic Learners Need Visual, Auditory, and Kinesthetic Instruction?', *American Educator*.
95. Hirsch, E, D. (2016) *Why Knowledge Matters: Rescuing Our Children from Failed Educational Theories*. Cambridge, Massachusetts: Harvard Education Press, p. 11.
96. Nuthall, G. (2007) *The Hidden Lives of Learners*. Wellington, New Zealand: NZCER Press, p. 34.
97. Brown, P, C, Roediger, H, L & McDaniel, M, A. (2014) *Make It Stick: The Science of Successful Learning*. Cambridge, Massachusetts: Harvard Education Press, p. 145.
98. Mccrea, P. (2017) *Memorable Teaching: Leveraging memory to build deep and durable learning in the classroom*. Scotts Valley, California: CreateSpace, p. 34.

The Education Endowment Foundation, known widely as the EEF, is an independent charity dedicated to breaking the link between family income and educational achievement to raise progress for all learners, regardless of their socio-economic background. The EEF also provide teachers and Senior Leader Teams (SLTs) with a variety of research summaries and practical tools that have been designed to improve classroom practice and boost learning. It is worth visiting this website and viewing their toolkits and summary reports, all are free to access and do not require any registration.

The EEF have stated 'there is very limited evidence for any consistent set of 'learning styles' that can be used reliably to identify genuine differences in the learning needs of young people and evidence suggests that it is unhelpful to assign learners to groups or categories on the basis of a supposed learning style'.[99] It also adds that 'labelling students as particular kinds of learners is likely to undermine their belief that they can succeed through effort and to provide an excuse for failure'.

Finally, below is the abstract from an article written by Paul A. Kirschner (2017) entitled 'Stop propagating the learning styles myth'.

We all differ from each other in a multitude of ways and as such we also prefer many different things whether it is music, food or learning. Because of this, many students, parents, teachers, administrators and even researchers feel that it is intuitively correct to say that since different people prefer to learn visually, auditively, kinaesthetically or whatever other way one can think of, we should also tailor teaching, learning situations and learning materials to those preferences. Is this a problem? The answer is a resounding: Yes!

Broadly speaking, there are a number of major problems with the notion of learning styles.

First, there is quite a difference between the way that someone prefers to learn and that which actually leads to effective and efficient learning.

Second, a preference for how one studies is not a learning style. Most so-called learning styles are based on types; they classify people into distinct groups. The assumption that people cluster into distinct groups, however, receives very little support from objective studies.

---

99. Education Endowment Foundation. (No date) 'Learning styles'. (Education Endowment Foundation) Available at: https://educationendowmentfoundation.org.uk/evidence-summaries/teaching-learning-toolkit/learning-styles/

Finally, nearly all studies that report evidence for learning styles fail to satisfy just about all of the key criteria for scientific validity. This article delivers an evidence-informed plea to teachers, administrators and researchers to stop propagating the learning styles myth.[100]

The debate is not about whether people have a preferred style or not, it focuses on whether learning this way improves or impacts learning. Researchers Harold Pashler, Mark McDaniel, Doug Rohrer and Robert Bjork published a literature review of learning styles research where they outlined that their review of the literature 'disclosed ample evidence that children and adults will, if asked, express preferences about how they prefer information to be presented to them.

There is also plentiful evidence arguing that people differ in the degree to which they have some fairly specific aptitudes for different kinds of thinking and for processing different types of information'.[101] They concluded in their review, that there is not an adequate evidence base to support or justify the use of learning styles assessments, into general educational practice.

The evidence against using learning styles for lesson planning and to improve student attainment appears staggering. I have admitted that I personally dislike the theory so, therefore, my personal bias could be viewed as influencing the research that I am selecting and presenting. I have also searched for arguments that defend the use of learning styles in the classroom. I tried to do so with an open mind. Whilst searching for literature defending the learning styles theory, the support I found predominantly came from teachers.

These teachers have argued that they believe their experiences in the classroom show that students respond well to an activity linked to their preferred style of learning. Teachers are clearly well intentioned. They want to provide enjoyable, personal and individualised experiences for their students, but the argument is that this can detract from how effective learning strategies actually are.

Currently, learning styles is still an area where teacher experience and research can clash. There are a large and growing amount of teachers who have welcomed the debunking of many myths in education, notably learning styles. I value the role of teacher experience, instinct and professional judgment and they should not be dismissed in the name of

100. Kirschner, P, A. (2017) 'Stop propagating the learning styles myth', Computers & Education, 106, pp. 166–171.
101. Pashler, H, McDaniel, M, Rohrer, D & Bjork, R. (2008) 'Learning Styles: Concepts and Evidence', 9(3). Available at: https://www.psychologicalscience.org/journals/pspi/PSPI_9_3.pdf

educational research, but we have to consider and combine the evidence that we have with all of those factors.

I have had the privilege of attending a workshop session and listening to a keynote presentation delivered by author and educator Ian Gilbert. He is incredibly knowledgeable, experienced and well-respected within the profession. In his second edition of *Why do I Need A Teacher When I've Got Google: The essential guide to the big issues for every teacher*, Gilbert argues that 'the idea of VAK has proven itself useful as a tool, not for labelling students, never do that, but for helping them learn quickly and in a way that works for them. Especially when plan A hasn't.'[102] This once again made me reflect on whether or not we dismiss learning styles completely, or instead view it as a tool to support learning as Gilbert suggested.

I discovered a blog post by teacher, writer, filmmaker and director Carol Black where she puts forward various arguments in defence of learning styles. Black writes that, 'the concepts of learning styles, rather than rigid pigeon holes or stereotypes, can be seen as a flexible heuristic device for stimulating creativity and problem solving in learning and teaching'.[103] A different blog post that was shared online became a hot topic of discussion on Twitter. This post focused on seven different learning styles, including tailoring lessons to suit interpersonal or solitary learners and mathematical learners.[104] This blog argues that 'while there is no evidence to support learning styles... we can assume that categorising students into the above styles is only helpful practice'. This illustrates that despite people being aware of the research (or lack of research supporting learning styles) they are still choosing to promote and encourage learning styles in the classroom. Should this topic continue to be up for debate and discussion when it so clearly seems to be dismissed by educational researchers?

Author and editor, Dr Christian Jarrett has explored why he believes the learning style theory continues to linger in education despite the debunking by leading experts in cognitive psychology. Jarrett writes that although it feels as though we learn better by using our preferred learning style, we don't.[105] He also warns that another issue with students using their preferred learning style and feeling that they learn

102. Gilbert, I. (2010) *Why Do I Need a Teacher When I've got Google? The Essential Guide to the Big Issues for Every 21st Century Teacher.* Abingdon, Oxfordshire: Routledge, p. 172.
103. Black, C. (No date) 'Science/Fiction'. (Carol Black) Available at: http://carolblack.org/science-fiction/
104. Avado. (13 August 2018) 'What are the 7 different learning styles and do they work?' (AVADO) Available at: https://blog.avadolearning.com/the-7-different-learning-styles-and-what-they-mean
105. Jarrett, C. (5 October 2016) 'It feels as though we learn better via our preferred learning style, but we don't'. (The British Psychological Society) Available at: https://digest.bps.org.uk/2016/10/05/it-feels-as-though-we-learn-better-via-our-preferred-learning-style-but-we-dont

better, when that might not be true, is that it can create a false sense of confidence in what students have actually learned or what has been transferred to long-term memory.

Nuthall suggests that the learning styles idea became so widely accepted for cultural reasons, 'we live in a culture that emphasises individual freedoms – where choice is increasingly seen as a basic right. The idea that everyone is fundamentally different and has the right to be treated as different fits well with our modern culture.'[106]

Nuthall further added that learning styles are about motivation and management, not learning and that it is an important distinction that teachers should be aware of. Whilst searching for literature about learning styles I found far more papers, articles and books that denounce learning styles than promote it, but it is still being widely shared in education as an effective learning strategy.

Many educators initially believed learning styles was supported with scientific research, it is a theory that seems very plausible. American educator and blogger Blake Harvard has expressed his concern about the spread of learning myths in education.[107] Harvard warns: 'These myths are not harmless. They shape the training of our teaching methods incorrectly and can create aversive conditions for our students.'[108] Educators can learn from the learning styles debate and realise the importance of engaging with research carefully, through various papers and reviews before fully embracing or embedding a new idea or theory in the classroom. A popular concept today could be the next debunked myth tomorrow.

The literature referencing scientific studies and research, explicitly explaining that using a student's preferred learning style does not improve academic attainment or achievement, is overwhelming. There is also a consensus that providing variety and different types of tasks and activities can be good practice in the classroom. It is also important that when challenging ideas and beliefs held by others regarding education and how children learn that we do so in a respectful and professional manner. When it comes to debate it is important to remember that we are in this profession together and we want the very best for the students in our care, despite our differences. It is clear that there is a need to

106. Nuthall, G. (2007) *The Hidden Lives of Learners*. Wellington, New Zealand: NZCER Press, p. 34.
107. Theeffortfuleducator. (17 July 2017) 'Learning Myths vs. Learning Facts'. (The Effortful Educator) Available at: https://theeffortfuleducator.com/2017/07/17/learning-myths-vs-learning-facts/
108. Harvard, B. (2017) 'But... We Do Learn From People We Don't Like'. (Psych Learning Curve) Available at: http://psychlearningcurve.org/learn-from-people-we-dont-like/

challenge the idea in schools that students will learn more efficiently using their preferred learning style, we can do this by using the wealth of evidence we have at our disposal.

A student once refused to complete a task I had set that was focused on retrieval practice because he argued it did not suit his preferred learning style. Parents have also become aware of learning styles, with some expecting or demanding the teacher to cater for their child's individual learning style and preferences. Students and parents are familiar with this theory and believe it to be scientifically supported by research when it is not. Students and parents also need educating about metacognition, which refers to students thinking about thinking or learning and be informed as to what the most effective strategies to support learning actually are.

The EEF teaching and learning toolkit has rated metacognition – described as 'learning about learning' – and self-regulation, where learners are aware of their strengths, weaknesses and are able to set realistic targets to focus on and motivate themselves, as being 'high impact for very low cost'. This explicitly suggests these are very important areas teachers and students should be investing in. Bjork and Bjork have written about the importance of students being able to manage their own learning activities and that learning how to learn is the ultimate survival tool.[109] Instead of focusing on what type of preferred style of learning students have we should focus on what are the most effective methods of supporting learning and long-term memory.

109. Bjork, E & Bjork, R. (2011) 'Making things hard on yourself, but in a good way: Creating desirable difficulties to enhance learning', *Psychology and the Real World: Essays Illustrating Fundamental Contributions to Society.*

Summary

- Short-term memory (working memory) is limited in capacity in relation to how much information we can store and for how long.

- Long-term memory is unlimited in its capacity. Our aim as educators should be to ensure information is stored in and can be retrieved from long-term memory.

- There are different types of long-term memory: episodic, semantic and procedural. All are important in the learning process, but the focus should be on semantic (meaning).

- Cognitive Load Theory by John Sweller explains that teachers need to limit the amount of new information they provide to students so that they do not overload working memory.

- Teachers do not need to plan lessons or activities to cater for individual preferred 'learning styles'. There is a plethora of literature explicitly stating that this does not improve academic attainment or achievement.

Recommended reading

Why Do I Need a Teacher When I've Got Google? The essential guide to the big issues for every teacher by Ian Gilbert (2014)

What Every Teacher Needs To Know About Psychology by David Didau and Nick Rose (2016)

Memorable Teaching: Leveraging Memory to Build Deep and Durable learning in the classroom by Peps Mccrea (2017)

Psychology in the Classroom: A Teacher's Guide To What Works by Jonathan Firth and Marc Smith (2018)

The Ingredients for Great Teaching by Pedro De Bruyckere (2018)

CHAPTER 3:
TEACHING WITH TECHNOLOGY FOR IMPACT

'Technology can amplify great teaching but great technology cannot replace poor teaching.'
Andreas Schleicher (OECD)

Not surprisingly, nine out of ten households in the United Kingdom have internet access and daily internet usage has more than doubled since 2006 (Office for National Statistics Internet Access 2018). We are all aware that technology has become more important and dominant in the lives of young people. I discovered some surprising statistics about screen time that teachers should be aware and mindful of. OFCOM reported that:

- 43% of three and four-year old children use YouTube and 53% go online for nearly eight hours a week.

- 79% of children aged five to seven go online for around nine hours a week.

- 94% of children aged 8 to 11 go online for nearly 13 and a half hours a week.

- 99% of children aged 12 to 15 go online for nearly 21 hours a week.

In addition to this 83% of children between the ages 12 to 15 have a smart phone and 74% have a social media profile.[110] This further highlights the importance of e-safety teaching. Online safety is an area where senior leaders, teachers and parents all need to collaborate, to ensure the safety and wellbeing of children using the internet and new technologies. This issue is being recognised by governments, the media, schools and parents.

---

110. Ofcom. (2017) 'Children and Parents: Media Use and Attitudes Report'. London, England: Office of Communications. Available at: https://www.ofcom.org.uk/___data/assets/pdf_file/0020/108182/children-parents-media-use-attitudes-2017.pdf

The new iOS 12 update will now include a feature where Apple device users can monitor and become more aware of their own screen time and parents can monitor their children's usage of Apple technologies. There is also a free app by YouTube suitable for children age four and above called YouTube Kids. This app ensures that children can be engaged, entertained and educated in a simple and secure way, providing safer online experiences for young children. Google also have a fantastic set of resources for young children to learn about responsible use of technology called 'Be Internet Legends' with associated resources, lesson plans and website: https://beinternetlegends.withgoogle.com/en-gb/toolkit.

There are regular claims that we are in the midst of a digital revolution – an on-going process of social, political and economic change that has been brought about and influenced by new digital technologies.[111] Despite the growing importance of technology in society I won't suggest that we should prepare students for jobs that don't exist yet. Whilst there is certainly truth in this statement we also know that there are many careers and professions that will continue to exist in the near future too.

Also, how can we prepare students for jobs that don't exist yet if we don't know what these jobs are? We can prepare students by ensuring they are literate with a wide range of skills and knowledge at their disposal. The rate that technology is developing is exponential and even more impressive are the skills young people are adopting to utilise these new technologies to their advantage.

I am an ambassador for the purposeful use of technology in the classroom. I can also be sceptical about the use of technology in an educational setting. I think it is important as educators that we do not become focused on a specific device or brand, especially with the increase in branded ambassadors across schools. The safety of our students online should always be the priority. This is not to say that brand ambassadors do not carefully consider e-safety, but the focus can be shifted onto the device instead of the learning and that is concerning.

Research about the impact of technology in the classroom is available but is still in the early stages. The OECD (2015) report points out that 'we have not yet become good enough at the kind of pedagogies that make the most of technology'[112] and this is not surprising when we

111. Kaye, L. (Ed.) (2016) *Young Children in a Digital Age. Supporting learning and development with technology in early years.* Abingdon, Oxfordshire: Routledge, p. 13.
112. OECD. (2015) 'Students, Computers and Learning: Making the Connection.' Paris, France: OECD. Available at: https://read.oecd-ilibrary.org/education/students-computers-and-learning_9789264239555-en#page6

evaluate teacher support and professional development. According to the EEF 'evidence suggests that technology approaches should be used to supplement other teaching, rather than replace more traditional approaches'[113] which firmly echoes my own views about technology within education. The EEF report (2018) shows that evidence suggests 'it is unlikely that particular technologies can bring about changes in learning directly, but some have the potential to enable changes in teaching and learning interactions'.

The report further adds that technology can support teachers providing more effective feedback and motivate students to practice more. We need to have the right approach when using technology in the classroom ensuring implementation is successful, purposeful and effective. Technology should not be at the heart or centre of learning, the curriculum should be, but instead technology should be used as a tool to support learning and reduce teacher workload, where possible.

Teacher confidence and support with technology

The different levels of confidence using technology can vary widely amongst teachers. Technology is an area where schools can really struggle to maintain consistency amongst staff, perhaps because of rapid changes and advances. One teacher might be using the iPads every lesson or providing flipped learning opportunities for their students in their classroom, however the teacher in the classroom next door might consider himself or herself to be a 'Luddite' with no interest or intention of ever using technology, and seem happy with textbooks as the main learning resource. I am not critical of either teacher, although both teachers need to have the right mindset with technology; it is not all encompassing, but it is not the enemy either.

Matthew J. Koehler and Punya Mishra noted that 'many teachers earned degrees at a time when educational technology was at a very different stage of development than it is today. It is, thus, not surprising that they do not consider themselves sufficiently prepared to use technology in the classroom and often do not appreciate its value or relevance to teaching and learning'.[114] There is also the obvious issue that technology can often be an area where students are more knowledgeable than their teachers.

113. Education Endowment Foundation. (No date) 'Learning styles'. (Education Endowment Foundation) Available at: https://educationendowmentfoundation.org.uk/evidence-summaries/teaching-learning-toolkit/learning-styles/
114. Koehler, M, J & Mishra, P. (2009) 'What Is Technological Pedagogical Content Knowledge?', *Contemporary Issues in Technology and Teacher Education*, 9(1), pp. 60-70.

This is not always true as researchers have discovered that university students do not have deep technological knowledge but instead they have limited knowledge of basic office suite skills, email, text messaging, social media, and browsing the internet.[115] There are a range of variables that will impact teacher confidence with technology in the classroom. Mark Anderson has designed a model to describe teacher confidence with the use of technology, based on the work of Mandinach and Cline (1996). The flow chart describes the different stages of teacher confidence and competence ranging from 'survival' to 'innovation'. Where do you think you are according to this scale?

Teacher confidence in the use of technology
based upon the work of Mandinach and Cline

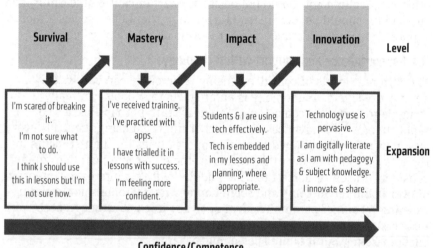

Technology is not always reliable and there can be a wide range of issues that some would prefer to avoid completely. If schools are keen to use technology – which a lot of schools are investing in – then regular training, support and guidance will be required for staff regardless of their confidence or ability with technology. Steve Wheeler, in his thought provoking and fascinating book Learning with 'e's: educational theory and practice in the digital age, identifies that 'introducing technology into schools is not difficult. Ensuring that it is used appropriately is another matter entirely'.[116]

115. Kirschner, P, A & van Merriënbowe, J. (2013) 'Do Learners Really Know Best? Urban Legends in Education', Educational Psychologist, 48(3), pp. 169–183.
116. Wheeler, S. (2015) Learning with 'e's: educational theory and practice in the digital age. Carmarthen, Wales: Crown House Publishing, p. 16.

This is so true! I am aware of many schools, both in the UK and internationally, that have spent considerable amounts of money purchasing technology, in the form of laptops or tablets and then simply handed them to staff – off you go! This is a missed opportunity. There has been the assumption that staff will know how to use this new technology when, in reality, they may or may not. This approach shows a clear lack of support, guidance and instruction. There is the expectation that a lot of money has been invested in this technology so teachers better use it. It does not have to be this way.

There are a few issues with this strategy. One is how to actually use apps, tools and hardware. The other issue is then how to apply these things in ways that can support or enhance learning or reduce workload. It does not just happen by giving someone a device.

If a school has decided to invest in technology, in the initial stages of this process senior management could ask for volunteers, perhaps from different departments, to trial the technology in the classroom and provide feedback. It would be useful to ask someone who is very capable when using technology, someone likely to enjoy using it and flourish in the classroom with minimal help or guidance, in addition to asking someone who lacks confidence using technology and may seem reluctant, so that they can provide feedback as to how they – a novice when using technology – found the experience. This will illustrate how experts and novices are represented in your trial.

Some schools invest in technology just for middle and senior leaders, what about the classroom teachers – the people delivering lessons day in and day out who could also really benefit from the technology. It can create a divisive, hierarchical system that classroom teachers are not worthy of the expensive device. It is not just money that needs to be invested when purchasing technology, schools need to be prepared to invest in time and support for staff too. This investment might be viewed as best being related to staff training, which of course is essential but significant funds will need to be put aside for ensuring sustainability and, equally important, the infrastructure that supports the use of technology such as technical support, Wi-Fi, broadband, and so on.

In their incredible book *What Does This Look Like In The Classroom? Bridging the Gap Between Research and Practice*, Carl Hendrick and Robin Macpherson discuss a range of topics linked to education and research. They also pose a selection of questions about how to implement this research into the classroom, to some of the world's leading experts in these fields. Macpherson addresses the issue surrounding staff training and professional development, focusing on the use of technology. Macpherson recognises that 'teachers need to be informed about the options, trained in how to use the software and hardware and supported as they begin to use it in the classroom. The delivery of this training needs to be research-informed on how students will learn, rather than tech-informed about how it runs. This is a strategic error that is all too common in schools' and I agree fully.[117]

Once again, we need to place the emphasis on the learning, not the tools. I have been able to learn a lot about technology by using social media to follow experts online, reading regular blogs about the latest developments and I also read books dedicated to 'EdTech'. I have also been fortunate to attend various educational events that have provided opportunities to learn more from others about new technologies.

Additionally, I have also received support in school and I have led sessions myself about how I use technology in the classroom. Colleagues have found it refreshing when I discuss technology in the classroom because I am not an ICT or computing teacher, although we should take advantage of their expertise and skills. I don't have any formal qualifications with computing or technology; I am a history teacher using technology confidently and appropriately to enhance learning – as any teacher can.

I haven't always been confident when it comes to using technology in the classroom. I didn't receive any training during my ITT year about how to use and navigate an Interactive Whiteboard (IWB). As an NQT, I had my own classroom for the first time along with my own IWB. I didn't know how to use it so I resorted to utilising it as a projector (a very expensive projector). I also had my whiteboard to write on, that I would use every lesson.

At the end of my third year of teaching my line manager asked if I had ever used the IWB in a lesson, I was honest and said no, although I quickly regretted being so open. She then decided that my professional development target for the following year would be to make full use of this equipment in my classroom to enhance teaching and learning, showing me how to use it in a variety of ways. I observed her and other colleagues use the IWB in their lessons and I was encouraged to do the same. I could never calibrate it or get it to work for me – they had made it look so easy! I did use it more but always reluctantly and sometimes with disastrous results.

117. Hendrick, C & Macpherson, R. (2017) *What does this look like in the classroom? Bridging the Gap Between Research and Practice*. Melton, Suffolk: John Catt Educational Ltd, p. 188.

Later that year my line manager asked to observe me using the IWB in a lesson, this filled me with sheer dread. I kept it simple, nothing too complicated and I had a solid plan B. The technology was not reliable in the lesson but I was glad my line manager could see this because then she could understand why I would rather not use it. This links with the TPACK model discussed below, which highlights that successful integration of technology does not equal using technology all the time. It should be within the professional decision-making domain of the teacher to decide whether or not to utilise technology based on their skills, confidence and whether or not the technology will support or enhance teaching and learning.

That wasn't the end of my IWB nightmare. That same year BBC Wales came to visit my school to find out how the leadership team supports staff with professional development opportunities. I was asked in advance if I would be interviewed. I purchased a new outfit and, more importantly, I had plenty to discuss about professional development. The BBC came and took some shots in my classroom, during an actual lesson, to include in the segment and then I was interviewed. The interview lasted about 45 minutes and I really enjoyed it. When the BBC segment was aired, my 45-minute discussion was reduced to two to three minutes. Although I was told in advance a lot of the content wouldn't be used, I still had no idea as to what would make the final cut. The programme that aired focused on how I had been developing my use of the IWB! I was gutted. After that everyone assumed I was the expert, I had been filmed by the BBC talking about my IWB, so I must be!

My friends and family wanted to know more about this piece of modern equipment. My colleagues were now seeking advice or asking to observe my lessons to see how I use this technology to innovate my classroom. Teachers from across Wales were contacting me online asking questions about the IWB and if I would be prepared to deliver CPD at their schools on this aspect of technology. I thought the IWB would haunt me throughout my teaching career, but luckily it didn't.

I still don't like an IWB but that's due to my personal preference and bad experiences in the classroom. My lack of knowledge and understanding about how it worked or how I should use it in my lessons contributed to my negative attitude and mindset. When I did observe colleagues they were making excellent use of this resource and I am not dismissing the IWB, I am only reflecting on and sharing my experience. Wheeler has commented that 'interactive whiteboards, when in the hands of an innovative teacher can enhance and enrich the entire learning encounter with students becoming actively involved in knowledge production as their teachers'. When it comes to using technology in the classroom, confidence is key. The right attitude and mindset are essential too, otherwise using technology will be detrimental to your teaching and, as a result, your students learning too.

Technology features in all chapters of this book, which illustrates how it has become embedded in my teaching practice, although I do regularly teach lessons without technology too. Technology will never replace teachers, despite some sensational claims in the media. Whilst technology can support teachers, the need for human interaction and other personal qualities will always be fundamental in a school environment. The attitude towards technology amongst educators is very mixed and I understand why. There are EdTech gurus who genuinely believe technology is the magic silver bullet answer to all the problems within education (it is not). Then there are others who view technology as a financial drain, a waste of time or an unwanted distraction in the classroom. Wherever you sit on your point of view about technology, it is clear that it is too expensive and, therefore, too important to get it wrong.

I am competent and self-assured using technology. I consider very carefully when and why I use it to support learning. If you do use technology in the classroom then hopefully some of the apps, websites or ideas I suggest will be of use to you. If you aren't using technology in the classroom then I hope there will be something in this book that encourages you to try and will result in a positive impact on your students learning and your workload.

The SAMR Model

I was reading the excellent book *Perfect ICT Every Lesson* by Mark Anderson when I was first introduced to the SAMR taxonomy. 'SAMR' is an acronym that stands for Substitution, Augmentation, Modification and Redefinition. Technology allows us to do things differently, more quickly or efficiently and it can also allow us to do things that would not be possible without it; this is essentially the concept behind the SAMR model, created by Dr Ruben Puentedura (2010). The SAMR model attempts to break down the different ways in which teaching and learning tasks can be transformed using technology.

Substitution: Tech acts as a direct tool substitute but there is no functional change.

Augmentation: Tech acts as a direct tool substitute, with some functional improvement.

Modification: Tech allows for significant task redesign.

Redefinition: Tech allows for the creation of new tasks, previously inconceivable.[118]

At the substitution stage technology directly replaces a traditional method, an example of this would be where writing notes becomes substituted by typing up notes. For this to be substitution, the activity has no functional change. The use of spell checker and other features can be considered augmentation as there would be some functional improvement. Some research suggests that taking notes electronically is less effective than writing, when focusing on retention and learning.[119] This is due to the distractions that can occur when using laptops or devices. This can be offset in the classroom through the use of device management solutions that help to keep learners focused upon only using one tool at a time.

Self-regulation, however, and good behaviour for learning can impact on this if attitudes towards learning in a classroom are good. Studies have also shown a direct comparison between students that record notes on a laptop and those that take notes longhand. Those that write down information performed better answering conceptual questions and people who made notes using a laptop tended to 'transcribe lectures verbatim rather than processing information and reframing it in their own words'.[120] Although, we do know that there are specific students who benefit greatly from typing. Substitution and augmentation are classed as providing enhancement to tasks rather than transforming them.

The modification and redefinition categories are both linked to transformative tasks in the classroom, things that could not be done without the aid of technology. There are lots of examples of modification and redefinition in this chapter. Virtual Reality (VR) has the ability to completely transform activities by allowing students to carry out experiences that would be not possible without that technology. The transformation category can provide unique opportunities to support learning, but ultimately if the same outcome can be achieved without technology then we need to consider whether it is necessary or not.

---

118. Puentedura, R, R. (2009) 'Learning, Technology, and the SAMR Model: Goals, Processes, and Practice'. Available at: http://www.hippasus.com/rrpweblog/archives/2014/06/29/LearningTechnologySAMRModel.pdf
119. Mueller, P, A & Oppenheimer, D, M. (2014) 'The Pen Is Mightier Than the Keyboard: Advantages of Longhand Over Laptop Note Taking', *Psychological Science*, 25(6), pp. 1159–1168.
120. Ibid.

Anderson, amongst many other educators and bloggers, have warned that SAMR should not be viewed as a ladder.[121] One interpretation of the model is that it promotes a series of stages, aspiring and progressing towards redefinition. It has also received criticism because some teachers interpreted the transformation phase as being more effective for learning, while others have highlighted that is not always true and the focus should be task redesign. This view can shift the focus of lesson planning onto technology, focusing on how we can transform learning tasks rather than focusing on the content of the learning.

Mark Samberg, educator and blogger, has pointed out a problem that can occur when using technology and focusing too much on redefinition. Samberg writes, 'A redefinition lesson may be shiny, it might be engaging, it may be interesting and it may be effective. But it might also take five days for the same instructional benefit that could be achieved in a substitution lesson in an hour.'

This is a very valid point; if a significant amount of time will be required to provide instruction and guidance with how to use the technology, but the same outcome can be achieved quicker without technology then that will be more beneficial. Anderson regularly shares that if the time required to prepare a lesson with technology would take longer than the lesson itself, we should carefully reflect upon whether or not its use can be justified. In a world where teacher workload is high and time is tight, whilst technology can make us more efficient, if it means we end up spending large amounts of time just preparing our lessons so we can use technology we should think carefully about whether it is worth the effort.

We need to reflect on our use of technology. Why are we using the technology in the classroom? Is it quicker, more effective or is it being used just to do something that requires technology? Could the same outcome be achieved quicker and more effectively without the (or minimal) use of technology? The SAMR model is not supported by evidence but I don't think that is a valid reason to dismiss SAMR. The SAMR model has helped me greatly when it comes to using technology as it helps me to reflect about when I use technology, how I use technology and why I have decided to use technology with my students.

121. Anderson, M. (25 May 2015) 'SAMR Is Not a Ladder, A Word of Warning'. (ICT Evangelist) Available at: https://ictevangelist.com/samr-is-not-a-ladder-purposeful-use-of-tech/

The evolution of TPACK

The TPACK model Koehler and Mishra (2006) builds on the work of Lee S. Shulman (1986) where he developed the PCK model. Shulman has written about the importance of both content and pedagogical knowledge within education in a journal.[122] Shulman posed the following questions in his article: 'whether in the spirit of the 1870s, when pedagogy was essentially ignored, or in the 1980s, when content is conspicuously absent, has there always been a cleavage between the two? Has it always been asserted that one either knows content and pedagogy is secondary and unimportant, or that one knows pedagogy and is not held to account for content?'

Shulman provides an overview of previous testing and examinations that teachers have had to complete which focused on one aspect more so than the other and the failure to recognise the importance of both content knowledge and pedagogical methods. Shulman became frustrated with literature focusing on certain aspects of teaching such as classroom management, activities and planning lessons but neglected the content of the lessons taught and quality of explanations.

Shulman and his colleagues wanted to readdress this imbalance that he refers to this as the 'Missing Paradigm'. Teachers will have their necessary qualifications that represent their knowledge in a specific domain and teaching qualification, but Shulman was concerned about the transition of teachers from being expert learners to novice teachers. He stressed the importance of blending content with different elements of the teaching process.

---

122. Shulman, L, S. (1986) 'Those Who Understand: Knowledge Growth in Teaching', *Educational Researcher*, 15(2), pp. 4-14. Available at: http://www.fisica.uniud.it/URDF/masterDidSciUD/materiali/pdf/Shulman_1986.pdf

PCK – Pedagogical Content Knowledge

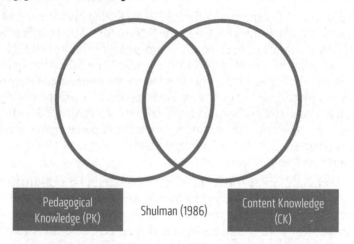

Pedagogical Knowledge (PK)   Shulman (1986)   Content Knowledge (CK)

TPACK focuses on the combination of 'Technological, Pedagogical and Content Knowledge' and the first article about this was published in 2006, titled Technological, Pedagogical Content Knowledge: A new framework for teacher knowledge by Koehler and Mishra. Since 2009 it has been recorded that TPACK has featured in over 1100 journal articles and book chapters and almost 300 dissertations and over 25 books have written about TPACK as the central theoretical construct.[123] This illustrates how influential this model has become in education.

It is a conceptual framework that claims the successful integration of technology to support students learning requires a teacher to have the following:

- Strong content knowledge of the specific subject being taught.

- Solid understanding of effective pedagogy.

- Knowledge and experience of different methods of teaching and learning.

- A good grasp of the technology that could be used.

Koehler and Mishra write, 'at the heart of good teaching with technology are three core components: content, pedagogy and technology, plus the relationships among and between them.'[124]

123. Mishra, P. (10 September 2018) 'The TPACK diagram gets an upgrade'. (Punya Mishra's Web) Available at: https://www.punyamishra.com/2018/09/10/the-tpack-diagram-gets-an-upgrade/
124. Koehler, M, J & Mishra, P. (2009) 'What Is Technological Pedagogical Content Knowledge?', *Contemporary Issues in Technology and Teacher Education*, 9(1), pp. 60-70.

A teacher can use their experience and knowledge of effective teaching methods to consider how to incorporate the technology into these methods. If the teacher lacks the knowledge and understanding of how the technology works, then this will cause problems and end up being a barrier to learning. In the same way, if a teacher knows how to use technology and has a good comprehension of teaching and learning approaches but has limited knowledge of the subject content then this can also have a negative impact on learning. Knowing subject material but having a lack of knowledge on how to communicate that information through pedagogy will also be unsuccessful.

When using technology, all three aspects are very important and need to complement one another. If a teacher has deep subject knowledge, is able to use effective pedagogical strategies combined with a good understanding of the technology being used, then all of this can lead to greater success in the classroom. It is also important to recognise that this is not about using technology more. Probably the most important element of the technological element is that it is down to the professional choice of teachers whether to use or not use the technology. Koehler and Mishra write, 'TPACK is truly meaningful, deeply skilled teaching with or without (because sometimes this can be the best choice) technology.'[125]

---

125. Ibid.

TPACK – Technological, Pedagogical and Content Knowledge

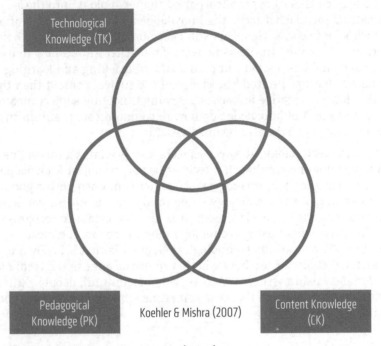

Technological Knowledge (TK)

Pedagogical Knowledge (PK)

Koehler & Mishra (2007)

Content Knowledge (CK)

The TPACK diagram gets an upgrade (2018)

In September 2018, Mishra revealed the final version of TPACK, which includes a focus on contextual knowledge. Mishra writes 'contextual knowledge would be everything from a teacher's awareness of the kind of technologies available for them and their students; to their knowledge of the school, district and state policies that they have to function within'.[126] This is clearly all encompassing taking into consideration a wide range of factors teachers have to consider when integrating technology successfully into the classroom, some that are out of the control of the teacher. The creators did not want to add another CK for contextual knowledge as the original CK represents content knowledge. Instead, the new revised model has an outer circle or section that is referred to as XK for Contextual Knowledge, as shown below.

---

126. Mishra, P. (10 September 2018) 'The TPACK diagram gets an upgrade'. (Punya Mishra's Web) Available at: https://www.punyamishra.com/2018/09/10/the-tpack-diagram-gets-an-upgrade/

TPACK – Technological, Pedagogical, Contextual and Content Knowledge

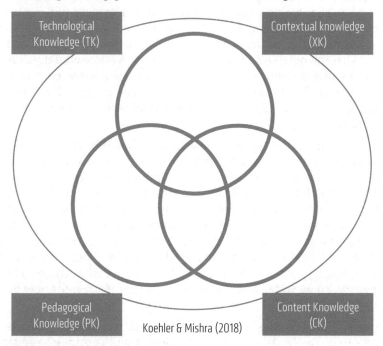

Koehler & Mishra (2018)

TPACCK – the new TPACK perhaps?

I discussed combining subject knowledge and pedagogical knowledge with knowledge of cognitive psychology in Chapter 2. The creators of TPACK didn't want to add an extra C but the extra C, in my proposed TPACCK model, refers to cognitive knowledge and understanding. Essentially, we should combine our content and pedagogical knowledge with our understanding of cognitive psychology when using technology. I know this sounds complex, but it really is not.

I have previously discussed using quizzing to support retrieval practice. To create a challenging and appropriate quiz for students to complete requires subject knowledge. Using quizzing as a method to support learning is a pedagogical strategy and demonstrates our understanding of cognitive psychology and the benefits of retrieval practice. Finally, we are using technology efficiently to create, deliver and record quizzes. Without the subject knowledge we would be unable to write questions that cover a wide breadth and depth of content. Without pedagogical knowledge we would not consider effective techniques such as quizzing.

Being unaware of the impact of retrieval practice for supporting learning would mean that we only use quizzing as an assessment tool instead of a learning tool. Attempting to use technology but failing to understand how to create a quiz online or instruct students how to respond and engage with the quiz will also cause problems. A successful quiz on Kahoot or Quizizz requires the teacher to have solid knowledge of all factors involved in the learning process and task design. This does not just apply to quizzes, this is relevant to all tasks involving, or not involving technology.

It could be argued that cognitive psychology should be considered as part of our pedagogical knowledge (PK) or even the new addition of contextual knowledge (XK) as it focuses on how memory works and how we can use this information to support learning. Since the TPACK model was introduced however, our understanding of cognitive psychology has become better known, respected and worthy of inclusion in the debate to help move it forwards. It is important that we embrace the findings of this important field of research and think carefully about how we choose to use technology based upon what we know about what works. The findings we know so far and the research taking place right now delve into the complex area of how children learn.

There are still many questions left unanswered in this field. There is still progress to be made. Just as new technologies will continue to advance in the future and teachers will continue to need support to improve their technological knowledge, the same can be argued of cognitive psychology. As new research develops explaining what does and does not work or what works best, teachers need to stay informed and then apply this to their practice.

I believe my TPACCK model will encourage teachers to carefully consider how different aspects can impact teaching and learning and recognise the value and importance of cognitive psychology and science. My aim is that by ensuring depth of knowledge in all four of these factors is strong, by knowing about what works or works best, teachers can look to technology to see how it can best achieve those goals. TPACK supports integration of technology but TPACCK focuses on how effective that integration of technology is on learning.

TPACCK – Technological, Pedagogical, Cognitive and Content Knowledge

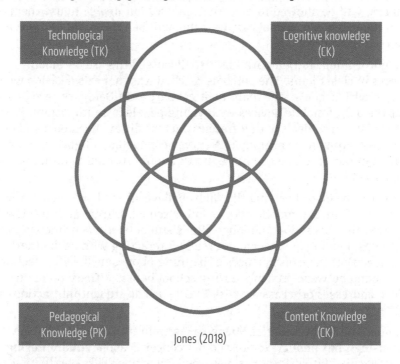

Jones (2018)

The BYOD Debate

The BYOD (Bring Your Own Device to school) debate has been a topic discussed in the global news. BYOD has grown in popularity with schools in recent years but there are also many critics who strongly oppose the idea. The French government for example made the decision to ban students from using their own personal mobile devices on school property from September 2018. Previously a law was passed in France that children should not use their phones in class but this new law extends to any time of the school day including breaks and lunchtime.

This has been referred to as a 'detox' law because there are serious concerns about the increasing amount of screen time with young people. Emmanuel Macron believed it was such an important issue that he made several promises during his election campaign, insisting he would outlaw the use of phones across schools from nursery to secondary. Jean-Michael Blanquer, Education Minister in France, has stated that the new law would 'make us all reflect on our phone use in society'.[127] In France, children will be allowed to have their phones but unable to use them until the end of the school day, how this will be implemented has not been made clear yet.

The government in Denmark has also discussed the use on mobile devices in classrooms. The outcome reached was that this decision would remain with schools. The main political parties in Denmark recognised that the use of mobile devices with young people is an important issue but that it can be dealt with differently across different schools and even from year group to year group.[128] A survey conducted in Denmark showed that eight out of ten people in Denmark are in favour of banning phones from schools.[129]

In the UK, headteacher Timothy Gibbs believes there have been many benefits of banning mobile phones in his school. During an interview he reported that his school 'no longer finds students at lunchtime standing in groups, looking at screens, not really interacting with each other'. He added that the consequences of banning phones included a 'decline in bullying between students during school hours'.[130] These points from Gibbs, addresses other issues with BYOD such as student interaction and bullying.

Founder and headteacher of Michaela Community School, Katharine Birbalsingh has publicly expressed her concerns about children using smartphones. Birbalsingh has described smartphones as destructive and damaging, she believes that children should not own a smartphone until the age of 18. Although she realises this is an extreme view, she feels very strongly and passionately about this issue.[131]

BYOD has been described by many within education as a great way to use digital tools in the classroom and keep up with the interests of students.[132] It allows technology to become part of lessons when financial budgets do not allow schools to purchase devices.

127. Chrisafis, A. (7 June 2018) 'French school students to be banned from using mobile phones'. (The Guardian) Available at: https://www.theguardian.com/world/2018/jun/07/french-school-students-to-be-banned-from-using-mobile-phones
128. No author. (1 August 2018) 'Schools can decide own smartphone rules in Denmark: MPS'. (The Local) Available at: https://www.thelocal.dk/20180801/schools-can-decide-own-smartphone-rules-in-denmark-mps
129. Ibid.
130. Wright, K. (2018) 'To ban or not to ban: Should phones be allowed in schools?' (BBC) Available at: https://www.bbc.com/news/uk-44546360
131. Barton, C. (17 July 2018) 'Slice of Advice: What did you learn this year?' (Mr Barton Maths Blog) Available at: http://www.mrbartonmaths.com/blog/slice-of-advice-what-did-you-learn-this-year/
132. Beach, M. (No date) 'How Schools Are Implementing 'Bring Your Own Device'. (Teach Mag) Available at: http://teachmag.com/archives/7706

It seems like a win-win situation in one sense, using new and exciting technologies, but without the cost! There is an argument that schools can still enforce specific rules and guidelines within a BYOD policy, it is crucial that they do. Many schools will state that mobile devices are allowed to be used in a learning environment with permission from a teacher, not allowing the personal use of devices outside of lessons and only used at dedicated times within lessons. BYOD can also allow students to continue a piece of work they have been working on and do so outside of the classroom.

Supporters of BYOD have argued that students can be distracted with pens and pencils, doodling or writing inappropriate material on books or desks. There have always been dangerous distractions in a classroom environment. This should be dealt with by a school behaviour policy in the same way misuse of personal devices should be. An article by Brian Lewis entitled *6 Advantages of BYOD In The Classroom* highlights that BYOD can become the norm in schools, 'students are asked to carry their own mobile device just as they carry a pen and pencil in their bag.'[133]

BYOD can also make sharing digital resources and materials with students easier such as via email, Bluetooth or AirDrop. It is clear that BYOD needs to be supported with a clear and concise policy linked to other policies such as behaviour and e-safety.

Headteacher Carolyn Roberts does believe phones have a place in schools and as a supporter of BYOD she says, 'we believe that one of the things you do in schools is give children the skills for adult life, and one of the things adults have to know is how to manage and moderate their mobile phone use.'[134] Roberts addresses the issue of confiscating phones with such large numbers of students, this could prove to be very difficult. The school policy Roberts discusses states that mobile phones are allowed until they become a nuisance and then if they get in the way of learning teachers confiscate them.

Howard-Jones echoes the beliefs of Roberts about providing students opportunities to be responsible with phone usage. He puts forward the argument that 'if school and education is about preparing us for that world, then learning how to use your mobile phone – when it is not appropriate, is a very important part of that.

133. Lewis, B. (1 October 2017) '6 Advantages of BYOD In The Classroom' (eLearning Industry) Available at: https://elearningindustry.com/byod-in-the-classroom-6-advantages
134. Wright, K. (2018) 'To ban or not to ban: Should phones be allowed in schools?' (BBC) Available at: https://www.bbc.com/news/uk-44546360

Children need to learn to self-regulate. They're not being given the opportunity to do that if their phones are taken away at the start of the day.'[135]

Macpherson and Hendrick posed the question: Would you ban mobile phones in the classroom? This was asked to Jill Berry and Tom Bennett, in the behaviour chapter and again to José Picardo and Neelam Parmar in the technology chapter, to gain different perspectives. Parmar argued that 'whether the mobile phone is part of the BYOD programme or not, an outright ban on all mobile phones for older students is unrealistic. Indeed, to do so will only encourage students to lie and become deceptive.'[136]

Wheeler also echoes this message that if schools ban devices 'students will use them anyway, most probably for unscholarly purposes'.[137] It is a very complex and challenging problem to tackle. As with most things, context is paramount and so it is incumbent upon schools and their leaders to engage with their communities to work out what is best for their school and what best supports teaching and learning.

This is an important debate and rightfully so, there is a lot of conversation and dialogue taking place about BYOD. People have such strong yet differing views regarding this controversial topic. The decision regarding BYOD does not always lie with the classroom teacher; senior leaders and even national governments are making the decision about the use of devices in schools. I am fortunate to work in a school that does have access to a broad cross-section of devices, including tablets and laptops. In addition to this, there is flexibility for students to use their own devices in lessons with the permission and supervision of the teacher.

I find BYOD works well with older and mature students that can use technology appropriately. My experiences of BYOD have been very positive. I have also heard stories about students taking photos or recording video footage without permission, potentially involving Snapchat (the app where you can take and send photos or videos that later disappear and then sharing those images online), which is totally unacceptable. I do not allow my younger students to use their own devices. The school devices are connected to the school Wi-Fi – although personal devices can do this

135. Ibid.
136. Hendrick, C & Macpherson, R. (2017) *What does this look like in the classroom? Bridging the Gap Between Research and Practice.* Melton, Suffolk: John Catt Educational Ltd, p. 188.
137. Wheeler, S. (2015) *Learning with 'e's: educational theory and practice in the digital age.* Carmarthen, Wales: Crown House Publishing, p. 10.

too – and can be easily monitored if needed. I can also ensure all of the apps I require in the lesson are downloaded and available ready to use. An issue I have with BYOD is that if I plan to use a specific app because I believe the app can support or enhance learning, not all students in the class might be able to access or download this app on their device. Some apps are only available on iOS or Android, other apps that cost can be purchased on the school iTunes account, but we cannot ask students to buy apps as that introduces even more complications, not to mention the suitability of apps and their age ratings.

iMessage, email and other communication methods can be disabled from school devices easily, teachers do not have the authority to do so with student devices and therefore this can lead to behaviour issues. There is a clear difference between banning mobile devices and banning technology altogether from schools.

Case study

Apple Classroom with Noel Tuohy, Head of Year 5, and Ciarán Kelly, Head of Primary IT, at Jumeriah English Speaking School (JESS) in Dubai.

One of my biggest concerns about using devices and the internet in the classroom is that of trust; can we trust our students to being do what they should be? Carl Hendrick wrote, 'allowing kids to browse the internet in a lesson and then expecting they will work productively is like bringing them to McDonald's and hoping they will order the salad.'[138] Fair point! So how do we tackle this problem? I believe there is a solution. I first discovered the answer to this question at the JESS Digital Innovation Summit in Dubai, October 2017. I was listening to a very entertaining and memorable presentation by primary teachers Noel and Ciaran. Below they explain how they use Apple Classroom in their classrooms:

'Apple Classroom is currently being used at JESS in a variety of ways. With the younger year groups it is incredibly useful as a classroom management tool to gather the children's attention with the lock down function. What we have noticed is that with time, as the children become more competent users of the iPad, this becomes less necessary. For teachers that are new to Apple

---

138. Hendrick, C. (June 2018) 'Challenging the Education is Broken and Silicon Valley Narratives'. ResearchED Magazine, Issue 1, p.17.

products in the classroom this is a great feature to start with. As well as this, the ability to direct younger children and/or less competent users of an iPad, to a specific app or web page allows for lessons to flow without valuable time being wasted trying to navigate to a specific resource.

'With the older year groups where the children are more familiar with their device, Apple Classroom is utilised more to deliver content to children to access, annotate, create and submit to their teacher or peers to observe or assess. The ability to grab a snapshot of a child's work and share this amongst a class or group using the AirPlay function is invaluable, allowing children further opportunities to collaborate with one another. Another useful function that we have utilised is the ability to group the children. This makes task allocation to specific groups incredibly easy. Apple Classroom is run throughout the school using our MDM (Mobile Device Management) system which gives us greater control of the accessibility features on the children's iPads and the apps they can access whilst under our school servers.

'Whilst this is not essential to use Apple Classroom, it gives even greater control of how the devices can be utilised more effectively and efficiently.'

You can follow Noel and Ciaran on Twitter at @noelhtuohyedu and @ciaranakelly, respectively.

What if your school does not have access to Apple technologies and you want to have a similar lockdown function and control with technology in your classroom?

You can visit the website www.netsupportschool.com

NetSupport provide a software service for schools where teachers can provide instruction, collaboration and assessment tools in addition to classroom management and monitoring. This allows the teacher to view all student activity online, therefore supporting e-safety in the lesson. NetSupport School can be used with Windows desktops and tablets, Mac, Chromebook, iPads, Kindle and Android tablets, providing a good solution to a potential problem. I can highly recommend considering this as a possibility for your classroom and school.

Apps for the classroom

The majority of the apps and websites suggested in this chapter and throughout the book are free (unless stated otherwise and some may have additional features that cost to access). I do not have any affiliation, loyalty or connection to any website, company or brand mentioned. I am purely recommending each app or website based on my own experiences, preferences and the impact they have had on teaching and learning in my classroom. This chapter contains more case studies than any of the other chapters and all of the examples are from educators based in the United Arab Emirates (UAE). This is because it is a very exciting time in education and the UAE is a hotbed of innovative modern teaching and learning practice, which includes technology. Many educators are using technology to support learning in their classrooms. I believe it is important to share some of the amazing practice that is taking place in the region.

QR codes in the classroom

QR (Quick Response) codes are not new and certainly not just for the classroom, but they have so much potential for teaching and learning, I think they are great and quite underrated. There are a wide range of websites and apps to easily create and read/scan QR codes – I would recommend the app QR Reader. If you haven't created QR codes before then they are very easy to make. I was surprised by how straightforward and quick it was. If you haven't tried QR codes in your classroom then it is worth trying, it is very simple and can be very effective. The latest iOS actually has a QR reader built into the camera and iOS12 has added this to the shortcut feature so there is no need to download an app just hold the iPhone camera above the QR code.

They are great for supporting independent research, 'independence is a desirable outcome of teaching, not a teaching strategy in its own right'– a great quote from Allison and Tharby.[139] When students have to research a topic, some will think that a quick Google search, copy and paste will be sufficient. That is why explicit and clear success criteria are needed in addition to students understanding how to carry out independent research, especially online. To simply give students a device and then say 'go find out about X' is not enough. We have a responsibility to help students learn how to carry out independent research and read information online, check information online and, of course most importantly, ensure that they are safe online.

---

139. Allison, S & Tharby, A. (2015) *Making Every Lesson Count: Six principles to support great teaching and learning.* Carmarthen, Wales: Crown House Publishing, p. 25.

Kirschner (2008), has written about the 'butterfly defect', first coined by Salomon and Almog (1998) and this refers to how students can easily wander off task when online floating and fleeting across the web. Kirschner writes that 'learners at the computer behave as butterflies. They flutter across the information on the screen, touch or do not touch pieces of information, to quickly flutter to the next piece of information – never knowing the value of it and without a plan. This butterfly defect, signalled by Salomon and Almog, happens on pages with many hyperlinks. Learners are seduced into clicking the links, often forgetting what they are looking for.'[140]

This is where QR codes can help. The internet allows both teachers and students to access a vast range of subject materials well beyond textbooks (although I do champion the use of textbooks) in various formats. There is so much information available to us online at our fingertips, but this array of information can be overwhelming. We can guide our students to useful, reliable and informative websites using QR codes. I am not suggesting we carry out the research for them, but we can provide students with a choice of reliable and recommended websites sending them in the right direction and avoiding the butterfly defect. QR codes can provide students with links to websites that are appropriate for supporting their studies.

I embed QR codes into revision booklets and bookmarks for students to refer to. Another positive feature is that QR codes allow lengthy links to be shared easily. The students can use their devices to scan the QR code and be instantly directed to a website, video, text, image, and so on. Differentiation for some teachers can result in added workload and planning with lots of different activities happening in the same classroom, when it does not have to be that way.

As a profession, our attitude towards differentiation has been changing over recent years, 'it is not humanly possible to personalise planning for each and every child, nor as often suggested is it possible to create three levels of worksheet for every lesson'[141] wise words from Allison and Tharby that feel like music to an educator's ears. We do need to support and challenge our students, but we can do this without 30 different types of resources.

---

140. Kirschner, P, A. (2008) 'ICT Myth Busting: Education is Not a Question of Belief, I Believe!' Available at: http://www.academia.edu/2722346/ICT_Myth_Busting_Education_is_Not_a_Question_of_Belief_I_Believe_.

141. Allison, S & Tharby, A. (2015) *Making Every Lesson Count: Six principles to support great teaching and learning.* Carmarthen, Wales: Crown House Publishing, p. 19.

The better we know our students, the easier it becomes to support and differentiate. QR codes can be used to provide both support and challenge. QR code stations are useful because there can be areas of the classroom with QR codes on display for students to scan if they need further support or have finished work and need a relevant extension. For example, a QR code I have on display is a link to the Edexcel website with exam questions and another with the mark scheme. To challenge students, QR codes can link to further reading and subject-specific materials. As well as providing support and challenge, QR code stations encourage students to become more independent learners. I know a maths teacher that provides QR codes with links to tutorials to further explain methodology and QR codes providing answers for students to self-assess and correct their own work.

A lot of students are very savvy when it comes to technology and can create their own codes too. I am often impressed with how quickly students can grasp technology. They can create QR codes if they want to share research, information, videos or any relevant content with their teachers or peers. Files and documents can be too large to share via email so QR codes are a great alternative.

Another way of using QR codes to share work is through interactive displays. If students have created an excellent piece of work, such as a presentation or iMovie, it is harder to display for others to view, unlike written pieces of work. A QR code on displays allows for others to scan and see the work. I have seen students in the corridor scanning QR codes on display out of curiosity. I have seen an English classroom with an oracy display board that mainly consisted of QR codes. Scanning the code then allowed the user to watch different videos of students speaking and discussing different topics. For further ideas and inspiration, I suggest looking on Pinterest to see how other teachers around the world are creatively using QR codes in their classrooms.

Double-sided QR code revision bookmarks for IGCSE history students.

Break down the walls of your classroom with Virtual Reality!

Virtual Reality (VR) has become a popular phenomenon inside and outside of the classroom. VR provides the user with an interactive and 3D simulation experience. The user will wear a headset and can be transported into a virtual video game, back in time or even in to space; there are no limits! In an educational setting I have used VR headsets with my students to explore a virtual World War One trench using the immersive free app Trench VR. I know teachers that have used the VR headsets to visit and learn about different locations around the world. VR can create unbelievable and magical memories for students, but we need to ensure we don't just focus on developing episodic memories, as we know meaning is required to make learning stick.

VR does have its critics too as it is viewed by some as a very expensive gimmick in the classroom. The prices of VR equipment can vary dramatically. A Google Cardboard 3D VR headset can be purchased online for under £10, whereas a more advanced piece of equipment like the HTC Vive VR headset is listed on Amazon presently at £790, not to mention the computer you need in order to make it work. Budgets are being stretched with many schools so purchasing this equipment will not always be possible or a priority although some schools do have the funding. When purchasing VR equipment careful consideration and discussion must be had between senior leaders and teachers. I am an advocate for using VR in the classroom, but I am also fully aware of the challenges and potential issues regarding the use of this equipment too. Therefore, schools should not purchase this equipment unless several factors have been considered:

- Are there any teachers who know how to use VR?

- Will staff require extra time and training to be able to use this equipment?

- If so, what are the cost implications of this and is this the best use of our CPD time?

- How will VR be used across the curriculum?

- How will it enhance or transform learning tasks?

- How will teachers know that VR is having a positive impact on outcomes?

Case study

Steve Bambury Head of Digital Innovation at Jumeriah English Speaking School (JESS) Dubai has become a well-known expert and advocate for the use of VR within the classroom.

Across the UAE, Steve is highly regarded in the educational community. As a multi-award-winning educator recognised for his innovative practice, he is a world-leading expert on VR in education. He regularly reflects, writes and presents about VR in education and he is keen to share how VR is being used successfully amongst his students and colleagues. I am very grateful to Steve for sharing his passion and experiences using VR purposefully at his school.

'I have been exploring the potential of Virtual Reality in education at JESS Dubai since I got my first mobile VR headset in 2014. Since then we have expanded our hardware to include full class banks of mobile VR headsets as well as HTC Vive rigs (more advanced equipment). I have worked with staff from early years to sixth form to explore meaningful ways to integrate VR across the curriculum. This has taken many forms and incorporated the use of simple 360° video content from YouTube, a range of mobile VR apps and more immersive, room-scale VR experiences using the Vive.

'Students have stood in Trafalgar Square during The Blitz, they have built 3D models of buildings and then stepped inside them in VR, they have walked on Mars (and even taken a few selfies whilst they were there) and even stood inside a beating human heart. Some of our sixth form art students have begun to incorporate the Google Tilt Brush platform into their repertoire – allowing them to create works of art not possible in the physical world using fire, light or sound as a medium and the air around them as their canvas.

'VR has so many benefits in the classroom. It can transport students to other places or even out of this world. It can allow them to travel in time and interact with history in ways never before possible. It has the power to deliver empathetic experiences to students as they walk in the shoes of people from other cultures. Students are ultimately empowered by the autonomy to engage with learning in a visceral way that other forms of technology cannot accomplish.'

You can follow Steve on Twitter @steve_bambury and visit his website www.virtualiteach.com

Google Expeditions

It is hard to believe that this engaging app by Google is free. Everyone should check out Google Expeditions, whether you use it in the classroom or for your own personal use, because there's simply so much to learn using Google Expeditions. This app can be used with a VR headset or without, simply with a tablet device will suffice. To use the app in class all devices are required to be on the same Wi-Fi.

A login is required for the teacher who will be the virtual tour guide and then the students connect as explorers. This gives the teacher complete control and oversight of where the students are looking as the app can direct all explorers to one key point/feature/place. There is also an information section provided for the guide that the explorers are unable to read, so you can impress with some intricate and unusual facts.

My students have experienced virtual field trips that include exploring The Sheikh Zayed Grand Mosque in Abu Dhabi and the Palace of Versailles in France – very informative and memorable. You can also learn about the ocean or look inside a virtual human body. The majority of these experiences would not be possible or highly unlikely without this technology, therefore according to the SAMR model, this task would be categorised as redefinition.

Balloon Stickies Plus

Adding captions, speech and thought bubbles to images can be done with ease and simplicity using this app. Although this can be achieved using Word, PowerPoint or Keynote, the quickest method based on my experience is using the app Balloon Stickies Plus, which I refer to again in Chapter 8. There are a range of other apps available with similar or additional functionality, but this app is free and the app that I prefer to use. The app allows the user to insert speech and thought bubbles and captions onto images very quickly. Balloon Stickies Plus app also allows the user to convert spoken word through recording into text, this has a lot of potential in the classroom for SEN and/or EAL pupils.

This app can be used with tableaux and freeze frames, adding captions and thought bubbles. I was covering a Drama lesson for a colleague and the class were asked to create a series of freeze frames to illustrate different types of bullying. To take their freeze frames to another level I took photos of each freeze frame and asked the students to add a caption, what the bully or victim might be saying. They also added a thought bubble to show what the individuals in the freeze frame would be feeling and the emotions they would be experiencing. I was very impressed with the level of discussion and empathy that was captured so well through the freeze frames and the additional captions. This idea could also be adapted for recording key character quotes, either with images or freeze frames, to further explore relationships and key themes.

The Balloon Stickies Plus app can be used in Modern Foreign Languages, the app can be used to develop reading and writing by adding keywords, sentences or phrases on top of images. Maths teachers have used this app, combining an explanation caption with a problem solving task. In PE the app can be used to describe or explain a specific posture or technique. There are many uses for this app, I encourage you to download and try it out for yourself.

Balloon Stickies Plus is only available on iOS but there are alternative apps and sites that have a similar feature that are available on all devices. My suggestions include https://bookcreator.com which is a simple tool to create and publish eBooks on iPad, Chromebook and on the web and the speech and thought bubble are one of many features. Bubble: Comic Speech Captions app is also available on both iOS and Android devices.

Microsoft Office Lens

Microsoft Office Lens available on Android and iOS is a very useful app that should be in every teacher's digital toolkit! This app is used to take photographs in the classroom, which can include taking a photo of board work, student classwork or information within a textbook. The app provides high-quality and professional results. Again, it is easy to use.

Simply open the app using your device and then take the photo whilst in the app. Edge detection software illustrates the detected edges with red lines. This will it mean that it will focus on everything inside of the edges and anything outside will not be included in the photo, so you can position the camera carefully to achieve your desired outcome. The camera can also make the image appear flat and clearer; sometimes writing can be more legible.

Then the photo can be saved to your photo library or as a PDF document, OneNote, Word or PowerPoint file. It can also be sent as an email attachment. I regularly use Microsoft Office Lens as I have a collection of students' work that I will share with other students as examples of what a good one looks like (WAGOLL). I have used Microsoft Office Lens to take a photo of notes taken on the board to then print or digitally send to my students, it can also be used for quickly scanning individual pages.

Post-it Plus

Post-it notes are a much-loved resource for many teachers due to their versatility and simplicity in the classroom. Post-It notes can be used at the start or end of a lesson for daily review or at any point in the lesson for answers/questions on a Post-it note. Post-it notes can be great for teaching and learning activities, but they can be very annoying too as they are difficult to record, keep safe and, of course, they lose their stickiness! This is where the nifty app Post-it Plus can be useful. This app allows the user to take a photo of a large sample of Post-it notes for you to keep and refer to at a later date. They can be organised, annotated and shared with staff or students. If you use Post-it notes in the classroom then you need to download this app.

Visualiser

Visualisers have been around a while and can actually be purchased for a relatively cheap price. A visualiser is a digital camera device that can reflect images onto the screen in your classroom. If your school uses iPads, then you could use the mirroring function to project the image on an iPad or iPhone camera onto the screen using Apple TV too. A visualiser can have multiple uses in the classroom. Great for modelling – reading through answers, importing and drafting; a simple but versatile piece of equipment for every classroom.

Case study

Hudl Technique with Guy Schooley, House Master and teacher of PE at Brighton College Al Ain. I am very fortunate to work with Guy; he is a teacher bursting with energy and enthusiasm.

Guy introduced me to the app Hudl Technique. He demonstrated how it worked by carrying out a live presentation, using eggs! Whilst I have never used this app in my subject I recognise it as an amazing tool to support any subject with a practical element.

Guy has kindly agreed to share how he uses this app in his lessons.

'Hudl Technique is not a new app, however it has stood the test of time and proved itself a very valuable teaching aid.

'PE is a very dynamic and fast-paced subject and if you are going to use technology you need it to work with minimal effort; in terms of set up, explanation and delivery of reliable results that actually have an impact on the whole class and individual student level. In its simplest terms, Hudl Technique allows you to analyse performance with the use of video technology. It can be watched in real-time or by reducing the speed in order to annotate over the athlete. This can be done with colour lines, measuring angles and you can even overlay video on existing footage to compare and contrast performances and techniques in closed and open environments.

'AFL in PE I hear you cry! Absolutely, and it gives you tangible evidence that can be exported and viewed repeatedly. Hudl Technique is an everyday tool to bring sports science to life within your PE lessons; it is great for engagement, differentiation and explicitly showing students specific areas to improve upon in their sport. I have used it across different ages and gender in addition to many students with English as an additional language and it has proven to be a very effective tool time and time again.'

Creating and recording films and videos

Quik by GoPro has a very appropriate name as this app allows the user to very quickly create movie montage videos. If you or your students don't feel confident using iMovie or Apple Clips and want an easy-to-use app with great results then try Quik. Simply upload images from your Camera Roll and then place in the order of your choice, you can add music provided within the app or from your own iTunes collection, but if you plan to share your Quik video publicly then you should use the royalty free music provided within the app.

Other features include altering the speed and pace of your video, selecting a theme of your choice and you can add text to images or create text titles too. I have created Quick videos in a few minutes. During a training session with Teaching and Learning Assistants at my current school, I showed them the Quik app and they were surprised by how effortless it is to use but how professional the finished film looks.

There is a range of other good apps for creating movies, although I would advise to use these with caution. The problem that can occur when asking students to demonstrate their learning by creating a presentation or movie is that they become too focused on the process and presentation, with the actual subject content taking a back seat. Time can be wasted on clip art, fonts, transitions and other effects. However, if your aim for students is to develop their editing and presentation skills then that is different.

This is why I recommend Quik by GoPro because it does all the editing for the user, so the person creating the video needs to focus on the images and text they select, rather than the layout and design. I'm aware of lessons where children are handed iPads and told to research something then create an iMovie about this topic. That task itself can take a considerable amount of time and is not always the best use of lesson time. I have viewed many excellent videos created by students to consolidate and demonstrate their learning, we just need to consider a lot of factors, such as the amount of time dedicated to the task, the ease of the technology being used and what the focus and outcome of the task should be.

Finally, save the Pacific Northwest Tree Octopus!

Are you familiar with the campaign to save the endangered tree octopus? If you type into Google 'Pacific Northwest Tree Octopus' then the first website to appear in the search engine should be: https://zapatopi.net/treeoctopus/

I recommend you visit and explore this site. It contains a lot of background information about the tree octopus, including where it can be found, 'temperate rainforests of the Olympic Peninsula on the west coast of North America'. The site explains that 'because of the moistness of the rainforests and specialised skin adaptations, they are able to keep from becoming desiccated… but given the chance they would prefer resting in pooled water'. There's also a wealth of bizarre facts, did you know their eyesight is comparable to humans? There are a range of photos of different sightings, a help page where you can find out about the different ways you can support the campaign to save the tree octopus and there are also links to other sites and recommended literature on this topic.

In case you hadn't realised already, the tree octopus does not exist; it is an internet hoax that was created by Lyle Zapato in 1998. If you share this link with children they will see a professional looking website and lots of information, which to a child could seem credible. There are also a range of posters and photos of the 'tree octopus'. In a PSHE lesson where students were told to find out about this campaign using devices it was noticeable that some students were suspicious, whilst others were ready to embrace and support the mission to save the Pacific Northwest Tree Octopus; many students did believe this site was genuine. The students were then instructed to visit other sites to find out more.

The second site confirmed it was a hoax, much to their surprise and shock. We need our students to be aware that not all of the information on the internet is correct. They probably already know this, but how do they find out if information is accurate, reliable or credible?

'Fake news' has become a strong talking point in the media and there is a greater awareness of false information being shared online. We need to be tackling this in schools, with the support of parents too. Miller and Bartlett write that being able to use and navigate the internet effectively requires the ability to distinguish between good and bad information and they recognise that learners often trust the first thing they find online, which can make them vulnerable.[142] Students can learn a lot from the internet, but they need to learn how to evaluate the information online first.

When exploring technology in education, it is clear that it is being used by many teachers with confidence, purpose and ease to support learning and workload. There is a growing divide between those who champion technology in the classroom and those that believe technology is more of a hindrance than help for both teachers and students. It should be obvious that investing money into technology to enhance education is not enough. Teachers can seek out assistance from colleagues, online resources and blogs but senior leaders must provide for professional development in this area too.

I hope the ideas and information in this chapter have provided some insight and opportunity to reflect on how, when and why we use technology for teaching and learning.

---

142. Miller, C & Bartlett, J. (2012) ''Digital Fluency': Towards young people's critical use of the internet', *Journal of Information Literacy*, 6(2), pp. 35–55.

Summary

- Technology can support teachers and students when used carefully, purposefully and effectively.

- If your school is investing in technologies then continued training, guidance, support and professional development should be provided.

- Technology can be used to substitute other methods where appropriate or provide some functional improvement. Technology can also be used to redefine and transform learning, achieving things that would not be possible without technologies, although this should never be the aim of lesson planning. SAMR is not a ladder of progress.

- It is important teachers combine their technological knowledge with their content, cognitive and pedagogical knowledge (TPACCK).

- There are methods and strategies, such as Apple Classroom and NetSupport School, which can regulate the use of screen time and appropriate use of technology in our lessons.

- Keep it simple and don't spend too much time preparing lessons that incorporate technology. Keep your use of technology focused upon whether it can enhance your teaching, students learning or improve your workload.

Recommended reading

Perfect ICT Every Lesson by Mark Anderson (2013)

Learning with 'e's: Educational Theory and Practice in the Digital Age by Steve Wheeler (2015)

Young Children in a Digital Age. Supporting learning and development with technology in early years edited by Lorraine Kaye (2016)

Bloomsbury CPD Library: Using Technology in the Classroom by José Picardo (2017)

What Does This Look Like In The Classroom? Bridging The Gap Between Research And Practice by Carl Hendrick and Robin Macpherson (2017)

CHAPTER 4:
HOW TO EMBRACE LITERACY IN YOUR SUBJECT

'A literate student is one who is confident with reading, writing, speaking and listening in any context and able to use this to navigate adult life'
Sarah Findlater

It is very likely that you will have heard this before, probably during a back to school inset, that we are all teachers of literacy. A teacher of 'literacy' is not the appropriate term to use. We are all teachers of our phase at primary or subject at secondary. All teachers, regardless of phase or subject, will agree that we have a professional obligation and duty to promote and develop the literacy skills of our students. For teachers that do not have English as a subject specialism, this can at times seem daunting, but it should not be. Teachers are very literate, especially in our own subject areas. Literacy consists of reading, writing, speaking and listening, which I refer to as the big four, and this is practically everything that we do in the classroom.

In his invaluable book *The Secret of Literacy: Making the Implicit Explicit*, David Didau puts forward that there is no such thing as literacy, just good teaching and learning. He also believes that developing the big four are absolutely fundamental to every teachers approach to pedagogy,[143] I completely agree. Didau sums up the responsibility of individual teachers in relation to literacy with this quote, 'teaching pupils to read, write and communicate is not something special that you need to do on top of your job. It is your job'.[144]

Essentially, everything in this book will be linked to literacy, the big four. This chapter aims to focus specifically on improving literacy within

---

143. Didau, D. (2014) *The Secret of Literacy: Making the implicit, explicit.* Carmarthen, Wales: Independent Thinking Press, p. 2-3.
144. Ibid.

our subject or across different subjects taught. Improving literacy levels and standards must be part of a whole school approach. Teacher, leader and Senior Associate at the EEF Alex Quigley explains that everything we teach and learn is clothed in language, therefore language and communication is our responsibility as teachers.[145] E. D. Hirsch Jr. writes in his phenomenal book *Why Knowledge Matters: Rescuing Our Children from Failed Educational Theories* that 'in a modern democracy literacy entails the ability to communicate effectively with strangers and to understand rather complex texts'.[146]

The 2003 OECD report 'Literacy Skills for the World of Tomorrow – Further results from PISA 2000' states 'the acquisition of literacy is a lifelong process – taking place not just at school or through formal learning but also through interactions with peers, colleagues and wider communities'.[147] An individual teacher can make a significant difference to a student's literacy skills and confidence, but even more so when done in collaboration with all staff and parents/carers too.

There is another viewpoint that literacy and numeracy lend themselves better to some subjects more than others, which certainly does have truth. The big four however occur in every classroom, every lesson, every single day. If your school has a literacy coordinator, lead teacher or designated leader then take advantage of their leadership, knowledge and expertise. The English department can also help with any specific language queries or questions. You are the expert with literacy in your subject and it is up to you to communicate and share this with your students.

The next chapter is also linked to literacy, as I believe in the importance of explicit vocabulary instruction and there was simply far too much to share in one chapter! I do love literacy, language and literature (and also alliteration).

145. Hendrick, C & Macpherson, R. (2017) *What does this look like in the classroom? Bridging the Gap Between*
146. Hirsch, E, D. (2016) *Why Knowledge Matters: Rescuing Our Children from Failed Educational Theories.* Cambridge, Massachusetts: Harvard Education Press, p. 80.
147. UNESCO. (2003) 'Literacy Skills for the World of Tomorrow – Further results from PISA 2000'. Paris, France: OECD.

The big four: Writing
Stop students rushing with a speeding ticket!

I created the 'Speeding Ticket' using Typorama app. It can be downloaded for free at my TES page[148].

Most teachers have encountered, much to our frustration, students that rush their work. The reasons for rushing written work can differ. There are the eager students that are so keen to please their teacher that they rush to complete tasks. It is important that we educate our students that completing written work needs to be more like a marathon than a sprint. We do not want our students to rush, but instead to create a high-quality piece of work that has been improved over time. If you want to show your classes an example of improving a piece of work then I highly recommend showing the inspiring video *Critique and feedback – the story of Austin's butterfly* with teacher and author of *An Ethic of Excellence: Building a Culture of Craftsmanship with Students*, Ron Berger. I have learned so much from Berger and 'Austin's butterfly' can be found and viewed on YouTube. Another factor that can lead to rushed written work is the desire to progress to an extension task, which some students are desperate to reach.

---

148. K8SUE. (29 June 2016) 'Speeding Ticket.' (TES) Available at: https://www.tes.com/teaching-resource/speeding-ticket-11309566

Extension activities can be common to promote student independence. When their work is finished, they know to complete an additional task. That should not be their goal and we need to encourage our students to redraft, reflect and self-correct to produce high-quality written work. In the opposite camp are the students that finish a task quickly because they simply just want to get it over and done with! The speeding ticket resource in the classroom aims to prevent students from rushing their written work and ultimately support their progression with their writing.

There are several obvious issues with rushing work. The presentation can become poor or even illegible when written too quickly. This is an issue I noticed when I was a GCSE examiner, students are answering questions in timed conditions and they don't consider presentation but it is still important. When rushing it is more likely students will make mistakes. We do need to create a classroom culture were mistakes are welcomed and embraced but often the mistakes that occur from rushing are those errors that students should not be making. Misspelling words that they do know how to spell but due to rushing and a lack of concentration an error has occurred.

Mistakes are different to misconceptions, teachers can predict misconceptions but students have a greater control (to a certain extent) over the mistakes they make in the classroom. Rushing work could also be a result of underlying issues such as a lack of understanding or problems with the level of difficulty and challenge. Rushing can also show a distinct lack of effort. The Growth Mindset by Carol Dweck, ideology tells us that through having the right mindset, focus and determination students can achieve fantastic progress. Taking time, care and effort links in with having that growth mindset.

In my classroom I have a small amount of speeding tickets printed and laminated. A class set simply is not needed because this resource never applies to all of the individuals in the class. The speeding ticket could also be printed as a sticker, to stick in books when it becomes obvious a student has rushed their work. The ticket can be given out in the lesson if it becomes noticeable that someone is speeding away. This clearly reinforces that they must slow down, take more time and care.

I have also issued the speeding ticket at the start of the lesson to one student, this was due to him rushing his work for a previous written task and ignoring my feedback regarding this. This ticket illustrated that I was aware of his bad habit of rushing and I wanted him to address and tackle this issue in the lesson. I informed him that when this was no longer a problem then I wouldn't issue him with a ticket. This also tells students they won't be rewarded for finishing work first and that it is not a class competition to do so. The speeding ticket is not meant to be harsh or come with any punishment, like an actual speeding ticket does! The aim is to act as a reminder and help the student focus and improve their writing. It may appear a gimmick or trick, but the speeding ticket acted as a prompt that helped my students to stop rushing and that led to an obvious improvement in their written work.

Case study

After sharing the speeding ticket resource online, Louise Connarty, head of geography and assistant headteacher, adapted this idea to use in her classroom and she has enthusiastically agreed to share her experience and idea below:

'Ever since I started teaching I have always been at a bit of a loss when it comes to those eager beaver students. On the one hand, I have never wanted to crush their enthusiasm for my subject, however I have always felt it was important to instil the qualities that produce pieces of work that students are proud of rather than something that is rushed and never looked at again.

'When I came across Kate's idea on Twitter of a speeding ticket I thought I had found just the 'ticket' to the problem of my students rushing their work. Rather than just handing my students a warning card to advise slowing down, I wanted to create something that was a part of the feedback cycle in my classroom – from this was born my adaptation of Kate's speeding ticket.

'The ticket I created contained a 'speed awareness course', where students were given specific feedback on the areas they had rushed and were given the opportunity to make improvements with a mini DIRT (Dedicated Improvement Reflection Time) exercise, they then stuck the ticket into their books.

'Within the classroom the speeding ticket was effective at making students think more carefully about what they were writing and how they were presenting it. I found that it was a great high-impact, low-workload strategy. I was able to give live feedback in the classroom that had an immediate impact on what students were producing. I would mainly give out on the spot fines when students were producing extended pieces of writing when consolidating their learning. I feel the strategy could be easily adapted to be used consistently during all lessons.'

SPEEDING VIOLATION

You have been caught speeding. Reason for violation:

☐ Presentation ☐ Punctuation ☐ Communication

☐ Spelling ☐ Grammar ☐ Organisation

Speed awareness course. Rewrite the highlighted violation.

P U R P L E

P E N

Teacher feedback:

☐ Presentation ☐ Grammar

☐ Spelling ☐ Communication

☐ Punctuation ☐ Organisation

| Date | Issued by | Pass ☐ | Fail ☐ |

You can follow Louise on Twitter @Geoisamazing and download her speeding ticket for free on the TES.[149]

SPaG Watch

Spelling, punctuation and grammar are an essential part of learning and communication. An idea I came up with to focus specifically on spelling and punctuation is 'SPaG Watch'. SPaG Watch has worked well with my students supporting their peers and highlighting SPaG errors in their written work. Metacognition is a massively important element of successful learning. By stressing the importance of certain elements of learning such as spelling, grammar and punctuation, children are able to ensure that it is at the front of their mind when learning in class. This

149. 88collinsl. (11 July 2016) 'Literacy speeding ticket.' Available at: https://www.tes.com/teaching-resource/literacy-speeding-ticket-11317997

is why, whilst on the face of it seemingly 'gimmicky', the SPaG Watch activity really is an integral part of learning in my classroom.

SPaG Watch acts as a form of peer assessment or support. Originally, the idea was intended for the more able and gifted students to help others in the class. Due to its popularity, I have adapted the task, because most of my students want to be SPaG Watch.

I certainly don't use this activity every lesson, but if the class are completing an extended piece of writing then the Hi Vis jackets come out. There are always keen volunteers on hand to take on the roles of Spelling Squad and Punctuation Police. This has to be very structured so that the SPaG Watch does not spend too much time helping others, as they obviously need to be focused on their own learning in the lesson too. The person in the role of the Spelling Squad will be armed with a dictionary and a whiteboard pen to write correct spellings on the board. When they are on patrol their duty is to check their peers work ensuring that they have spelt keywords correctly.

Punctuation Police purely focus on the punctuation, naturally. This could be punctuation in general, but that can depend on the volunteer, class and ability. I may ask the student to check specifically that capital letters and/or full stops are being used accurately. It may be more complex, such as checking parenthetic commas are being used correctly.

At certain points in the lesson I will play a short music clip; this has varied from The Bill theme tune to the A–Team, progressing to the Avengers Assemble soundtrack, as it was pointed out my choice of music was very out of date. The music is used as a cue for SPaG Watch to go around the class. The music will often only last three to five minutes and I will probably play it twice in a lesson. The music does add another element of fun, but this is mainly to ensure SPaG Watch stick to their allotted time to help others. The music stops and they stop, returning to their seats and they continue with their work.

Students have been very vocal that they like this activity, whether they are SPaG Watch or not, because they can see that it is helpful. I use this with Key Stage 3, but primary school teachers have also used this too. The Hi Vis jackets were a purchase from a pound shop and used simply to identify who the SPaG Watch are, although some students love wearing the jackets. Who knew correcting spelling, punctuation and grammar could be so exciting!

This activity could be deemed as distracting with music playing and the fluorescent jackets worn. Supporting peers with spellings and punctuation can easily be achieved without the music and Hi Vis jackets if you do not want to include those things. I have used it without the music and vest with older students where they appreciated their peers highlighting errors that they could correct. Remember: try, refine or ditch.

Spot the SPaG mistake

Continuing with the SPaG correction theme is an idea that involves showing students an example of writing with some form of literacy mistake that they have to identify and correct. This can be a Tweet or Facebook post from a celebrity they are familiar with, as an example of bad spelling or punctuation displayed (there are plenty to choose from online). Alternatively, if you notice a public sign or display with a literacy or numerical mistake then take a photo to show your students so they can spot the mistake and correct. You will be surprised how many literacy and numerical mistakes you can find!

After sharing literacy mistakes with my class, in the following lesson one of my students showed me a photo of a shop sign with errors that she had noticed outside of school. This really can make students aware of the mistakes around them, with both literacy and numeracy.

This is also a good way of encouraging students to use the marking policy/codes if you use them. Codes are great for focusing on specific targets and can support teacher workload with marking and feedback. To check they understand the codes being used, encourage them to use the codes with self and peer assessment. I believe that marking codes should be used as a whole school approach to ensure consistency. Although marking codes can be a great time saver, it is important students actually understand where they have gone wrong. If the teacher writes 'Gr' next to a sentence to illustrate a grammatical error, can that student identify and self-correct the error? Do they know what a grammatical error is?

The marking codes can be supported with verbal feedback in class too (although you should not need a verbal feedback stamp to show you have had a discussion with a student). Here are some suggested literacy and marking codes that are commonly used:

Sp – Spelling error

C – Capitalisation error

P – Punctuation error

Gr – Grammatical error

Np or // – New paragraph required

WW – Wrong word (when students have used the wrong homophone eg. there/their/they're)

WT – Wrong tense

? – Unclear/explain further

FS – Write in full sentences (although some schools use FS for full stop which is more specific than P)

Ex – Explain, further explanation required

^ – Missing a word

WWW – What went well...

EBI – Even better if...

Case study

Rachael Bethell, English teacher at Castell Alun High School. Planning in the palm of your hand!

I had the privilege of working with Rachael in her role as senior leader and whole school literacy coordinator. I learned so much from Rachael and she played a huge role inspiring my love of literacy. Rachael shares her creative and useful planning in the 'palm of your hand' activity and how it works in the classroom. This activity is designed to support persuasive speech writing with the objective to focus on planning content, sequencing and developing ideas.

'Firstly, students need to explore the content, organisation and language of speeches through deconstructing models and evaluating 'What a Good One Looks Like' (WAGOLL). Individuals then begin the process of planning their own speeches, exploring a specific topic. For example, a task could be to write a speech for a Year 9 assembly to persuade students to support a charity of your choice. A hand template is required because each finger on the hand represents the planning for each paragraph of their speech. Here are my step-by-step instructions to planning in the palm of your hand:

■ Students draw around their hand on a plain A4 piece of paper.

Top tip: tell them to stretch their hand to create the biggest span possible.

- In the palm of their hand, students create an emotive topic sentence to address and hook the audience.

- They then use the little finger to plan emotive language, hyperbole and imagery to support their opinion. Students are also encouraged to add key personal reminders, such as first and second person pronouns.

- The ring finger should include biased statistics. To encourage students to engage with the statistics and develop some form of analysis, they can also include the rhetorical question 'why?'

- The middle finger is used to plan an emotive anecdote. This includes bullet pointed information to develop an account. Before the actual written planning, students complete a paired oracy task, creating an anecdote through discussing key questions: Who? What? When? Where? Why? How?

- Ample planning time should be given for students to develop sophisticated vocabulary and imagery.

- Students use the index finger to plan statements from influential figures linked to their topic and analysis. For example, Members of Parliament, media figures or subject specialists.

- Finally, students plan their conclusion on their thumb. They should be encouraged to reflect on the topic sentences they have planned, reassert their opinion and use a few imperatives to sound assertive.

'This quite rigid structure was used to support lower ability students using a 'step-by-step' approach. All students had planned the content, organisation and language aspects of a speech that was at least six paragraphs long. More able students should be given far greater independence in all aspects of planning and they may want to extend their arguments to offer alternatives; additional paragraphs can be planned on the reverse of the hand.'

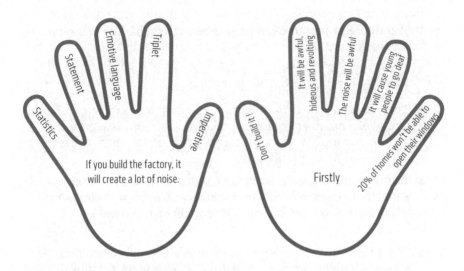

The big four: Reading

'One of the most important skills parents can teach their children is make them into readers from an early age.' – Geoff Barton, *Don't Call it Literacy! What Every Teacher Needs to Know about Speaking, Listening, Reading and Writing.*

Reading is essential to a student's development. Barton also adds that reading is a crucial life skill – although that sounds dramatic it is, of course, true. Quigley passionately argues that 'there is no more important act in education than helping children to learn to read',[150] and this really struck a chord with me. The OECD report (2000) note that PISA define reading 'as the ability to understand, use and reflect on written texts in order to achieve one's goals, to develop one's knowledge and potential and to participate effectively in society. This definition goes beyond the notion of reading literacy as decoding written material and literal comprehension. Reading incorporates understanding and reflecting on texts. Literacy involves the ability of individuals to use written information to fulfil their goals and the consequent ability to use written information to function effectively in complex modern societies',[151] illustrating the sheer weight and significance of reading.

150. Quigley, A. (25 June 2017) 'Why Whole-School Literacy Fails!' (The Confident Teacher) Available at: http://www.theconfidentteacher.com/2017/06/why-whole-school-literacy-fails/
151. UNESCO. (2003) 'Literacy Skills for the World of Tomorrow – Further results from PISA 2000'. Paris, France: OECD.

As teachers we have a responsibility to support students with their reading and to also promote a love of reading, within our own subjects as well as in general. Reading is not just for the English department to deal with, again reinforcing the message of a whole school focus and approach. We need to ensure that parents fully embrace and support their child's development with reading too.

Reading or library lessons, when I was at school, were often a lesson we would look forward to as we could relax and not do any work whilst the teacher would insist on silence to catch up on their marking. That is not to suggest that students should not have opportunities to read in school; I teach history so reading plays an integral role in this subject. We can also be reading with our students in lessons so that we are able to stop, elaborate and expand on specific points. This allows us to explain keywords that might be unfamiliar to students and model pronunciation when needed.

I previously considered reading in class, especially with older students, to be a waste of valuable lesson time if the information/content could be read outside of the lesson for homework as part of a flipped learning approach. Then when I did incorporate reading into my lessons I was never sure how effective this was. So how should we carry out reading in our lessons?

Put the popcorn away

'Popcorn reading' is a very popular whole class strategy for reading aloud. Popcorn reading is where a student will read a section of text and then stop at a certain point and say 'Popcorn Jessica'. Jessica will then read out loud until she metaphorically passes the popcorn onto someone else and so on. There are many students who enjoy this and hope the 'popcorn' is passed to them, as they want to have the opportunity to read out loud in front of their peers. Not all students share the same enjoyment and confidence when reading in front of others.

There are several issues with this strategy. Popcorn reading does not allow the student to read the text in advance. Reading the text in advance helps with confidence as they are able to find out the meanings of any words they are unsure of or check their pronunciation. I recall a lesson where a student was reading to the class and she mispronounced a word that most of the class were familiar with. She was very embarrassed and it is likely that it knocked her confidence. The danger with that type of experience is that it can put students off reading and speaking in front of their peers, both of these we wish not to discourage.

Another problem with popcorn reading is that students can become stressed, anxious or too focused about whether they will be picked next, that they are thinking about that instead of following the text and concentrating on the actual content.

Students also often pass the 'popcorn' (the reading) to their friends and it stays within the friendship group and the teacher does not have control as to who is reading out loud. We can probably remember either as a student or doing so as a teacher, where someone was not reading along with the rest of the class and was singled out by the teacher and asked to read. That person wouldn't know what point in the text the class had reached and then had to admit they weren't concentrating. If the teacher uses reading out loud as an opportunity to highlight someone not concentrating then this can create the impression that reading is a punishment, which it certainly is not.

To support students reading text out loud in front of the class we need to give them time to read the text first. This can be set the previous lesson or dedicated time in the lesson. Also, in our planning we can check the text in advance and identify keywords that students may struggle with so that we are prepared to address this in the lesson. Before the text is read the teacher can introduce and explore new vocabulary, explaining the definition with concrete examples and modelling the pronunciation clearly.

Taking time to read together as a class should not be considered a waste of time, but instead an opportunity to explore, discuss and analyse text together. Barton recommends that a teacher should read from the back of the classroom, as students can't see the teacher but the teacher can see if everyone is following the text.[152]

Reading should be associated with rewards. When the teacher has control over who is reading out loud, rather than asking students to pass it amongst themselves, the teacher will know who the confident and reluctant readers within the class are and can direct accordingly. The teacher can also differentiate, giving a piece of text that is more challenging and demanding to a student that will be able to cope with that rather than a reluctant reader or student with English as an additional language (I have also encountered many EAL students who are able to read with confidence and fluency).

---

152. Barton, G. (2012) *Don't Call it Literacy!* Abingdon, Oxfordshire: Routledge, p. 68.

Create your own book club

Author Matt Haig Tweeted about the importance of reading for pleasure:

'Reading is not important because it helps get you a job. It is important because it gives you room to exist beyond the reality you're given. Reading makes the world better. It is how humans merge. How minds connect. Dreams. Empathy. Understanding. Escape. Reading is love in action.' – @matthaig1

A book club for your students can be linked to your subject or purely reading for pleasure. There will be students who will want to attend your book club because they are avid readers, and there will be other students who imagine a book club to be dull and boring. I would suggest inviting those students who you know to be disengaged with reading. Encourage them with rewards or by inviting some of their friends too so they are more likely to attend. I know lots of students enjoy reading the bestselling Horrible Histories series, so that could always be a good option; reading a book for pleasure but also to support their studies in a specific subject.

You could ask the students themselves to recommend books, as much as we try to keep up-to-date with what young people are interested in, we don't know as well as they do what is relevant or of interest to them. Consider how often you meet and how realistic it will be that all the students in your book club will have read the book or section of that book in the time given.

This can also provide a lovely opportunity to get to know your students outside of the classroom but still within a school environment. When students discovered I had read the Twilight series they were really surprised, they asked me questions about whether I was Team Edward or Team Jacob (obviously I'm Team Jacob). This discussion went on for many years as the books and films were released and led to many corridor conversations during my weekly duties. If we can support students developing a love of reading that lasts for the rest of their lives, then that truly is something special.

The big four: Speaking and listening

Green screen is no longer for the Hollywood movies; it can have a purposeful place within the classroom setting too. Initially, I was reluctant to use green screen because I thought it was much more complicated than it actually was. If you don't have an actual green screen you can paint a section of your classroom or corridor green or use green backing paper. Alternatively, you can purchase a large green screen cloth very cheaply. It does not have to be expensive. You will also need a device to carry out the filming and editing process. There are a wide range of apps available to use with green screen, but after trialling and testing many, my personal recommendation has to be DoInk Green Screen.

DoInk Green Screen is an exception to the majority of suggested apps in this book as it does cost, but it is not costly. There are free green screen apps available, but I recommend this app above the other apps because it is user friendly, simple and quick to use as it does not demand much effort, attention or time, as should always be the case when using technology in the classroom.

Green screen – or blue screen, which works in the same way, as blue and green are regarded as the best colours to use as they are the furthest colours away from human skin tones – allows the editor to remove the green background and replace the back drop. Green screen can provide opportunities for students to discuss, evaluate or reflect on their learning using their imagination and digital skills. Using green screen is another example of using technology to do things that would not be possible without technology, as per the SAMR model.

I have used the green screen with students ranging from Foundation Stage 1 (FS1) to A-Level. Older students are able to film and edit using the technology independently, whereas with the little FS1 students I carried out the filming and editing. Different green screen videos/clips can be linked together by importing into iMovie. Some examples of how I have used green screen with my classes to support or consolidate learning include the following:

Creating a news report. This can be to feedback news from your school or local area for an assembly. A green screen news report could be used to show students discussing local or global current affairs. I have seen it used in geography, creating a news report focusing on natural disasters. I have used this in history to recreate a news broadcast of a key historical event. Although, if the event occurred before the second half of the twentieth century, then the task becomes an anachronism – an anachronism is something placed in the wrong time period for example an iPhone being used during World War One. A weather report, similar to an actual televised weather report where presenters use green screen as they deliver the weather forecast. This idea works well in geography and also MFL when learning terminology linked to the weather.

Student presentations can be supported with green screen. If students are presenting to the class, either individually or in pairs/groups then a green screen background can enhance their presentation. Green screen can be for the teacher too.

Below you can see me standing in front of the Bayeux Tapestry. Teachers can create revision tutorials or videos that can be used in the teacher's absence. If you have a planned absence you could film a short video with an explanation or demonstration that can be shown to your class. Other suggestions include creating a music video for a student performance, sporting commentary, or even travel back in time or into a fictional setting.

Some quick tips and tricks to help your green experience are to make sure students aren't wearing green or brown. If green is the colour of your school uniform then watching the green screen video back will show your students as floating heads and missing bodies! Ensure that the shot focuses on the green screen and does not go beyond the edges, as this will impact the quality of your finished film. A corridor or extra room is a useful space to avoid background noise in your video. When searching for your background images encourage students to use sensible sites, as suggested in Chapter 1, that provide images and videos which can be used without any copyright or royalty issues. A tripod will stop the unwanted shaky hand effect!

Public speaking skills and confidence with Virtual Reality

If you or your school have access to a VR headset, there are a wide range of apps that can be used to support, practice and develop public speaking skills. My recommendation would be VirtualSpeech – a free app that can be downloaded by iPhone and Android users and also Oculus Go, Gear VR and Merge VR. The app is free, although extended features and options can be purchased too. This app combined with a VR headset allows the user to practice public speaking in a wide range of scenarios.

The user can select a setting and room that can include an interview presentation, conference room, classroom or even a TedX style presentation – the user can even select the size of their audience too. There are different features for different rooms that include voice recognition and speech analysis to provide feedback about clarity and hesitation. The user/presenter can also be rated on different aspects of their presentation such as eye contact with the audience and the user can even listen back to their presentation. Slides can be uploaded so that they can be used in conjunction with the presentation and there are hints and tips to develop further. This app is great for building confidence and tackling a fear of speaking in front of others.

'It is my perspective that the most important thing you learn in school is how to communicate',[153] observes Phil Beadle in his intelligent and witty book *Literacy: Commas, colons, connectives*, part of the *How To Teach* series. The powerful quote by Beadle stresses the importance of communication in all forms. As the majority of examinations and standardised testing assess a student's subject knowledge and skills through writing, it is natural that a lot of emphasis is placed on written communication in the classroom. Very few exams, with the exception of some like English language and MFL, are assessed verbally.

The ability to be able to communicate verbally is of great value and importance. Every day teachers model the importance of verbal communication with our explanations, instructions, guidance, feedback and interaction with staff and students. It is vital that students can communicate clearly and confidently across all subjects and outside of the classroom.

Ko et al report that effective teachers communicate to their students what is expected of them and why, in addition to being able to

---

153. Beadle, P. (2014) *How to Teach: Literacy across the curriculum – semantics, stanzas and semi colons...* Carmarthen, Wales: Independent Thinking Press.

communicate knowledge and information fluently and clearly.[154] Lots of the activities in this book have provided opportunities for students to discuss subject matter with one another. I really enjoy walking around my classroom and listening to the student conversations to support students staying focused. During classroom discussions it is important to always be visible. Nuthall revealed some of the personal conversations that took place between peers in the classroom and he explores the impact peer culture can have on their learning.

Nina Jackson shares a wide range of strategies for effective group work and communication in her book *Of Teaching, Learning and Sherbet Lemons: A Compendium of Advice for Teachers.* Jackson believes that one of the worst things we can do as teachers is to stop students talking to each other about their learning.[155] I agree with this sentiment. This can link back to using green screen during the planning, preparation and presentation stages.

Questioning

Wragg and Brown (1993) have identified that teachers ask up to two questions every minute in the classroom, which can total up to 400 questions a day, 70,000 over a year or two to three million in the course of a teaching career! Not all of the questions asked are linked to learning as teachers regularly ask managerial questions.

'Is your name on that?'

'Have you glued that sheet into your book?'

Nevertheless, this does mean that questioning accounts for up to a third of lesson time, second to teacher explanation, so it is one of the most important practices a teacher can develop and focus on. Wiliam has written about the significance of questioning in his accomplished book *Embedded Formative Assessment.* Wiliam suggests that 'there are only two good reasons to ask questions in class: to cause thinking and to provide information for the teacher about what to do next'.[156] I find that very useful when planning, considering and reflecting on questioning in the classroom.

During an observation as an NQT, my line manager commented on my use of questioning and suggested this was an area I needed to improve.

154. Ko, J & Samons, P, Bakkum, L. (2013) 'Effective teaching: a review of research and evidence'. Education Development Trust. Oxford, Oxfordshire: Oxford University Department of Education.
155. Jackson, N. (2015) *Of Teaching, Learning and Sherbet Lemons: A compendium of advice for teachers.* Carmarthen, Wales: Independent Thinking Press.
156. Wiliam, D. (2011) *Embedded Formative Assessment.* Bloomington, Indiana: Solution Tree.

She was right and the feedback was very constructive and helpful. I was fortunate to visit another school, to observe a teacher who was renowned for his questioning in the classroom. I felt that the experience helped me greatly. Not only did I learn a lot from another experienced practitioner, it also made me aware of and reflect on the questions I was asking in the classroom.

The report on 'Effective Teaching' by Ko et al discussed the importance of questioning, explaining that 'the skilful use of well-chosen questions to engage and challenge learners and to consolidate understanding is an important feature of good teaching'.[157] Questioning is also a central element of Rosenshine's Principles of Instruction. Teachers can naturally improve their questioning techniques, but it is an area we can, and should, continually discuss and develop.

Communication is key in a classroom and plays a crucial role in learning. I know teachers have often felt concerned about how much time in a lesson should be dedicated to teacher talk, but instead of focusing on the duration Wiliam resolves that 'it would appear that how much students learn depends more on the quality than the quantity of teacher talk'.[158] Students should have plentiful opportunities to develop their communication skills in different forms and contexts. Teachers also need to be aware of and reflect on our communication in the classroom too.

157. Ko, J & Samons, P, Bakkum, L. (2013) 'Effective teaching: a review of research and evidence'. Education Development Trust. Oxford, Oxfordshire: Oxford University Department of Education.
158. Wiliam, D. (2011) *Embedded Formative Assessment*. Bloomington, Indiana: Solution Tree, p. 79.

Summary

- Literacy consists of reading, writing, speaking and listening. Skills we develop every single lesson.

- Developing a student's literacy skills should not be the sole responsibility of the literacy coordinator and English department. Every teacher has a role and duty to support students with this.

- Rushing work can have a negative impact on the quality of students work for various reasons. We should encourage our students to become careful, considerate and reflective learners.

- Students need to develop an awareness of their own SPaG mistakes and be able to recognise errors when they encounter them.

- Reading in the lesson is not a waste of time, although there are some strategies that can be deemed more effective than others.

- Clear communication is essential in a successful classroom. We should think and reflect about how we communicate information, knowledge and instructions to our students. We also need to provide plentiful opportunities for students to communicate with their peers.

Recommended reading

Don't Call it Literacy! What Every Teacher Needs To Know about Speaking, Listening, Reading and Writing by Geoff Barton (2012)

An Ethic of Excellence. Building a Culture of Craftsmanship with Students by Ron Berger (2003)

The Secret of Literacy: Making the Implicit Explicit by David Didau (2014)

How to Teach Literacy across the Curriculum – semantics, stanzas and semi-colons by Phil Beadle (2014)

Why Knowledge Matters: Rescuing Our Children from Failed Educational Theories by E. D. Hirsch (2016)

CHAPTER 5:
VOCABULARY INSTRUCTION AND CONFIDENCE WITH KEYWORDS

'It is clear that a large and rich vocabulary is the hallmark of an educated individual.'

Isabel L. Beck, Margaret G. McKeown & Linda Kucan.

Every subject has its own collection of specific terminology and keywords. Students are regularly introduced to new vocabulary; it is a key feature and skill of each discipline. Robert Bjork stresses the importance of vocabulary learning, which he describes as 'fundamental to our initial and continued learning in almost every domain' and he further adds, 'our primary concern as teachers, for example, may be increasing students' higher-level understanding of concepts in some domain and increasing their ability to generalise those concepts to new situations where they are relevant, but achieving those goals rests on students having acquired the basic vocabulary of terms and labels in that domain.'[159] Vocabulary instruction is essential within every classroom.

As experts in our fields, it is important that we don't use these words without ensuring students understand them fully, it can be easily done. We should not assume students understand keywords just because we are very familiar with them or because we have used them in the lesson before, as the Heath brothers highlight, it is easy to lose awareness that we're talking like an expert[160] and this can happen in the classroom. The 'Curse of Knowledge' is a cognitive bias where you assume that

---

159. Bjork, R, A & Kroll, J, F. (2015) 'Desirable Difficulties in Vocabulary Learning', *The American Journal of Psychology*, 128(2), pp. 241-252.
160. Heath, D & Heath, C. (2008) *Made To Stick*. London, England: Arrow, p. 115.

other people know the things you do, or that they have the background to grasp what you are discussing. Some students can become easily confused when we use subject-specific terminology without exploring and explaining these keywords in the correct context first. This is why explicit vocabulary instruction is necessary.

Receptive vocabulary consists of words that we know and understand when we hear them and expressive vocabulary includes words that we are able to use confidently when we speak or write.[161] Ultimately, we want to expand both receptive and expressive vocabulary. All teachers play an important role in developing the vocabulary of our learners. There are some words that students will pick up naturally from their surroundings, which may include their peers, teachers and parents. Students can be introduced to new vocabulary from screen time such as films, television, social media and, obviously, through reading.

Encountering words naturally does not always secure a strong grasp and understanding of vocabulary. Authors Beck, McKeown and Kucan address that relying on learning word meanings from independent reading is not an adequate way to deal with students' vocabulary development.[162] There are a wide range of words that require support and explanation to ensure deeper understanding.

Author Daniel Rigney delivers an uncomfortable but realistic message in his well-known book *The Matthew Effect*, which is that the 'word rich will get richer while the word poor will get poorer'.[163] The phrase the rich will get richer and the poor will get poorer, derives from the gospel of Matthew 25:14-30 Parable of the Talents, 'For to everyone who has will more be given and he will have an abundance. But from the one who has not, even what he has will be taken away. And cast the worthless servant into the outer darkness'.

The reasons behind this growing vocabulary gap is that those who are good at reading are more likely to enjoy reading and, as they continue to read, will progress, moving from learning to read to reading to learn.[164] The word rich will become stronger readers and, as a result, increase their vocabulary. They are also more likely to associate with those who

161. Hutton, T, L. (2008) 'Three Tiers of Vocabulary and Education'. (Super Duper Handy Handouts!) Greenville, South Carolina: Super Duper Publications. Available at: https://www.superduperinc.com/handouts/pdf/182_VocabularyTiers.pdf
162. Beck, I, L, McKeown, M, G & Kucan, L. (2002) *Bringing Words to Life: Robut Vocabulary Instruction (Solving Problems in the Teaching of Literacy)*. New York City, New York: Guildford Press.
163. Rigney, D. (2010) *The Matthew Effect: How Advantage Begets Further Advantage*. New York City, New York: Columbia University Press, p. 76.
164. Ibid. p. 76.

are literate and word rich too. In contrast are those who struggle to read, they can become disengaged with reading and not find it a pleasurable experience and avoid reading completely. The word poor or reluctant readers will not have the same opportunities to develop their vocabulary as a confident reader would and cannot progress further thus widening the gap between the word rich and the word poor. Regardless of their social or economic background or ability, we want all of our learners to become 'word rich' and we need to support them with this and create word rich classrooms.

The three-tier model of vocabulary instruction

The three-tier model, designed by authors Isabel L. Beck, Margaret G. McKeown and Linda Kucan, is very useful and explored more fully in their magnificent second edition of *Bringing Words To Life: Robust Vocabulary Instruction*. The concept is that vocabulary can be categorised into one of the three tiers and this is designed to illustrate which words require specific instruction and attention. Quigley has written about several myths that surround vocabulary in schools and he argued that the belief that vocabulary will naturally develop in school as a result of simply being in school is not true. Thinking that vocabulary development does not require any explicit instruction is simply a myth.[165]

I have found the three-tier model helpful, as it made me realise the importance of vocabulary instruction. As such, I now ensure this is an integral part of my lessons.

First tier: words consist of basic vocabulary such as cat, dog, book, walk, and apple. Words that children learn at a young age. They are relatively easy with understanding, pronunciation and often appear in daily speech.

Second tier: words are more sophisticated. They will appear in adult conversation and can be words that have a multiple meaning. The authors and creators of the model explain that the second tier contains words that are of higher utility for mature language users and they are found across a variety of domains.[166] Examples of second tier words appear in literature and mature conversations such as fortunate, circumstance, and characteristic.

As you can see, tier two words are more complex than tier one words, but not limited to a specific subject like tier three words. Beck, McKeown

---

165. Quigley, A. (21 April 2018) '5 Vocabulary Teaching Myths' (The Confident Teacher) Available at: https://www.theconfidentteacher.com/2018/04/5-vocabulary-teaching-myths/

166. Beck, I, L, McKeown, M, G & Kucan, L. (2002) *Bringing Words to Life: Robut Vocabulary Instruction (Solving Problems in the Teaching of Literacy)*. New York City, New York: Guildford Press, p. 9.

and Kucan add that due to the large role tier two words play in a language user's repertoire, rich knowledge of words in the second tier can have a powerful impact on verbal functioning.[167]

Third tier: words will be the focus of this chapter, as they are often words within the domain of specific subjects and not as commonly used as tier one and two words. For example, in history there are keywords that I know students are unlikely (although possible) to have encountered before that could include: segregation, abdicate, heir, excommunication or revolution. Examples from science can include ion, reproduction or photosynthesis.

It is likely that students will only be exposed to these words in the context of their lessons, therefore the responsibility for developing the vocabulary of tier three words does not rely on teachers of English – although, of course, there are tier three words linked to English language and literature such as stanza, sonnet and so on – but rather, subject-specific teachers. Daniel Kahneman author of *Thinking Fast, Thinking Slow* highlights that 'learning medicine consists in part of learning the language of medicine'[168] and we can apply this to every subject studied in school.

This does not mean we need standalone lessons focused on vocabulary instruction, but instead it should become part of our lesson routines. Instruction for tier three words needs to focus on building content knowledge rather than isolated vocabulary knowledge.[169] This illustrates how subject knowledge and vocabulary knowledge are beautifully intertwined and reliant upon each other.

Hirsch argued one of the main reasons that reading scores for 17 year olds in the USA had decreased in 2012 was a result of too little time being spent on gaining the wide knowledge required for a broad vocabulary. He believes a knowledge driven curriculum will improve vocabulary as, during lessons, learners will be exposed to a wide variety of subject-specific vocabulary (tier three words). We should not shy away from using sophisticated vocabulary in our lessons; instead, we should introduce new vocabulary with support and scaffolding.

---

167. Ibid.
168. Kahneman, D. (2011) *Thinking Fast, Thinking Slow.* New York, NY: Farrar, Straus and Giroux, p. 3.
169. Ibid. p. 29.

The three-tier model of vocabulary instruction

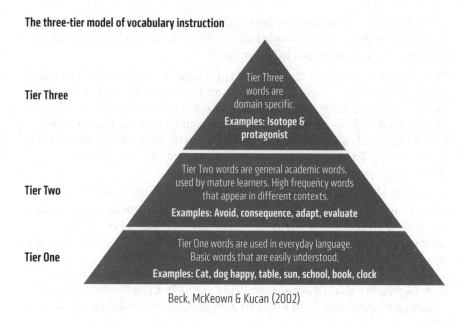

Tier Three

Tier Three words are domain specific.

Examples: Isotope & protagonist

Tier Two

Tier Two words are general academic words, used by mature learners. High frequency words that appear in different contexts.

Examples: Avoid, consequence, adapt, evaluate

Tier One

Tier One words are used in everyday language. Basic words that are easily understood.

Examples: Cat, dog happy, table, sun, school, book, clock

Beck, McKeown & Kucan (2002)

How to apply tier three techniques

I regularly dedicate time in lessons to ensuring students have a confident grasp and understanding of terms (tier three words) linked to the topics studied across the curriculum. I have several strategies and resources that I use to do this. The ideas shown in this chapter can be used and adapted for different subjects and key stages, as shown with my examples from history, geography, RE and MFL. Fully grasping subject-specific terminology naturally increases expressive vocabulary and provides students with a deeper level of subject knowledge and understanding.

Subject-specific vocabulary can be very challenging for students for many reasons. Difficulties can occur with reading and pronouncing the keywords, which is why modelling is an excellent starting point, for example repeating the words for students out loud. Also, understanding the terminology in a contextual setting can be a struggle for some, hence the need for concrete examples.

Definitions

People can often assume that being able to define a word illustrates depth of understanding. Daniel Willingham explains that if a vocabulary word or concept is missing from your long-term memory, you will likely be confused. But the need for background knowledge is deeper than the need for definitions.[170] We need to be very careful when designing tasks focusing on definitions of tier three words. I have a love and loathe relationship with dictionaries; I believe dictionaries should be used with caution and guidance. It can promote independence with students searching for a word in a dictionary to double check or self-correct spelling errors. Using a dictionary to support spellings is a good strategy. When students search for a dictionary definition this can result in the student feeling confused and none the wiser. Below is an example of the Oxford English dictionary definition of the word: Peasant

'A poor smallholder or agricultural labourer of low social status (chiefly in historical use or with reference to subsistence farming in poorer countries).'

Would that definition support a Year 7 student, with English as a first or second language, with their understanding of the term peasant? I would suggest a teacher explanation would be clearer and more student friendly, yet still ensuring understanding of this word.

'A peasant is a term used to describe a person in the period we are studying who worked for other people on the manor (land) and didn't have much freedom, money or own many possessions.' This explanation of the new term is supported with tier one and two words, as I try not to include other tier three terminology in a definition, as this could potentially confuse students. This could then lead to further discussion and explanation around the terminology and other historical context.

Anti-Semitism: Hostility to or prejudice against Jews.

This dictionary definition of anti-Semitism relies on the student having a good grasp of tier two terms – hostility and prejudice.

In contrast, some dictionary definitions can be suitable for some learners, take another example from the Oxford English dictionary:

Dictator: A ruler with total power over a country, typically one who has obtained control by force.

When it comes to dictionary definitions context is key, older students may be able to cope much better. Quigley raises the valid point that actually using a dictionary successfully requires a lot of background knowledge.[171] There are child-friendly dictionaries available that are

170. Willingham, D, T. (2010) *Why don't students like school? A Cognitive Scientist Answers Questions About How The Mind Works And What It Means For The Classroom.* San Francisco, CA: Jossey-Bass, p. 29.
171. Quigley, A. (21 April 2018) '5 Vocabulary Teaching Myths'. (The Confident Teacher) Available at: www.theconfidentteacher.com/2018/04/5-vocabulary-teaching-myths/

designed to have definitions and explanations more suitable for younger students. Dictionaries include the multiple meanings of words that can add further confusion. Hirsch has observed that 'in the time it took children to find a dictionary word and construe the meaning, they usually forgot the original context and never found their way back!'[172]

I am not trying to abolish the dictionary from the classroom, as in the right context it can be beneficial to support learning. Searching words in a dictionary either on paper or digitally is not an effective way of learning new words. If a dictionary were being used, I would advise a teacher or peer explanation to support understanding and trying a range of the activities below to check for understanding and the ability to use new vocabulary correctly and confidently.

Keywords within our subject area can also be particularly challenging for students with additional needs such as SEN (Special Educational Needs) and/or EAL (English as an Additional Language). A useful starting point with EAL students is to encourage them to translate the word using a bilingual dictionary to check if they are already familiar with the term in their first language. It is easier to learn a new concept by tying it to a concept you already know[173] and this can be applied to vocabulary with concrete examples.

My Year 9 class had studied the Civil Rights Movement in the USA. Segregation was a key focus of this unit. The same class were later studying life in Germany during the Nazi occupation and the students were able to apply the word segregation in a different, but correct, context when discussing the Nuremberg Laws of 1935. They made the connection that the Jewish people had been isolated and separated, as African–American people had been with the Jim Crow Laws. This links with Willingham's point that 'we understand new things in the context of things we already know and most of what we know is concrete'.[174]

Marzano's six-step process (2004)

Robert J. Marzano is a renowned educational researcher and author that devised a precise process to support teaching academic vocabulary. This has been well received by many teachers of different age ranges and subjects.

---

172. Hirsch, E, D. (2016) *Why Knowledge Matters: Rescuing Our Children from Failed Educational Theories.* Cambridge, Massachusetts: Harvard Education Press.
173. Heath, D & Heath, C. (2008) *Made To Stick.* London, England: Arrow, p. 54.
174. Willingham, D, T. (2010) *Why don't students like school? A Cognitive Scientist Answers Questions About How The Mind Works And What It Means For The Classroom.* San Francisco, CA: Jossey–Bass, p. 88.

The six-step process involves:

1. The teacher provides a description, explanation or example of the term.

2. Ask students to provide their own description or explanation, in their own words. Marzano encourages teachers to allow EAL students to write this explanation in their native language, as this checks their understanding of the word in their first language.

3. Students are instructed to draw an image, picture or symbol that represents that specific term.

4. Regularly carry out classroom activities that allow repeated exposure to that word and further build on their knowledge of that word. Marzano encourages the use of vocabulary notebooks.

5. Ask the students to discuss the term/s with their peers during classroom conversation and discussion.

6. Allow students to play games that require them to repeat and use the terminology to reinforce their knowledge of the term.

This six-step process by Marzano has inspired a lot of the ideas below. They are either similar to the six-step process or can be used as one of the classroom games or activities (step six) to practice using vocabulary.

Keyword Spotlight

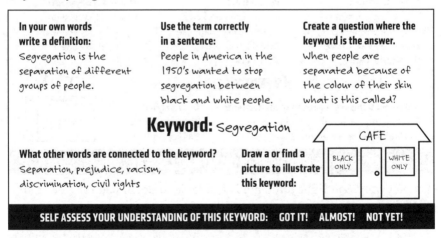

The concept of this task is to spend time focusing and exploring one specific keyword, putting the keyword under the spotlight.

First students have to provide a definition of the keyword in their own words, not regurgitated from a dictionary. The keyword under the spotlight should be a word that has already been introduced to students, a word they are familiar with. In addition to the definition, students then have to show they can use the word in the correct context by including the keyword in a sentence that differs to the definition.

Beck, McKeown and Kucan inform us that a learner might know the definition of a word but be unable to produce a context for it, or be able to use it in seemingly appropriate ways, but actually have a misunderstanding of its meaning.[175] This task aims to go beyond a definition but instead focus on the context of the word too. To further assist putting the term into context students must list other words that have a connection to the specific keyword being analysed, this illustrates their range of vocabulary connected to the topic. Students also have to include an image or drawing that they think represents or illustrates that keyword.

The task that students can find most challenging is to create a question where the keyword is the answer – this can really get them thinking! Finally, there is the opportunity for students to self-assess their level of understanding of the keyword. In my experience, after completing this task, most students are very honest selecting 'Got it!' or 'Almost!' This can then inform future planning and differentiation.

In your own words write a definition:	Use the term correctly in a sentence:	Create a question where the keyword is the answer.
Democracy: A system with a government chosen by the people for the people fairly.	Countries that have a democracy include Britain, USA and Australia.	What is the system where a government is chosen by the people?

Keyword: Democracy

What other words are connected to the keyword?	Draw a or find a picture to illustrate this keyword:	
Election, equality, politics, democrat, political parties, government		VOTES

SELF ASSESS YOUR UNDERSTANDING OF THIS KEYWORD: GOT IT! ALMOST! NOT YET!

The Keyword Spotlight template is available to download for free from my TES page.[176]

175. Beck, I, L, McKeown, M, G & Kucan, L. (2002) *Bringing Words to Life: Robut Vocabulary Instruction (Solving Problems in the Teaching of Literacy)*. New York City, New York: Guildford Press, p. 12.
176. K8SUE. (20 September 2016) 'Keyword Spotlight.' (TES) Available at: https://www.tes.com/teaching-resource/keyword-spotlight-11372156

Keyword Spotlight Grid

This task works in the same format as the Keyword Spotlight task above, the key difference is that the spotlight is on a range of keywords not just one. This will obviously require more time as it includes more words.

Keyword Spotlight Grid

Keyword	Definition	Use the term correctly in a sentence	Create a question where the keyword is the answer	Draw a picture to show the keyword	Other keywords linked to keyword

Keyword Challenge Grid

Manifesto	Campaign	Election
Democracy	Vote	Candidate
Parliament	Constituency	Referendum

This is a grid with nine keywords (often a combination of tiers two and three). Again, these will all be words that have been exposed to students before, because we know that repeated encounters with words can lead to rich word knowledge and understanding. This task provides students with another opportunity to engage and interact with vocabulary. A simple resource, but one that my students have responded well to and enjoy the challenge. Here are 11 different ways this simple keyword grid can be used in the classroom:

1. Provide a definition of the keyword. Project the grid onto the board or simply write out nine words. Students have to write definitions, explaining in their own words the meanings of the different terms that are connected to the subject, topic or lesson.

2. Use the keyword in a sentence (as before with the Keyword Spotlight task).

3. If this is the answer, what is the question? A popular and well-known quiz with a twist, where students have to come up with different possible questions where the keyword would be the correct answer.

4. Tell me what you know! Students have to write key facts or information linked to what they know about each word, no notes allowed to encourage students to recall using retrieval practice. This goes further than providing a definition, as it can include examples, statistics, information, and so on.

5. Keyword paragraph. Students have to write a paragraph, with the aim to include as many of the keywords from the grid as they can.

6. Think and link. Ask students to make links between the different keywords. Students make the links then explain the connection. This helps when providing an overview of a topic and analysis. This task can be used verbally, as well as written.

7. Literacy grid. The grid can be used in different ways connected to literacy such as listing synonyms or antonyms for each of the words.

8. Revision activity. The keyword grid can be adapted for different subjects and year groups. I have a lot of examples at Key Stage 3, but it can also be used with GCSE and A-Level to encourage students to include these terms in their examination answers.

9. Narrative. The keywords can be used to act as a prompt for students writing a story. Each keyword will lead to the next part of their story. Students could use the keywords in a specific sequence or any order depending on your/their choice.

10. As a former teacher of MFL I have used the keyword grid in various ways, with the ideas mentioned above, such as include in a sentence in the correct context, create a paragraph with the keywords, translate keywords or link the words using past and/or future tense.

11. Create your own Keyword Challenge Grid. Students create their own grid and have to select the nine keywords to include based on what they have been learning. Then they can swap with peers to complete some of the suggested tasks above.

YSGOL	CELF	RYGBI
HANES	NOFIO	HOFFI
CYMRAEG	GYMNASTEG	MATHEMATEG

An example of keywords in Welsh connected to the topic Ysgol/School.

The Keyword Challenge Grid can also be easily differentiated. This could be by colour, so that words in blue (tier three) for example are more difficult and aim to challenge learners. Another colour could include words that all students should be able to access (challenging tier two words) but to reinforce, revise and practice. The grid can vary in size, depending on how many keywords you wish to include. The idea is to once more check understanding of key terms in a variety of ways.

Go for Gold

Aim to include the following keywords in your answer and go for gold!

Bronze	Christian	Sex	Believe/Belief
Silver	Bible	Roman Catholic	Chastity
Gold	Celibacy	Adultery	Contraception

The 'Go for Gold' task has become a regular activity in my lessons. It is similar to the tasks previously mentioned, as it provides repeated exposure to tier three words. This idea is helpful because once again it is simple – not simple in the sense of making a task easy for learners, but the focus and challenge can be on the vocabulary rather than the activity. This resource can be adapted for any subject or year group, encouraging students to use sophisticated vocabulary in their writing. The task can be differentiated with the different colours, with the level of challenge increasing from bronze to silver to gold.

We want to ensure challenge for every learner, so everyone in the class has the opportunity to be stretched and encouraged to use sophisticated vocabulary in their writing. Bronze words should be terms that students are familiar with, possibly relevant tier two words, or the level of difficulty can depend on the spelling, content, mark scheme or other requirement. I have used this strategy with Year 5 social studies and Year 13 history.

Vocabulary Chase

USA Divided: Keyword board game!

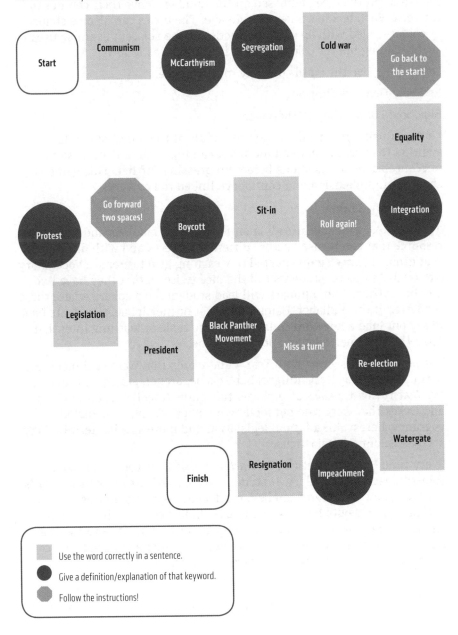

A straightforward game, but again the focus is on subject-specific keywords. Dice and counters are required to play vocabulary chase. Students roll the dice and based on the number, move their counter to that box. Each box has a keyword inside. The boxes can also be shape or colour-coded with specific instructions. The adjacent example uses shape-coding but for colour-coding it would be as follows:

Yellow box: Use the word correctly in a sentence.

Red box: Give a definition.

Blue box: Follow the instructions.

I suggest using this task during the middle of the topic/course. In addition to checking understanding, it can highlight any confusion, misconceptions or questions before progressing further. This game checks comprehension and confidence linked to keywords.

Vocabulary 6x6 Grid

Learning 6x6 grids, as already mentioned, are a fabulous and flexible resource that can be used across different subjects and with different year groups. I once again adapted the learning grid to create a Vocabulary 6x6 Grid. As before, students roll the dice twice so that they have two numbers. Those two numbers will lead students to a square where there is a letter of the alphabet. Using that letter of the alphabet students have to say out loud a keyword connected to the topic or learning intention. Then their partner rolls and does the same.

I have played this game with Year 7 and words that were said included; Saxon, Viking, tapestry, knight, heir, battle, archer, shield and cavalry. My Year 13 history class also played this game (much to their delight) and words that were said out loud by members of the class included; vagrancy, heresy, dissolution, legislation and more specific terminology such as Valour Ecclesiasticus.

Every time I use this activity in class I always hear very impressive subject-specific vocabulary. If students were asked to write these words – which is an option and can be done depending on your class – then perhaps some would be reluctant to use challenging vocabulary. This simple game provides an enjoyable opportunity to practice retrieving and pronouncing keywords, as suggested by Marzano step six. You can download the vocabulary grid for free from my TES page.[177]

---

177. K8SUE. (9 June 2016) 'Vocabulary Learning Grid.' (TES) Available at: https://www.tes.com/teaching-resource/vocabulary-learning-grid-11296189

Vocabulary Learning Grid: Roll dice and come up with keywords connected to our topic beginning with...

	1	2	3	4	5	6
6	A	J	I	D	F	B
5	H	K	B	W	R	I
4	Y	J	O	F	S	U
3	L	C	A	M	T	N
2	G	O	V	P	C	D
1	R	Z	S	E	S	T

Apps to support vocabulary instruction

Below are some of my favourite apps with explanations and examples on how I have used them within my subject, focusing on developing knowledge and understanding of key terms.

Militarism

Militarism is when a country puts great importance and investment into a strong and powerful army and navy. Before WW1 Militarism was common and countries became very tempted to go to war to prove their army was the best!

Created by a Year 9 student using Adobe Spark Post app.

Adobe Spark Post and Typorama

Adobe Spark Post and Typorama are ingenious apps, both free. Adobe Spark Post is available on both iOS and Android, in addition it can also be used in browser at https://spark.adobe.com. Typorama is only available as an app, but again for both iOS and Android.

I regularly use these two apps to create visually impressive resources and do so speedily and effortlessly. Both apps allow the user to create single image graphics with text overlays, with a variety of fonts and styles available. The images can be selected from the app library (all royalty free images) or you have the option to upload from the photo library on your own device. I have introduced these apps to my students and they have proven to be really useful with vocabulary development, either in the lesson or outside of the classroom using a device.

WordFoto

WordFoto, which will be referred to again in Chapter 8, is a marvellous app that can be used in a variety of contexts. The central focus of this app is the combination of the selected image and chosen keywords. WordFoto allows the user (either teacher or student) to embed a selection of keywords onto an image connected to the topic, helping to further make connections.

I created the example below at the start of a topic focusing on recruitment during World War One.

The WordFoto image acted as a prompt for discussion and questioning, asking students:

Do you recognise any of the words?

What do the words have in common?

What are the links between the keywords and the image?

Many students recognised the propaganda poster although some confused it with the Uncle Sam 'I want you for the US army' poster. Students were able to use their prior knowledge to deduce the poster was from the same period and linked to WW1.

Encouraging students to make their own WordFoto can be a useful method to practice using subject-specific vocabulary. The WordFoto app is another way to introduce students to tier three words too. It can combine a wide range of words and combine them within a picture, allowing the student to make connections between tier three terms and the image. Year 9 students, using images and words to describe life in the Trenches, created the WordFoto below.

Freerice.com

I was first introduced to this website at a TeachMeet event in Manchester, by teacher, Chris Mayoh who you can follow on Twitter at @chrismayoh. This website has two clear aims:

1. To support students develop their range of vocabulary and understanding.

2. To fight against global hunger.

How are these aims achieved? If you visit the website freerice.com it is very self-explanatory and obvious to navigate. Freerice.com is essentially a literacy game where a single word will be shown and three words will be provided as answers, with only one word representing the correct meaning. Students have to click on the correct definition.

The website lists this following example:

'Scare' means:

- Wed

- Frighten

- Laugh softly

Students click on the correct answer – in this case, frighten. As students progress through higher levels, the words become more challenging. For every correct answer the World Food Programme donates ten grains of rice to help end hunger. Students can create an account that they can return to and login if they wish to track their results (there is also a global scoreboard for those that are competitive). Students enjoy the competitive nature of the online game in addition to the fact that they are contributing to improving the lives of others. Freerice.com also has different categories and subjects to select from.

There are different questions connected to different subjects such as humanities, chemistry, geography and other languages: German, Spanish, French, Italian and Latin.

Our classrooms can become vocabulary rich learning environments and we can work towards closing the vocabulary gap between the word rich and word poor. This focus and emphasis on the importance of subject vocabulary must be consistent as a whole-school priority. It's a difficult question to answer when people ask how do you know if a resource or task has worked?

When using strategies to widen a learner's repertoire, you know the approaches are working because you hear the students using tier three terms during peer discussions or whilst answering a question and you read tier three words in their writing. Tier three terminology becomes embedded in their vocabulary with confidence and students are able to apply key terms in different contexts. Explanations become richer with subject-specific vocabulary.

It is truly wonderful when you hear your students talk like a historian, mathematician or a scientist! Vocabulary instruction should be an integral and important element of our subject, at all ages and we play a crucial role supporting our student's vocabulary development.

Summary

- Students are regularly exposed to subject-specific terminology in lessons. We need to ensure students have a good grasp and understanding of this vocabulary.

- Supporting students with explicit vocabulary instruction can help close the gap with the 'Matthew Effect'.

- The three tier model of vocabulary designed by Beck, McKeown and Kucan explains that tier one includes basic vocabulary, tier two contains higher frequency words and tier three focuses on low-frequency and subject-specific vocabulary. All tiers are important, teachers will have a duty to promote the use of tier two words and provide explanation of tier three words in their subject.

- Strong understanding of key terms is linked to strong content knowledge and understanding.

- Dictionaries have a place and purpose in the classroom. Dictionaries are not always suitable for providing students with appropriate definitions and explanation.

- There are a range of classroom activities, tasks and apps that we can include in our lessons to support development and recall with vocabulary.

Recommended reading

Building Background Knowledge for Academic Achievement. Research on What Works in Schools by Robert J. Marzano (2004)

Teaching Children To Read: An Evidence-Based Assessment of the Scientific Research Literature on Reading and It is Implication for Reading instruction by National Reading Panel (2000)

Bringing Words to Life, Second Edition: Robust Vocabulary Instruction by Isabel L. Beck, Linda Kucan and Margaret G. McKeown (2013)

The Matthew Effect: How Advantage Begets Further Advantage by Daniel Rigney (2010)

Closing the Vocabulary Gap by Alex Quigley (2018)

In addition to his book, Quigley also very generously shares a range of high-quality resources for free on his website to support the explicit teaching of vocabulary. These resources can be found at https://www. theconfidentteacher.com/resources

CHAPTER 6: HOW TO BE REVISION READY

'If you're good at learning you have an advantage in life'
Peter C. Brown, Henry L. Roediger & Mark A. Mcdaniel, Make it Stick: The Science of Successful Learning.

When it comes to learning, the authors of *Make It Stick: The Science of Successful Learning* warn that 'people are generally going about learning in the wrong ways'.[178] That can seem quite alarming and disheartening to both educators and students. Luckily, it is not all doom and gloom as the authors also add 'much of what we've been doing as teachers and students is not serving us well, but some comparatively simple changes could make a big difference'.[179] When teachers and students become research-informed, as to what revision strategies are effective (and which aren't) then we can be creative and clever when it comes to consolidation.

This chapter is not just aimed at teachers of older students, learners should understand effective revision strategies from a young age, so that it becomes embedded as part of their learning habits and routines. All teachers have been through the examination process, so this is an area we can fully relate to, understand and empathise.

There is a debate and concern about schools turning into exam factories. When data and results are heavily scrutinised, both students and staff can feel this pressure. Celebrity scientist Brian Cox has publicly criticised the effect of schools when they drill teenagers for tests. The article in The Times quoted Cox as saying that he wants teenagers to develop a real understanding of their studies, not to carry on being 'exam-passing machines'.[180] Cox also discussed the increasing pressure to pass exams

---

178. Brown, P, C, Roediger, H, L & McDaniel, M, A. (2014) *Make It Stick: The Science of Successful Learning.* Cambridge, Massachusetts: Harvard Education Press, p. 9.
179. Ibid.
180. Griffiths, S. (26 August 2018) 'Stressed teenagers should think about Mars, not exams, says star physicist Brian Cox'. (The Times) Available at: www.thetimes.co.uk/article/stressed-teenagers-should-think-about-mars-not-exams-says-star-physicist-brian-cox-c8vx58vdp

and expressed a concern for the rise in mental health problems amongst young people.

Whilst I have been enthusiastically encouraging the 'testing effect' and regular quizzing, I know there is much more to schooling and education than retrieval. All educators are driven by far more than examination results and school means much more to students, teachers and parents than a set of grades, although that is not to dismiss the importance of qualifications. Cox was not critical of teachers, his views were more directed at current polices and systems in place.

The importance of student wellbeing is paramount to all teachers. Exam stress is a common problem throughout all stages of education. We can't ignore it. We may not be able to remove the stress completely, but we can do all we can to support and reduce the trauma. I think the best way we can do this is by ensuring our students are using the most effective, evidence-informed revision methods to give them the best chance to succeed and the confidence to achieve their potential.

A key component linked to student success is consolidation and revision. This is an area the teacher can support but the student must be motivated and able to carry this out independently. Students are responsible for their own learning, despite the accountability and scrutiny that teachers have to experience. Willingham points out that motivation alone is not enough; sadly a desire to want to remember information has little or no effect.[181] Therefore, effective strategies are needed alongside motivation, independence and determination from learners.

Popular and common revision methods used by students are highlighting, re-reading or cramming the night before the exam. They are not the most effective strategies for supporting long-term memory. It is unlikely students will suddenly stop using these methods. Despite this, we can educate learners about strategies that have been supported by research and deemed more effective.

A masterful quote from Professor John Dunlosky, taken from his thought-provoking and informative article 'Strengthening the Student Toolbox. Study Strategies to Boost Learning' published in the *American Educator*: 'Teaching students how to learn is as important as teaching them content, because acquiring both the right learning strategies and background knowledge is important for promoting life-long learning.'[182]

---

181. Willingham, D, T. (2010) *Why don't students like school? A Cognitive Scientist Answers Questions About How The Mind Works And What It Means For The Classroom.* San Francisco, CA: Jossey-Bass, p. 60.
182. Dunlosky, J. (2013) 'Strengthening the Student Toolbox: Study Strategies to Boost Learning', American Educator, 37(3), pp.12-21.

This is a must read for both teachers and students as it provides an overview of the research in terms of effective revision strategies and is a student friendly read (for older students). I have shared this article with colleagues and the students in my examination classes. I remember some of my students were astonished by this report because they genuinely believed the strategies they had been using for years had been scientifically proven to be effective, but in fact it was the opposite.

The 'testing effect' or quizzing with the use of retrieval practice, as discussed in previous chapters, are clearly very good strategies to support learning and long-term memory. A lot of the ideas and resources explained throughout this book can be used during the revision period. These strategies can be embedded into regular classroom routines rather than used a month before examinations begin.

Start with why

Simon Sinek, inspiring TedX speaker and author, often encourages people to start with why. His target audience are usually leaders, businesses and corporations, but this can be applied to our students too. What's their why? Why do they want to be successful in their examinations? The typical response could be, no one wants to fail! When you discuss and think about this question with your class you will find out different students have their own motivations to succeed. It can be powerful to remind students of their why. When I have had these conversations with my classes, their responses have varied and surprised me.

I remember a student told me she wanted to do well because she had envisioned results day, she could see herself celebrating with her mum. I found a lot of students wanted to make their parents proud with their results. Other students wanted to do well in a specific subject because they were continuing to study that subject at A-Level or university. A student in my Upper School House told me she really disliked maths but she wanted to be a teacher when she was older, so she already knew the importance of doing well in this subject, regardless of her personal preferences.

CAT4 data and other assessment tools can be very rigorous and informative, but they do not take all relevant factors into account such as attendance, work ethic and effort, which we know can play a very significant role in student outcomes. I know many students that have felt their CAT4 predicted grades were far too low and this motivated them to show that they could do better. This can have the opposite effect with other students who are predicted low grades, lowering their own aspirations and targets. For students to be aware of their 'why' can really motivate and inspire them. It could be a good idea to write down their 'why' so they can refer to this on days when they may be lacking self-motivation and struggling. Everyone would like to achieve success, but when you delve into individual reasons why, we can learn a lot about our students.

Spaced practice

We hope that our students prepare in advance so that they don't need to resort to last minute cramming, but we know many still do. This can be a result of low confidence, the failure to revise as much as they should have, or it can be linked to feeling anxious about an upcoming high stakes exam. Despite the fact that many students will pull an all-nighter, staying up late and drinking too much caffeine because they believe last minute revision works best for them, we can demonstrate and explain using plenty of relevant examples to show how cramming is not effective.

If you have a student in your class who has achieved a high grade playing a musical instrument, then ask that student to share their steps to success with the rest of the class. Will that musician have been up all night before the exam practising? No. Instead, they will have been practising over a considerable amount of time to prepare and be ready. The same can apply with a dance recital, a football trial, swimming gala, and so on. Cramming does not work with a physical form of assessment or competition. Students need to grasp that this applies to all types of testing.

To avoid cramming or massed practice – which involves the constant practice of one specific concept, term or fact before moving onto another element – introduce students to spaced or distributed practice. The Learning Scientists, a group of cognitive psychological scientists interested in research on education, explain that studying five hours spread across two weeks is actually better than studying that same five hours right before the exam.[183]

This is known as spaced practice, spacing learning and retrieval over a period of time. The effectiveness of this strategy is echoed in *Make It Stick: The Science of Successful Learning*, as Brown et al wrote that if 'learners spread out their study of a different topic, returning to it

---

183. The Learning Scientists. (19 September 2016) 'Study Strategies: Spaces Practices.' (YouTube) Available at: https://www.youtube.com/watch?v=3WJYp98eys8

periodically over time, they remember it better'.[184] Bjork and Bjork also emphasise the benefits of this approach: 'Although massed practice, (for example, cramming for exams) supports short-term performance, spacing practice (for example, distributing presentations, study attempts or training trials) supports long-term retention. The benefits of spacing on long-term retention, called the spacing effect, have been demonstrated for all manner of materials and tasks, types of learners (human and animal) and time scales; it is one of the most general and robust effects from across the entire history of experimental research on learning and memory.'[185]

Bjork and Bjork help us to understand why this is a strategy teachers and students must be aware of and apply to their own practice. If we explicitly tell this to our students, hopefully they will act on this scientific advice. Students can plan spaced practice into their revision timetable and schedule in the same way teachers can with their planning and delivery of a curriculum. Instead of turning to cramming and coffee the night before the exam, they can focus on sleep!

In addition to their wonderful website www.LearningScientists.org you can also follow them on Twitter @Acethattest. I can also recommend visiting www.scienceoflearning.com created by leading expert in the field of educational neuroscience Dr Jared Cooney Horvath.

To highlight or not to highlight?

You probably have the answer to that question, or your own views about highlighting. When we consider the purpose of this technique, it is to highlight information, but that does not mean or suggest it should be used to learn information – there is a distinct difference. An actor would highlight their lines in a script, because this would show the actor the lines that they need to learn. The highlighting wouldn't actually help them learn the lines. The actor will need to practice and rehearse, but the highlighters simply show the actor the sections they need to learn/ memorise. The highlighters can help the actor refer to their lines in a script with greater ease. This is a good use of highlighting.

Yet, this idea and purpose has become confused with people assuming the act of highlighting will help us to learn.

184. Brown, P, C, Roediger, H, L & McDaniel, M, A. (2014) *Make It Stick: The Science of Successful Learning.* Cambridge, Massachusetts: Harvard Education Press, p. 10.

185. Bjork, E & Bjork, R. (2011) 'Making things hard on yourself, but in a good way: Creating desirable difficulties to enhance learning', *Psychology and the Real World: Essays Illustrating Fundamental Contributions to Society.*

Dunlosky describes highlighters as a security blanket for students when revising.[186] Ironically, the first time I was reading his article about the problems with this, I was actually highlighting this information – it is a hard habit to kick. Dunlosky also adds that highlighters could be a starting point, but should not be the main revision strategy for students to use. Clearly, highlighting notes will be better than no revision at all. Students will eventually learn from re-reading and highlighting, they were probably the methods we used to revise as students. Those strategies are not effective when we consider how long it takes to do and how long you can retain than information for.

Willingham often stresses that whatever students have to think about, they will remember.[187] Do students really think about content when they are highlighting text? This activity does not require anyone to think hard, in contrast to the testing effect. Answering questions requires more challenge and thinking; testing is more effortful, so we can understand why students would prefer to highlight – it is easier. We know that better and stronger recall is achieved through mental effort, where's the effort with highlighting?

Brown et al explain that highlighting can give students 'a satisfying – but deceptive – feeling of fluency and familiarity with material'.[188] Highlighting can give students a sense of achievement and satisfaction. This can be linked with the learning styles debate, as students may prefer a specific style because it gives them a false confidence about how much information they have learned or retained. Preferred learning styles and highlighting may feel good but that does not equate to being a good learning technique. I prefer pizza over apples, but we know pizza is not good for me!

Quigley has made no secret of the fact that he does not like his students using highlighters. His blog post 'Why I HATE Highlighters!' shows how he feels about this approach. Quigley has noted in his blog that 'highlighting looks like good work, it looks just like visible learning, but the more objective evidence states that it is little more than colouring in'.[189] I have found this to be true, with students creating beautiful revision notes with all the colours of the rainbow. Highlighting looks

186. Dunlosky, J. (2013) 'Strengthening the Student Toolbox: Study Strategies to Boost Learning', *American Educator*, 37(3), pp.12–21.
187. Willingham, D, T. (2010) *Why don't students like school? A Cognitive Scientist Answers Questions About How The Mind Works And What It Means For The Classroom*. San Francisco, CA: Jossey-Bass, p. 54.
188. Brown, P, C, Roediger, H, L & McDaniel, M, A. (2014) *Make It Stick: The Science of Successful Learning*. Cambridge, Massachusetts: Harvard Education Press, p. 15.
189. Quigley, A. (17 January 2015) 'Why I Hate Highlighters!' (The Confident Teacher) Available at: https://www.theconfidentteacher.com/2015/01/hate-highlighters/

impressive, it suggests that a lot of revision has been carried out and students can be proud of their multi-coloured notes. Although presentation is important and highlighting shows evidence of material being read, it does not mean that this method is actually supporting learning.

A lot of the arguments against the efficiency of using highlighters can be applied to re-reading. Re-reading does not require hard thinking or any challenging recall. Bjork and Bjork explain that 'rereading a chapter a second time, for example, can provide a sense of familiarity or perceptual fluency that we interpret as understanding or comprehension, but may actually be a product of low-level perceptual priming'.[190] The strategies that students find the most enjoyable and satisfying are often those deemed as the least effective.

I have encountered arguments defending highlighters, how bad can they be? Dunlosky and his colleagues reviewed 1000 scientific studies looking at the top ten revision strategies. Surprisingly they found eight out of the ten techniques didn't work or even hindered learning. Highlighting, underlining, re-reading and summarising fared low in regard to how effective they were, in comparison to practice testing and spaced practice which fared high.[191] That research would make for a very useful CPD session with staff and an informative assembly for students. A lot of my students have embraced and acted on the research-informed advice. It is not easy and I am still taking on the battle of the highlighter with some students.

Case study

All of the case studies in this book have been written by teachers and leaders. I wanted to include student perspective and voice so I asked two of my A-Level students Lauren Ashworth and Daniel Leo.

In August 2018 my students achieved their GCSE examination results. Daniel and Lauren are both very motivated and hardworking historians who have embraced the research-informed revision strategies. These revision strategies weren't

190. Bjork, E & Bjork, R. (2011) 'Making things hard on yourself, but in a good way: Creating desirable difficulties to enhance learning', *Psychology and the Real World: Essays Illustrating Fundamental Contributions to Society.*

191. Dunlosky, J, Rawson, K, A, Marsh, E, J, Nathan, M, J & Willingham, D, T. (2013) 'Improving Students' Learning With Effective Learning Techniques: Promising Directions From Cognitive and Educational Psychology', *Psychological Science in the Public Interest*, 14(1), pp. 4-58.

used just before the examination period but instead over the two-year course. Lauren and Daniel have reflected on how these strategies supported their learning.

Lauren 'I think that a combination of different revision techniques helped me to do as well as I did. Reading through the textbook and rephrasing in my own words was useful for me because I personally found it tested my comprehension of the information and how I could simplify it in a way that was easier to remember. I believe retrieval practice was one of the most useful techniques because it draws from your memory and constantly exercises the thought process that is the same as the actual exam. Retrieval is good as it shows where you need to focus your revision and for someone who struggles with how to begin revision, I found this very useful.

'The combination of using retrieval practice and answering past exam questions were very beneficial for me. Retrieval helped me understand historical events and contextualising the topic. Answering the past exam papers was also useful as it improved my subject knowledge. Completing past papers showed how much depth was required and understanding how to actually answer the question was important too.

'Not only was retrieval useful, but the repetition of using it in our lessons generally at the beginning of every lesson we would answer retrieval questions, helped keep previous lessons in memory so that key information would not be forgotten. Regular retrieval meant it didn't actually feel as though I was doing as much work as I was. I didn't need to revisit everything again at the end of the course because I had been doing that throughout the two years'.

Daniel 'One of my favourite revision techniques was definitely Kahoot. The Kahoot Miss Jones created helped me to recall key historical dates and events that I can even remember now! Repeating the Kahoot quiz helped me to remember the correct answers next time. I could use Kahoot using any device such as on my iPad or computer and on top of that, it was fun. Other helpful type of revisions included the flash cards and past papers throughout my two years studying history. When Miss Jones told me how great a resource flash cards actually were with memory my initial thoughts were, 'really I thought that's only for younger kids?' But unexpectedly, I realised how beneficial and important this was for my learning.

'Miss Jones taught us how to write questions on one side and the facts, information and answers on the other side. I could then self-test and absorb information easier. Finally, the use of repetitive past papers helped me perfect my technique in actual answers. I found the four mark questions in the exam the hardest rarely getting more than two per question but with regular practice and revision I was able to focus on getting this question right. I really enjoyed watching helpful videos online from www.mrallsophistory.com/revision and www.historychappy.com. In addition to the videos, the use of retrieval practice helped me continually see what I was doing wrong or what I couldn't remember so I knew how I could continue to improve.'

I would like to thank Lauren, Daniel and their families for agreeing to feature in this book.

Tried and tested tasks from my classroom

The revision task at hand must focus on subject content or the required skills. If a student is creating a revision poster or PowerPoint, which they tend to do, it is likely they will be devoting attention to design or animations distracting from the actual content and relevant skills. I have discussed this in Chapter 3, illustrating the problems with creating presentations or videos. The challenge should not be on the actual activity itself, unless that alone will aid learning and revision. Another problem that can occur with revision happens when students are told to revise and then left to do so independently.

Independent study without structure, guidance or instruction may be suitable for some capable students that can cope with this but there will be other learners who cannot and will struggle.

I have used these activities in this chapter to consolidate knowledge or check understanding before introducing new subject content. These tasks are designed for experts rather than novices when it comes to the content and skills. If you have time prior to the examination period then take the opportunity to share effective revision strategies with students and carry out practice testing and quizzing.

We can skilfully use our understanding of effective strategies combined with our in-depth subject knowledge to be creative when it comes to revising. Staying focused with so many distractions around for young people can be very difficult – especially with mobile devices! This is where students and parents have to be disciplined monitoring screen time at home.

Making revision appeal to students as fun or engaging is not the priority, learning takes priority but the build-up to the examination period is often a very stressful time. I believe revision can be very rewarding and enjoyable too, hopefully making the process less stressful.

BUG that question

It is absolutely essential that students understand examination questions in order to be able to access and attempt the examination paper. The layout of the question should become familiar. Despite recent changes to examination boards and specifications, students should be prepared as to what the examination paper will look like and the type, style or amount of questions they will be required to answer. Once students are familiar with the layout of the examination paper they then need to be able to independently grasp what the question requires of them – basically what is it asking them to do? A useful examination technique used with students includes 'BUG' an examination question. BUG means to:

Box the instructions, this shows students have fully understood what they need to do; this could be explain, evaluate or describe, etc.

Then **underline** key ideas/ focus of the question, again ensuring full understanding of what content will be needed in their answers.

Finally, students **glance** over the question once more. This is to make sure that they don't rush and miss out any important information or read the question wrong, which can easily happen especially under exam pressure. A common mistake that has happened in several mock examinations is that students ignore the stated date, therefore if they provide historical information that is not in the correct time period that can deem their whole answer as 'no relevant material provided'. After many years teaching and four years as a GCSE examiner, it became easier to identify and predict where students can go wrong, especially when reading the question.

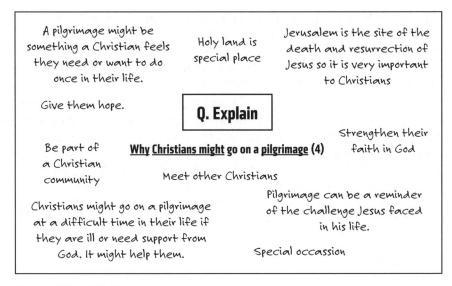

A pilgrimage might be something a Christian feels they need or want to do once in their life.

Holy land is special place

Jerusalem is the site of the death and resurrection of Jesus so it is very important to Christians

Give them hope.

Q. Explain

Strengthen their faith in God

Be part of a Christian community

Why Christians might go on a pilgrimage (4)

Meet other Christians

Christians might go on a pilgrimage at a difficult time in their life if they are ill or need support from God. It might help them.

Pilgrimage can be a reminder of the challenge Jesus faced in his life.

Special occassion

Students 'BUG' a GCSE RE question and plan an answer.

The Zone of Relevance

Another resource I have used regularly with my classes, not just during the revision stage, once students have grasped subject content, is the 'Zone of Relevance'. The idea focuses on what information is relevant for a specific question. Students will be given an examination question and, without their notes or reading material, they have to retrieve from memory, relevant and correct information. When students have spent a lot of time revising information there can be the temptation to include all of their knowledge in their exam answer. I remember memorising several key dates for my A-Level examination and I was bitterly disappointed that I didn't have the opportunity to include them all in my essay answer, but I understood the mark scheme and the importance of staying focused on the key question to include the correct relevant material. This activity can help students understand, as well as being able to recall information; it is an important skill to select the appropriate and relevant information that specifically addresses the examination criteria.

The example below is from my previous GCSE class studying crime and punishment. The question asked how abolishing the death penalty was a turning point in punishment in the 20th century. We discussed this question as a class and then looked at the mark scheme. Students then filled in the outer circle; it can also work with concentric squares too.

The largest zone must be for the relevant information, which is the most important because it is the content of the answer. Students include the relevant information with supporting detail and justification. In the middle zone students write extra information they could add to their answer, such as examples or statistics.

The final and smallest zone focused on what not to do! Students should be able to refer back to previous answers and learn from mistakes they had previously made. In this specific unit, there was a common error that students made, they would often express their views on the death penalty despite the fact the question did not ask for opinion or offer any marks for that either. The question also specifically asked about England and Wales, yet students would often write about the USA, again there were no marks available for this. The question was asking about the 20th century so discussion of any other periods was not required or rewarded.

Zone of relevance

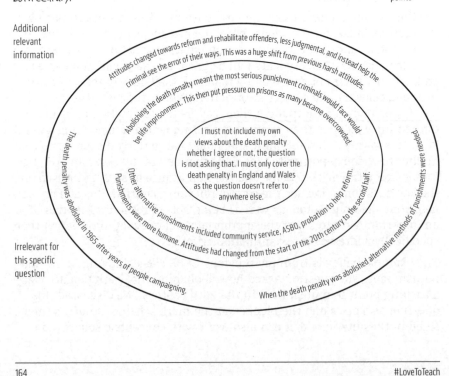

Exam question: Why was the abolition of capital punishment a turning point in changing attitudes in the 20th century?

Most important & relevant key points

Additional relevant information

Irrelevant for this specific question

Attitudes changed towards reform and rehabilitate offenders, less judgmental, and instead help the criminal see the error of their ways. This was a huge shift from previous harsh attitudes.

Abolishing the death penalty meant the most serious punishment criminals would face would be life imprisonment. This then put pressure on prisons as many became overcrowded.

I must not include my own views about the death penalty whether I agree or not, the question is not asking that. I must only cover the death penalty in England and Wales as the question doesn't refer to anywhere else.

The death penalty was abolished in 1965 after years of people campaigning.

Other alternative punishments included community service, ASBO, probation to help reform. Punishments were more humane. Attitudes had changed from the start of the 20th century to the second half.

When the death penalty was abolished alternative methods of punishments were needed.

Walkabout Revision Bingo

Walkabout Bingo is one of my favourite resources. It is very adaptable, so I will refer to it again in Chapter 8 with icebreaker walkabout bingo. The concept of the game is that students will be given a sheet with different questions linked to the topic or subject. They cannot answer those questions themselves. Students need to ask their peers each of the questions. They can only ask someone a question once, encouraging everyone to interact and get involved. It is an enjoyable activity that focuses on recall and retrieval.

On the sheet, students record the answers and the name of the person who has provided the answer. The first person to get all their boxes completed by different members of the class shouts 'bingo' and wins the game. Students could create their own version with questions that their peers will have to answer. Walkabout Bingo can be used as a starter activity to recall prior learning.

Crime and punishment walkabout bingo

Q. What is the name of a person accused of committing heresy? A: Heretic Name: Abby	Q. Describe the crime of treason A: Plotting against monarchy Name: Katie	Q. Name an item that was smuggled in the 17th & 18th century? A: Brandy, Silk Name: Sophie
Q. Give a cause of crime. A: Poverty Name: Beth	Q. State one reason highway robbery increased. A: Cheap guns Name: Owen	Q. State on reason highway robbery declined. A: Banks Name: David
Q. Who was the fictitious leader of the Luddites? A: Ned Ludd Name: John	Q. What did the Luddites damage? A: Textile machinery Name: Charlotte	Q. What was the name of the riot that happened in South Wales and men dressed as women? A: Rebecca Riots Name: Megan
Q: Describe living conditions in the 18th & 19th century. A: Awful Name: Robert	Q. Name a crime associated with technology. A: Hacking Name: Courtney	Q. Give an example of terrorism. A: 911 Name: Chloe
Q. Name a crime associated with motoring. A: Speeding Name: Miss K Jones	Q. Give a cause of crime from both the Tudor period and 20th century. A: Poverty Name: Graham	Q. How has technology helped prevent or solve crime. A: DNA Name: Adam

Roll, recall and revise

Another way the versatile 6x6 learning grid can be used is to revise or check understanding of a topic. Students roll the dice twice; to give them a number they can use for the horizontal and vertical line (for example 2 across and 4 down) and then answer the question in that specific box on the grid. A former colleague, Jade Lewis-Jones, with her class, used the example below during a math lesson. This was used as a consolidation and retrieval activity with Key Stage 3.

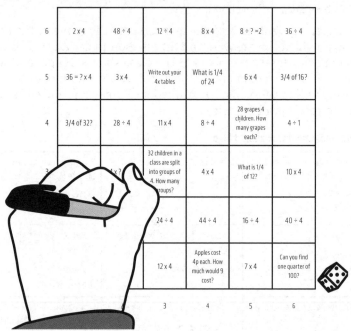

	1	2	3	4	5	6
6	2 x 4	48 ÷ 4	12 ÷ 4	8 x 4	8 ÷ ? =2	36 ÷ 4
5	36 = ? x 4	3 x 4	Write out your 4x tables	What is 1/4 of 24	6 x 4	3/4 of 16?
4	3/4 of 32?	28 ÷ 4	11 x 4	8 ÷ 4	28 grapes 4 children. How many grapes each?	4 ÷ 1
3		4 x ?	32 children in a class are split into groups of 4. How many groups?	4 x 4	What is 1/4 of 12?	10 x 4
2		24 ÷ 4	44 ÷ 4	16 ÷ 4	40 ÷ 4	
1		12 x 4	Apples cost 4p each. How much would 9 cost?		7 x 4	Can you find one quarter of 100?

Revision clock by Becky Russell

Revision flash cards can be great for helping students to break down information to make a whole subject or topic more manageable. Flash cards can also be great for quizzing and testing. An imaginative resource that will support retrieval practice of different topics and units is the revision clock. I discovered this resource online, created by geography teacher, Becky Russell who teaches in Manchester and can be found on Twitter @ TeachGeogBlog. Thank you to Becky for sharing her great idea in this book.

The purpose of this activity is to give students a selected amount of time, usually five minutes, to recall information from memory on one aspect/

topic/keyword then move onto another. This resource is dedicated to one hour of revision, for those students who rush or spend far too long on a task this structure can be very beneficial. Students enjoy this revision clock challenge and it is a good way to revisit previous learning. This activity can combine written text and illustrations, such as symbols or diagrams.

There are more examples of the revision clock that can be found on Twitter using #RevisionClock. It is a very effective resource that you can download for free on the TES.[192]

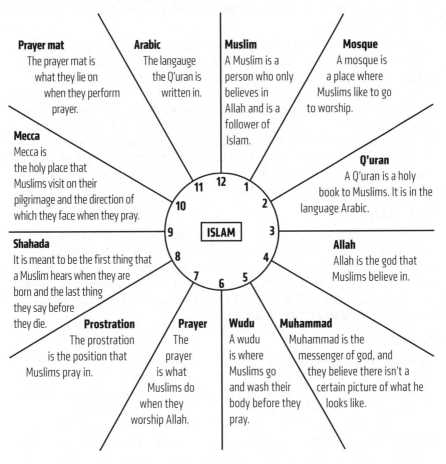

192. Teachgeogblog. (15 October 2018) 'Revision Clock'. (TES) Available at: www.tes.com/teaching-resource/revision-clock-11141536

Revision ready bags

The revision ready bag idea has been popular with teachers online for a few years. You can search Twitter and Pinterest for different variations of the revision bag. I have thoroughly enjoyed creating the revision ready bags for my students and they always appreciate them too. The revision bags are a kind gesture and final token of support. I am not encouraging teachers to spend their own money buying their students leaving presents, which I have seen with some extravagant revision bags and I don't think that is a good idea. Also, this academic year I have very small classes, so creating the revision bags was easier and cheaper; class sizes should be considered.

The revision ready bags I create often include useful resources to further support students with their revision and wellbeing. I created the revision ready bags for the students in my examination classes and tutor group (my tutor group is based on a House system with students ranging from Year 9-12). Obviously, subject-specific revision bags can contain revision materials specific to the examination and pastoral revision bags can be more focused on wellbeing. I would suggest rather than students receiving revision bags in all, most or some subjects that introducing the idea as a whole school approach would be even better. Here are the items I include in the revision ready bag:

Post-it notes

The reliable Post-it note appears again! Check in your department store cupboard or with the procurement department or resources team, if there is a supply of Post-it notes that you are allowed to give to students. Students can use the Post-it notes to list the topics they need to revise/read/cover that day. Other students I know stick Post-it notes around them as reminders, prompts and cues.

Flash cards

As mentioned, flash cards are a very useful revision activity, which can be purchased as a pack or sections of cards cut and divided up – simple. When students create flashcards with questions on one side and answers on the other or keywords and definitions on the back make sure that they consciously recall the answer either verbally or through writing. The reason for this being is that many students can struggle to self-test; they may see a question and think they know the answer and before consciously recalling it they have turned over to read the answer and then told themselves they knew that! They should say the answer out loud or write the answer down, continue answering other questions then check their answers shortly after. This powerful strategy promotes retrieval and informs students what information they can and cannot recall.

Stationery

Any general stationery is also a good idea, one that students are grateful for. Extra pens, pencils, paper and subject-specific stationery/equipment for subjects like maths are obviously essential when revising.

Bookmarks

A bookmark will come in very helpful to students when revising. Students will be undertaking a lot of reading across all their subjects. The QR code bookmarks in Chapter 3 can also be included in the revision bags. The bookmarks do not take long to create and no cost involved other than the printing. A bookmark is also a good opportunity to provide a revision list/specification for students if they do not already have one.

Good luck postcard

A final warm and friendly touch. I made good luck post cards using the free apps Typorama and Adobe Spark Post. Fortunately, with small class sizes, I was able to write a short, personalised message with some advice and best wishes. A generic card wishing your students the best of luck with their examinations and future will also be much appreciated. You could add a sweet treat too, if you are feeling generous.

Study buddy

Revising can be a real struggle for some students whilst others embrace this time to fully prepare for upcoming examinations. Should we encourage students to revise together?

This is a difficult question because some students prefer to study alone. I understand this because it helps me to stay focused, I found with my friends that we could easily stray off topic and I did not like that. Firth and Smith address this as they comment that 'studying together can be motivating but also distracting, as the presence of others will divide our attention'.[193]

I think the best approach during lessons is to provide opportunities for students to work with others as well as independently too. Revision can be very intense, so variety can provide some relief. I know students who

---

193. Smith, M & Firth, J. (2018) *Psychology in the Classroom: A Teacher's Guide To What Works*. Abingdon, Oxfordshire: Routledge, p. 33.

revise alone outside of school, whereas other students have benefitted greatly from revising with their peers. During the examination process we learn a lot about ourselves as individuals and this is one area where the students will find out for themselves whether they prefer to work alone or in the company of others.

Students revising together can be very different from one student teaching another. 'The protégé effect' has been described online as 'the best way to learn'.[194] The concept of The protégé effect is that students will learn information better and with greater clarity when they teach or intend to teach others.[195] That is quite a sensational claim and one that I am very sceptical of. I have yet to find any conclusive research to support this, although of course it could be available. When students are revising together they can be quizzing and testing one another. When students are teaching one another content this can be very uncertain territory. Certainly, novice learners should not be providing new information to other novice learners so the suggestion must be that one student should become an expert in order to communicate knowledge and information to their peers.

Another educational phenomenon linked to The protégé effect, that has become 'debunked' or recognised as a myth in recent years is 'The Pyramid of Learning' or 'Learning Pyramid'. The Pyramid of Learning is based on the work of well-respected researcher Edgar Dale, Cone of Experience (1946). The main premise of the pyramid is that students will remember 5% from lecture, 10% of what they read, 20% of what they hear, 30% of what they see, 50% of what they see and hear, 70% of what they say and write and 90% of what they do or teach to others. You may be familiar with this as it has been widely shared within education and continues to be so. There are different variations of the pyramid online with numbers varying slightly but that is the most well-known.

The first issue researchers have addressed with this pyramid is that the original cone of experience by Dale has been misunderstood and altered. Will Thalheimer has written that 'Dale included no numbers in his cone. He also warned his readers not to take the cone too literally'.[196] Lalley and Miller also discuss Dale's Cone of Experience in their 2007 paper 'The Learning Pyramid: Does it point teachers in the right

194. Paul, A, M. (13 June 2012) 'The Protégé Effect'. (Psychology Today) Available at: www.psychologytoday.com/us/blog/how-be-brilliant/201206/the-prot-g-effect
195. No author. (No date) 'The Protégé Effect: How You Can Learn by Teaching Others'. (Effectiviology) Available at: https://effectiviology.com/protege-effect-learn-by-teaching/
196. No author. (No date) 'Mythical Retention Data & The Corrupted Cone'. (Work-Learning Research) Available at: www.worklearning.com/2015/01/05/mythical-retention-data-the-corrupted-cone/

direction?' where they write that the cone was 'designed to represent the importance of teaching methods in relation to student background knowledge: it suggests a continuum of methods not a hierarchy'.[197] The second issue with the pyramid links to the percentages provided; where do the percentages come from? A series of studies or experiments? This information is unclear, leading many to suggest that data is bogus.

De Bruyckere often describes The Learning Pyramid as the Loch Ness Monster of educational theory. De Bruyckere has written about this myth extensively on his blog and in his book *Urban Myths about Learning and Education* alongside his co-authors Casper Hulshof and Paul A. Kirschner. I have also seen Kirschner describe this as the Learning Pyramid Zombie on Twitter. De Bruyckere explains that it is 'strange to find such neat percentages in research, so we can assume the research percentages are made up even more because the research data that it allegedly is based on can't be retraced'.[198]

The Learning Pyramid - Averege student retention percentages

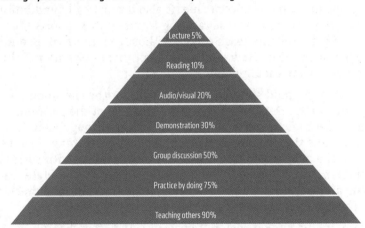

We already know this is where learning myths begin, when ideas, research or scientific evidence become misunderstood or miscommunicated to others and then it spreads. Thalheimer adds that researchers have been able to provide 'extensive supporting material necessary to present a comprehensive refutation of the aforementioned attempts to corrupt Dale's original model' and that 'there is no body

197. Lalley, J, P & Miller, R, H. (2007) 'The Learning Pyramid: Does It Point Teachers in the Right Direction?', Education, 128(1), pp. 64-79.
198. Pedro. (8 July 2016) 'From experience to meaning…'. (The Economy of Meaning) Available at: www. theeconomyofmeaning.com/?s=learning+pyramid

of research that supports the data presented in the many forms of the retention chart. That is, there is no scientific data – or other data – that supports the claim that people remember some percentage of what they learned.'[199] Lally and Miller reveal that 'no specific credible research was uncovered to support the pyramid'.[200]

Willingham has also contributed to the debate highlighting that 'so many variables affect memory retrieval, that you can't assign percentages of recall without specifying many more of them.'[201] For example, Willingham asked the following – what is being recalled? Age of the subjects? Delay between study and tests? How was memory tested? These questions illustrate that memory is much more complex than pyramid percentages suggest.

Whilst I don't think there is anything wrong with promoting a range of different teaching strategies and approaches, I have my own concerns about the pyramid percentages and hierarchy. To suggest students only retain 10% of what they read seriously undermines the importance and value of reading, which concerns me. It also dramatically undermines the role of the teacher too by suggesting lecture only supports 5% recall. How can novice students teach others without the information and knowledge themselves? How do they find out this information – through being taught by another student?

The Learning Pyramid simply is not practical for the classroom; it is a dangerous myth. Despite being wary, I was told of the pyramid after I had just spent four years at university learning through lecture and reading, so this theory completely went against everything I had been doing, but the people who told me of this theory did so with such faith and confidence in the model. The Learning Pyramid can dictate teachers planning and learning, which is too complex, important and precious to be left fully in the hands of learners to teach their peers.

Therefore, if students do wish to revise and study together, we should suggest effective strategies such as spaced practice and retrieval, rather than highlighting or teaching each other content.

199. No author. (No date) 'Mythical Retention Data & The Corrupted Cone'. (Work-Learning Research) Available at: www.worklearning.com/2015/01/05/mythical-retention-data-the-corrupted-cone/
200. Lalley, J, P & Miller, R, H. (2007) 'The Learning Pyramid: Does It Point Teachers in the Right Direction?', *Education*, 128(1), pp. 64–79.
201. Willingham, D. (25 February 2013) 'Cone of learning or cone of shame?' (Daniel Willingham – Science & Education) Available at: www.danielwillingham.com/daniel-willingham-science-and-education-blog/cone-of-learning-or-cone-of-shame

Sleep

Everybody knows sleep is important. We don't need any research or books to tell us that because when we are tired we can struggle with everyday activities. Being tired can make us feel emotional or irritable, and we can even become more vulnerable to illnesses. Although I was aware of this, I completely underestimated the importance of sleep until I read Matthew Walker's compelling book *Why We Sleep: The New Science of Sleep and Dreams*. Walker has spent over 20 years studying and researching sleep, in addition to working in various roles, including a sleep consultant to leading sporting teams.

This book really shocked me, and it provided a hard-hitting realisation about the power of sleep. It made me think about the importance of sleep for our students in addition to reflecting on my own sleep patterns. Sleep matters, both the duration and quality. Walker explains that 'routinely sleeping less than six or seven hours a night demolishes your immune system, more than doubling your risk of cancer'.[202] There have been many nights where I haven't had six or seven hours sleep and this will certainly apply to students (likely other teachers too). Walker explores other factors that are impacted by sleep such as major psychiatric conditions, depression, anxiety and suicidal feelings.[203]

Lack of sleep can be linked to weight gain, in both adults and children. The effects on both mental and physical health are truly worrying. Walker also reveals the rejuvenating health benefits that can occur as a result of simply better and longer sleep. Sleeping is an underestimated natural remedy, 'sleep enriches a diversity of functions, including our ability to learn, memorise and make logical decisions and choices'.[204] The quality of sleep can have a huge impact on learning and motivation in the classroom.

As teachers we do not have any control over the sleeping habits of our students, this is where parents are much more influential. If we can educate both students and parents about the significance of sleep and the impact this can have on their lives – both positive or negative depending on the quality of sleep – then this will be very valuable. Firth and Smith discussed the connection between sleep and memory, 'sleep deprivation can harm executive function, we need to be aware of the impact that fatigue can have on education in addition to its role in long-

---

202. Walker, M. (2017) *Why We Sleep. The New Science of Sleep and Dreams*. London, England: Allen Lane/ Penguin, p. 3.
203. Ibid.
204. Ibid. p. 7.

---

term memory.'[205] This is perhaps something teachers are aware of, but we don't consider it as much as we should. If you are up late reading this book then please go to sleep, if you are not reading this in the evening then aim to go to bed tonight and achieve your seven-hour sleep – although the appropriate amount of time can vary for each individual.

Summary

- There is a wealth of research to inform teachers and students about the most effective strategies for revision. We should share this information with students, about what they should and should not be doing.

- The most popular types of revision amongst students are generally not the most effective. We need to promote regular retrieval practice and the benefits of the 'testing effect'.

- Variety and engagement with consolidation tasks can help relieve the pressure and anxiety during this stressful period.

- Study buddies can work for some learners, as it will motivate and encourage them. A study buddy can have a negative impact on others, acting as a distraction.

- The importance of sleep should not be underestimated by students, teachers and parents.

Recommended reading

Make It Stick: The Science of Successful Learning by Peter C. Brown, Henry L. Roediger III and Mark A. McDaniel (2014)

How We Learn: The Surprising Truth About When, Where and Why It Happens by Benedict Carey (2015)

Why We Sleep: Unlocking the Power of Sleep and Dreams by Matthew Walker (2017)

Exam Literacy: A guide to doing what works (and not what doesn't) to better prepare students for exams by Jake Hunton (2018)

Understanding How We Learn: A Visual Guide by Yana Weinstein and Megan Sumeracki with Oliver Caviglioli (2018)

205. Smith, M & Firth, J. (2018) *Psychology in the Classroom: A Teacher's Guide To What Works.* Abingdon, Oxfordshire: Routledge, p. 47.

CHAPTER 7:
OWN YOUR OWN CPD

'Every teacher needs to improve, not because they are not good enough, but because they can be even better.'
Dylan Wiliam

Continuing Professional Development (CPD) across schools previously had a stigma associated with termly inset days that teachers would dread. These insets often involved a team building task (resented by teachers, who would rather be planning, marking or doing anything else to reduce their workload) or being introduced to the latest fad in education. Another issue with CPD is that schools have often adopted the one-size fits all approach. This whole staff approach can work, I have attended many sessions that I found useful and have also delivered many whole school professional development sessions to colleagues. Despite using subject-specific examples, I tried to ensure that the session aims and content were relevant to all staff.

Whole school training depends on the context and delivery. It is not always the best method as a staff body will often vary in levels of confidence, years of experience, different subjects taught, different age groups, and so on. CPD should not be limited to inset days or twilight sessions as it is an on-going process throughout our career and we should be taking leadership and ownership of our professional development.

Shaun Allison, author of *Perfect Teacher-led CPD*, has stated that leaders responsible for CPD need to get teachers excited about teaching, talking about teaching, planning and evaluating their teaching with other teachers, observing, learning and sharing what works with each other.[206] This book by Allison is a very good read for anyone leading CPD. It is clear and concise with lots of suggested strategies for schools. Responsibility for professional development as a middle leader with colleagues in your

---

206. Ibid.

phase or subject or as a senior leader is **so** important. Continuing to help teachers improve their practice should lead to greater improvements and value added success with student progress. Coe et al strongly emphasise in their report, titled 'What makes great teaching? Review of the underpinning research', that 'teacher CPD should lead to benefits for learners' and he believes that there should be a 'general recognition that teaching well is hard and needs to be learned'.[207]

There's a belief that some teachers are just better than others or that people are born to teach! There are people who are naturally stronger at communication or are naturally more confident. The idea that you are either a good or bad teacher, you have either got it or you haven't, demonstrates a very fixed mindset. As a profession, I believe that we don't accept this notion; if we did believe that then we could have an even bigger retention crisis. If we also had this attitude that you are either good or bad at something then imagine the negative impact that would have on the learners in our classroom!

Wiliam recognises and addresses the complex issue of teacher quality and examines the options to deal with this. Firstly, attempt to replace existing teachers with better teachers, although with reported figures of teacher retention,[208] this could lead to further problems. Replacing teachers is not always easy to do and the process can be slow. Another suggestion Wiliam refers to by Hanushek is to increase the threshold for entry into the profession. In Finland, teachers are regarded in high esteem and are well paid but all are expected to have completed further study to at least a Masters level. The alternative to both options is to improve the quality of teachers already in the profession. Wiliam writes, 'our future economic prosperity, therefore, depends on investing in those teachers already working in our schools.'[209] This is where on-going professional development becomes central and critical.

Coe in a different report entitled 'Improving Education: A triumph of hope over experience' suggests CPD should be intense with at least 15 hours but preferably 50 and the case study in this chapter shows an example of a school that requires teachers to undertake 50 hours through a strategy that has been well-received by staff. Coe adds CPD should be sustained, over at least two terms. The report recommends CPD should

---

207. Coe, R, Aloisi, C, Higgins, S & Elliot Major, L. (2014) What makes great teaching? Review of the underpinning research. (The Sutton Trust) Durham University, Durham: CEM.

208. Department of Education. (28 June 2018) 'School workforce in England: November 2017'. London, England: The Stationery Office. Available at: https://www.gov.uk/government/statistics/school-workforce-in-england-november-2017

209. Wiliam, D. (2011) Embedded Formative Assessment. Bloomington, Indiana: Solution Tree Press, p. 26.

be content focused on teachers' subject knowledge and how students learn. There should be opportunities for staff to try out ideas, discuss and evaluate and, of course, should be supported. Finally, it is no surprise that Coe promotes an evidence-based approach, sharing strategies that are supported by robust evaluation and evidence. Coe does realise that 'even if such training were offered, many school leaders would have serious concerns about allowing their teachers to spend so much time out of the classroom and their CPD budgets would probably not allow it anyway. Moving to a model like this would require big culture shifts.'[210]

A stand-alone single CPD session or inset day won't transform teaching practice. It might be useful, but the impact will be limited. I attended a course focusing on moving teaching from good to outstanding, the focus should have been about effective teaching, rather than using language associated with Ofsted (The English School Inspectorate – Office for Standards in Education). Perhaps my expectations were too high, but I was very disappointed. How can a teacher who has been teaching for six years progress from 'good to outstanding' during a one-day course? That course was very costly. This took place during the week, so I had to set cover and be absent for my classes.

This experience made me think very carefully about the CPD courses I would attend in the future, is the juice worth the squeeze? That is not to say that there aren't great courses available for teachers, because there are. For that specific event, I failed to do my research and I had unrealistic expectations. Professional development is an on-going and long-term process, not a short-term quick fix. One-off expensive courses in a hotel conference room with a free lunch won't change your life but taking control of your professional development can.

In recent years, teachers around the world have shown that they are leading the way, with ownership of their own professional development. This can be very empowering and enjoyable. Taking responsibility of your own professional development can enhance, and eventually even transform, your teaching practice.

Based on my own personal experiences, I feel that this approach towards my own professional development has been a major factor towards increasing my confidence and wellbeing. I certainly believe that I have progressed more so in the last three years of my career compared to the first five years, and that is not a criticism of the school I worked at

---

210. Centre for Evaluation & Monitoring. (2013) 'Improving Education A triumph of hope over experience. Inaugural Lecture of Professor Robert Coe'. Durham, England: Durham University. Available at: http://www.cem.org/attachments/publications/ImprovingEducation2013.pdf

because it was the leaders at that school that helped me truly understand how powerful professional development can be.

Jackson often shares this message that 'learning is a part of everyone's life – it's not just something that happens in the classroom'.[211] I believe as teachers we are excellent role models when we learn, progress and develop throughout our careers. Quigley offers some wise words which further echo this, 'We must never fall prey to thinking our learning has stopped. We should be the ultimate role models for continuous learning'[212] and Quigley links this to growing teacher confidence too. This chapter focuses on how teachers can take a firm hold of our own learning, progress and professional development.

Observe, observe and observe

The word observation can cause anxiety and fear for some teachers; I have certainly struggled with nerves during lesson observations. When lesson observations are developmental not judgmental they can be very helpful, insightful and useful to teachers. I really enjoy the opportunity to visit other teachers in their classrooms and inviting other teachers to my classroom. It is really important that schools create an open-door culture, I don't mean all teachers should have their doors open if they would rather not, but instead the idea is that others are welcome at all times to visit your lessons, as long it does not disrupt learning.

The key point here is the idea of being welcome. A middle or senior leader who is continually 'popping into a lesson' can cause the teacher stress and feel like they are being closely monitored and scrutinised. When the process becomes critical or focuses on grading then the impact of lesson observations can be very negative. When in fact, watching others should have a positive and beneficial impact, as we can learn a lot from each other in regards to behaviour management, communication, questioning and much more.

A strategy we use in my current school is the Green Light Classroom, also known by other schools around the world as Green Light Learning Walks or Spotlight Classrooms. This does not happen all the time, it takes place during one week every half-term. Teachers will metaphorically open their doors to all staff that want to visit. We have a shared document and a teacher will write on the timetable to show when and where they will be teaching, in addition to a brief summary of what they will be doing. If

---

211. Jackson, N. (2015) *Of Teaching, Learning and Sherbet Lemons: A compendium of advice for teachers*. Carmarthen, Wales: Independent Thinking Press, p. 11.

212. Quigley, A. (2016) *The Confident Teacher: Developing successful habits of mind, body and pedagogy*. Abingdon, Oxfordshire: Routledge, p. 69.

there are any teachers who would like to see that in action and they are available, they can go visit. We do carry out the Green Light visits during PPA time, but it is not compulsory so if a teacher is having a particular busy week there is no pressure to get involved with the Green Light Classroom. Teachers have to sign up to attend on the shared document so that a lesson is not disrupted with 12 members of staff watching the first 20 minutes of the lesson then leaving! This is informal, there's no paper work to fill out, but instead dialogue and reflection are encouraged after the visit. It also promotes opportunities for teachers to observe a lesson, or section of a lesson led by a teacher outside of their phase or department.

Other schools simply put up a sign outside their classroom with the days and times of the lessons that they wanted other teachers to visit. I think this is a great idea but this strategy can be viewed as a type of learning walk, so it is therefore worth being aware of union guidelines and classroom observation protocols. The NUT provide a 'Learning Walk and Drop-in' policy to advise schools how best to do this, for example it is stated that 'a maximum of two colleagues will be involved in learning walks at any time' and they should be 'conducted with minimum disruption to teachers and pupils'.[213] The difference between a green light classroom and a learning walk is the invitation to the lesson.

Learning walks can be helpful but they can also feel like SLT are checking up on teachers. If the feedback provided by SLT is school-wide, generic and vague then who does that help? How will that support an individual teacher to improve? It is a question that leaders and teachers should carefully consider and discuss.

Social media: Twitter

Twitter – that's right I am telling you that Twitter is a phenomenal source of inspiration, debate and discussion for educators around the world. Twitter was a complete revelation to me. Blogger Thomas Whitby, commented on the surprising impact of Twitter on the teaching profession, 'Nobody ever expected teachers to adopt Twitter as the backbone of the professional learning network. But it happened.' It certainly did. I was aware of Twitter for many years before I started using it professionally, if you are not using Twitter as a teacher, or 'Tweacher' on EduTwitter then you might be slightly confused, but trust me and stick with me. If you are using Twitter for professional

---

213. National Education Union. (No date) 'Learning Walks Model Policy' Available at: https://www.teachers. org.uk/learning-walks-model-policy

development, then my advice might help you gain even more from this platform.

My former deputy headteacher, Paul Williams, would regularly share slides, quotes and educational research during our morning briefings in the staffroom. Paul would also inform staff that his source for all this information was Twitter. He encouraged us all to look into Twitter as a form of professional development.

At first, I was very reluctant to use Twitter in this way. I thought teachers and social media can be a dangerous combination with students finding out about our personal lives or trying to connect with us online, but those issues can be easily prevented and managed through privacy settings. I decided to set up an account and find out for myself what the fuss was about. I then found other educators to follow on Twitter (when you connect with someone on Twitter you press the follow button, rather than sending a friend request as you do on Facebook).

I was able to find educators to follow online quite easily because I followed all the accounts that Paul was following. All of these educators had clearly been tweeting for a long time and had gathered a large following, which further opened up the online educational community to me.

How can Twitter help with your professional development? It can help in many ways. There are some teachers who use Twitter to gain support and inspiration. If you work in a school with a small department, it can be great to interact and communicate with other educators. Even if you work in a large school, perhaps you want to find support from a teacher who does not teach at your workplace. Twitter allows us to connect and interact with educators outside of our school or area. Anderson is another advocate for using Twitter, who describes it as 'the best staffroom in the world'.

There are lots of networking possibilities. You don't have to share anything on Twitter; you can simply follow others and provide feedback, you can ask teachers questions or seek informal professional advice. You could share a resource or useful website, anything that you think might be of help to other educators – if you find it useful, it is likely others will too. It is your account, you decide who you follow, who you engage with and what you share or don't share online.

If you are new to Twitter, here are my top tips to get started:

- Pick a Twitter handle that is simple and that you are happy with. I didn't give any consideration to @87History but it will do. I could of course change it, but I have had it a few years now so it has stuck! A Twitter handle that is easy to remember is also a good idea so that when you are networking at educational events, and so on, you can quickly share your handle to connect with others online, and a simple handle increases the likelihood of them remembering it.

- Share some information in your bio. It does not have to be too revealing; perhaps what subject you teach, your role or location. This is useful for other educators using Twitter. When I was considering moving to the UAE, I followed teachers that had Dubai or Abu Dhabi as their location listed in their bio so that I could find out more about teaching in that area.

- Upload a profile photo. This does not have to be a headshot or 'selfie' if you don't wish it to be, but the standard egg profile photo Twitter provides is not very exciting. Some users might be reluctant to follow you back, as they may assume your profile is a spam account. Use your bio to show who you are and that you have a genuine account and what you are interested in.

- Remember the **golden rule** about posting online. If you have a public account (a private account is locked and only people who request to follow you and who you accept can see everything) then anything you post could potentially be viewed by your colleagues, headteacher, governor, students, students' parents and potential future employers. Keep that in mind.

- Professional or private? What is the aim of your account? Is it to use as a platform for professional development, if so try to keep the content of your feed linked to that. Or are you using it personally posting holiday photos, photos of your children or cats? Some people do combine both aspects. I have found very clear separation helps me, but I have begun sharing some travel photos to show my other interests. We can be professional online and show our personality. Do I want my colleagues, headteacher, governor, students, parents or potential future employers viewing all of my holiday photos from Spain? No.

- Language and the use of appropriate language online has become a hot topic of debate. In the UAE, it is illegal to swear online so educators in the region don't (or should not) use bad language. Prior to my relocation I didn't use bad language on Twitter. I am not being so naive to suggest that teachers never swear outside of the classroom, but this comes back to the golden rule. If your profile is public or dedicated to professional development do you think it is acceptable to be swearing online? This is not for me to answer, every individual can make that decision for themselves; it is just something to consider in my humble opinion.

- Don't let the negativity put you off. There is a lot of educational debate on Twitter. Educators disagreeing, challenging or questioning each other, which is healthy for the profession to develop. There are times where I have observed very personal and nasty attacks and exchanges online. I have received some negative comments that I simply ignored, but nothing of a serious nature. You can ignore, mute, block or report. Generally, 'EduTwitter' is a delightful, friendly and supportive network.

Hashtags

Hashtags are words or phrases with no spaces that begin with the # symbol. If you are looking for something specific you can search a hashtag. If you want to share something with a wider audience than your followers, then including a hashtag is a good idea. Below are some useful hashtags that you can use or search anytime, and it is likely there will be something of interest or use to you.

#AppleEDUchat – A hashtag for the community of Apple Distinguished Educators, although anyone can join the discussion or use the hashtag.

#BameEd – This refers to Black, Asian & Minority Ethnic that aims to promote visible diversity in education.

#Bookcreator – For educators that use the app Book Creator.

#CogSciSci – A hashtag for science teachers interested in the study of Cognitive Science and how this can support teaching and learning.

#Edchat

#Edtech – Anything related to technology in the classroom, as is the same with the hashtag below.

#Elearning

#FEchat – The hashtag for educators in the Further Education sector.

#Historyteacher #Geographyteacher #RETeacher #PEteacher and so on.

#PrimaryRocks – The hashtag sharing and discussing primary education.

#ResearchEd – This is often used during various ResearchEd events, which take place around the world.

#ResearchSEND – The hashtag for educators to share research, linked to

Special Education Needs and disabilities.

#SEND – A hashtag to use when discussing Special Educational Needs and disabilities.

#STEM – The sharing of practice linked to STEM subjects.

#TeachUAEchat – A Twitter chat that I coordinate that explores education with educators from the UAE, although we are always joined by educators from around the world.

#TeamEnglish – You can find a wide range of English literature, language and literacy resources shared with this hashtag. The #TeamEnglish community are a powerful force of good in education!

#WomenEd – This promotes and celebrates women in education and leadership.

Twitter chats

There are regular Twitter chats that take place were someone, a host, will ask a range of questions linked to education or a more specific topic such as wellbeing, edtech, literacy, feedback, research, and so on. People answer using the hashtag, examples include #UKEdchat, which take place every Thursday at 8pm in the UK. Others can respond and the discussion usually carries on for about an hour. This is a great way to express your views, ideas or experiences and connect with other educators.

I created a hashtag for teachers across the UAE to use, #TeachUAEchat. In addition to this I launched a Twitter chat. I began by asking educators online that I knew, to join the chat. I usually ask three to four questions and I asked people for recommendations as to what they would like the next topic to be. I decided to host the Twitter chat every fortnight. Each time more people got involved. There are now other educators guest hosting #TeachUAEchat.

Guest hosts have included an edtech special with Mark Anderson (@ICTEvangelist). Tom Sherrington (@TeacherHead) hosted a great discussion about curriculum design. I was fortunate that British Olympian James Goddard agreed to host a chat, about the importance of swimming and sport with young children. Alex Quigley (@HuntingEnglish), hosted a Twitter chat discussing and sharing techniques to support vocabulary instruction. Dr Caroline Kuepper-Tetzel (@pimpmymemory), who works as a Lecturer in Psychology and as part of The Learning Scientists team also hosted a very special #TeachUAEchat too.

Two years ago, I had no idea what a Twitter chat was but I got involved with a chat one evening. After being involved with several Twitter chats I became a guest host for #UKEdchat and #MovingOnEdchat before I created my own regular chat. I always look forward to #TeachUAEchat because it is great to discuss and debate important issues in education, with other educators in a friendly and informal online environment. Be brave, try out a Twitter chat or even host your own when you are feeling more confident about it.

My top tips to host a Twitter chat

Create the questions in advance. It sounds obvious, but I know people who have tried to create the questions during the chat. A Twitter chat can get very busy with lots of people responding so it is better to engage with the other users during the chat instead of just posting out questions. My secret is that I create the questions and write the tweet but then save it in my drafts, so I can quickly hit post later! I have found that easier than scheduling tweets using sites such as TweetDeck (where you can automate Tweets in advance) but instead the tweet is there and ready.

Think carefully about the questions you ask too. I am based in the UAE and there are specific cyber laws all residents have to do adhere to, so I aim to keep the chat as positive as possible and avoid controversy. I don't think we should stop discussing challenging and difficult aspects of teaching, but asking teachers questions that might lead to criticism of their school or employer is not always a good idea.

Create images to accompany your questions. I have previously written about the excellent free apps Adobe Spark Post or Typorama, they are the apps I use to create images when I host a chat.

Don't forget the hashtag! This always happens, every single chat I have been involved with someone (I have been guilty of this too) forgets to use the hashtag. Send gentle reminders to people involved to remind them that in order for everyone to see and interact with their responses they need to include the relevant hashtag.

Promote the chat online in advance. Inform people what day and time the chat will be taking place. I let people know the topic in advance because it may or may not be something of interest to them. Ask your followers to share and spread the message far and wide. The wider the promotion, the more likely people are to get involved with the chat as they are aware of it. If you do host a Twitter chat, let me know @87history I'll do best my to join the conversation!

Below is a thorough list of Twitter chat timings (all timings are GMT and weekly unless stated otherwise). Thanks and credit go to Hannah Tyreman, she is the Online Learning Specialist at the Chartered College of Teaching, for collating and sharing this information and you can follow Hannah on Twitter @hannahtyreman.

Monday

#Primaryrocks – 8pm for primary schools educators.

#Behaviourchat – 8pm a chat focusing on behaviour management strategies.

#ASEchat – 8pm a chat for science teachers.

#Engchat – 8pm a chat for English teachers.

#ukREchat – 8pm (fortnightly from the first Monday of the month) for teachers of RE.

#LrnSciChat – 9pm (monthly) A chat led by the Learning Scientists @ acethattest related to cognitive science.

Tuesday

#bettchat – 4.30pm a chat focusing on technology in education.

#mathchat – 7pm a chat for maths teachers.

#caschat – 8pm a chat for teachers of computing and computer science.

#PDNReflect – 8pm a chat for educators to reflect on their practice with peers.

#MTPTchat – 8pm a CPD chat for teachers on parental leave.

#AppleEDUchat – 8pm an Apple technology education chat.

#TwinklTeach – 8pm (fortnightly) a general chat for all educators.

#BELMASchat – 8pm (monthly) a leadership focused chat.

#deabteED – 8.15pm weekly educational debate.

Wednesday

#ELTChat – 12pm and 9pm a chat for English Language teachers.

#TeachUAEchat – 4 or 5 pm UK time, always 8pm UAE time. A chat for educators across the UAE.

#2ndaryrocks – 7pm for educators in secondary schools.

#Geogchat – 7.30pm a chat for geography teachers

#ITTchat – 7pm a chat focusing on Initial Teacher Training.

#mathschat – 8pm another chat for maths teachers.

#SENexchange – 8pm a chat focusing on SEND.

#EYshare – 8pm a chat for early years in education.

#NQTchat – 8pm a chat for newly qualified teachers.

#mfltwitterati – 8.30pm a chat for teachers of MFL.

#UKPastoralchat – 8pm (monthly) a chat focusing on pastoral care and issues.

#RR_chat – 8.30pm (monthly) reading rocks chat focusing on literacy for primary school.

Thursday

#CCTbookclub – 7.30pm (monthly) The Chartered College of Teaching book club where authors discuss their books and answer questions from educators.

#UKEdchat – 8pm a general education chat for all.

#UKEdReschat – 8.30pm chat focusing on educational research.

#ScotEdchat – 8.30pm a chat for educators based in Scotland.

#UKfechat – 9pm a chat for educators working in Further Education.

Friday

#PedagooFriday – all day, every Friday teachers sharing their weekly highlights.

#coachinghe – 12pm (monthly) a chat focusing on coaching in education.

Saturday

#EdchatMENA – a slow chat throughout the day for educators across the Middle East and North Africa region, but welcome to all.

Sunday

#aussieEd – 11.30am Australian education chat, open to all globally.

#SGHour – 6pm a chat focusing on child protection.

#PlanningPanic – 7pm a lesson planning chat.

#mltchat2 – 7.30pm a chat for existing and aspiring middle leaders.

#NewtoSLTchat – 7.30pm a chat for new Senior Leaders.

#SLTchat – 8pm a chat for existing and aspiring Senior Leaders.

#UKgovchat – 8.45pm a chat for UK school governors.

Social media: LinkedIn

LinkedIn is the world's largest professional network. Unlike Facebook, Twitter, Instagram and other social media sites, LinkedIn is designed to be purely professional. LinkedIn was launched in May 2003 and, according to the LinkedIn, it has over 500 million members across 200 countries. Professionals set up an account that is essentially an online CV. Users then connect with other professionals in their field, using the site to assist them. LinkedIn does state that users should not connect with people they don't know, but clearly people do. LinkedIn can be another great source of professional development. I am referring to the free option, as you can join LinkedIn for free or pay a subscription fee for access to different features. I don't have a paid subscription as I didn't feel the need to do so, but I know other educators that have chosen to.

I regularly check LinkedIn to read different educational blogs and articles shared by educators that I am connected to. It is an excellent way to keep up-to-date with current affairs, latest updates and debates surrounding education (the same can also be said for Twitter). In addition to using LinkedIn for recruitment and networking, it can also be useful if you yourself are sharing resources, ideas or writing. I am a regular blogger and a quick analysis of my statistics page shows that many of my views come from LinkedIn. If you are a blogger, using LinkedIn can be another platform to share and increase your audience.

Another important feature of the site is the ability to endorse people. On the profile section you can list various skills and people you are connected with can endorse you for those skills. This is a good insight for employers, as other professionals can endorse your skills or write a recommendation for you. All recommendations have to be approved, so if someone did write something about you that you disagree with or are not happy with, you have the control not to make it visible on your profile.

A quick summary of the main benefits of using LinkedIn are:

- It is easy to use and navigate.

- It is available as a free app and can be accessed in a browser.

- LinkedIn provides access to a worldwide network of educators that you can connect with, interact, share and learn from. There is great potential when searching for a teaching position. I have seen teaching positions advertised on LinkedIn before being advertised on other sites (probably because it is much cheaper to advertise and recruit). It can be a great platform to showcase your skills, experience and passion for education. Finally, it is a professional site purely focused on professional development, networking and recruitment.

Podcasts

Podcasts have become one my favourite forms of professional development. CPD on the move! I listen to podcasts when I'm driving or at the gym. This might give the impression that I'm thinking about work all of the time – which isn't true – but I like listening to the podcasts and I learn a lot. There is now a wide range of educational podcasts available for teachers to download freely. There are subject-specific podcasts. I thoroughly enjoy Versus History, where teachers Dr Elliott Watson and Patrick O'Shaughnessy debate the importance or significance of key historical events and individuals. I listen to Dan Snow's History Hit podcast too. There are podcasts that provide a wider overview of education. I have become an avid listener of the Mr Barton Maths Podcast, some episodes are subject-specific but most are relevant for all teachers. Craig Barton hosts this and he has featured a wide range of well-known and accomplished guests including Robert and Elizabeth Bjork, Dylan Wiliam and Doug Lemov.

Here are an additional five educational podcasts I recommend, available to download:

TES – The education podcast

The Cult of Pedagogy Podcast with Jennifer Gonzalez

Education Research Reading Room with Oliver Lovell

The Edtech Podcast with Sophie Bailey

Dismissed – a podcast about expat life and education with Principal Jeremy Williams

Case study

I attended a leadership conference in Dubai, where I listened to primary school teacher and leader Ben Rothwell explain how his school has transformed CPD for all staff. I wanted him to share this experience in my book and I am very grateful that he has agreed to do so.

'Victory Heights Primary School (VHPS) is a relatively young primary school in Dubai, we opened in 2013, we currently have just shy of 800 students from FS1 through to Year 6. As a small school, we have a somewhat limited CPD budget and in the past this has restricted our ability to provide external CPD to our staff. It was possible, but ate away significantly at the budget. We also have a mixed cohort of staff; some seasoned pros, some NQTs, some English speaking, others Arabic speaking, not to mention a sprinkling of subject specialists, as is common in the region. This meant that providing CPD opportunities to that wide range of stakeholders was extremely challenging.

'In 2016, I, alongside some other senior colleagues, devised a new way of thinking, an approach to CPD that would go on to raise staff satisfaction levels significantly. This provided over 27 staff members the opportunity to lead sessions in 2018 and it led to a number of staff talking at local teaching conferences and seminars, as well as – the feather in the proverbial cap – a nomination for the 'Outstanding Strategic Initiative' at the British International Schools Awards. This brief commentary in this book is designed to show you why you should consider a similar approach and some of the tools and techniques you might use.

'We made CPD a key focus of our school development plan and, in a scheme dubbed the VHPS University gave our teachers full control of their own professional learning journey. Rather than run sessions to a blanket audience with the occasional external speaker, we instead invited staff to use their own professional expertise to run sessions on topics that they were interested in (and on most occasions expert.) We dedicated 90 minutes every Tuesday after school as 'VHPSu' time – where staff could attend sessions held by their peers, based on their own requirements and taste. Attendance at these sessions was not compulsory. Nothing about VHPSu is ever compulsory, save for issues of statutory compliance, such as child protection training. Instead, we ask our staff to dedicate 50 hours of their time towards CPD in any given academic year.

'This could be entirely constructed of attendance at training sessions in-house and for many of our younger staff, this is exactly what they need. Indeed, working in smaller groups led by experienced staff, who importantly know the context of the school, have given these staff a far more personalised learning experience.

'But for some staff, there are other avenues they want to explore. We reward those who run sessions with additional credit on their hours contribution, to recognise planning and preparation time. We have staff following Masters degrees and other accredited courses, who are able to gain credit for these. Staff have formed study groups exploring EdX and Coursera courses. Others have undertaken action research projects, have developed their own strategic initiatives by forming working parties and we even credit our intrepid educational book club.

'You may think it is a nightmare to manage, but we have developed some simple, but effective strategies to enable staff to log their hours. Most importantly, we use free in-house software, built on top of Google Apps, but replicable in Office365 or other office packages – there are no expensive subscriptions required!

'Staff log their hours using a simple form and with some query and filtering magic, we are able to get an overview of our staffs' progress. We are currently further developing our systems to allow staff to triangulate their VHPSu records with feedback from performance management, learning walks and other school data. We are extremely proud of our journey and our staff consistently tells us that they love the flexibility that VHPSu affords them. We work in an extremely competitive environment with yearly inspections and have progressed rapidly to achieve a 'Very Good' rating. But most of all, we measure our own success by extremely good staff retention rates and the continued smiles on the faces of our staff.

'If you are reading this book and can make a similar impact on your own school CPD strategy, I urge you to consider loosening the reins – if not removing them all together – and allowing your high-quality staff to develop themselves, whilst gently holding their hand and coaching them to enable them to develop.'

You can follow Ben on Twitter @VHPS_Innovation

TeachMeet events

A TeachMeet event is an organised but informal meeting of educators, across different sectors, to share good practice, practical ideas and personal experiences or insights into teaching. This phenomenon has become very popular in the last decade. It is known as a 'Spark' event in the UAE and an 'Unconference' in the US. After joining Twitter I kept reading about TeachMeet events, but I didn't know what they were. At this point there seemed to be no TeachMeet events taking place in my area, so during the Easter break – as Wales and England sometimes have different term dates – I travelled to London to attend my first TeachMeet. This was TMLondon 2015, hosted at Quintin Kynaston Academy by a group of educators. I didn't know what to expect but the experience was so liberating. The presentations were of such a high quality and I loved the atmosphere. Refreshments were provided and plenty of time encouraged for networking. I made two good friends Penny Rabiger and Alex Warner, who I have since been able to stay in touch with through Twitter. I learned so much and I felt totally inspired. I was at an event with teachers who were as passionate about education as I was. TeachMeet events are generally free, although sometimes they may charge a small fee.

After TMLondon, I attended many more events across the country from Cardiff and Manchester to Reading, to name a few. At every event I met new people and took something away to improve my practice. I was encouraged to present and share some ideas, I recall my first presentation at Liverpool and I was so nervous, it was only a three-minute presentation! The positive feedback and comments afterwards filled me with joy and confidence. Weeks later, it was great to hear from teachers who were using my ideas in their classroom. I am very grateful to all the educators that have hosted these events to benefit and support other teachers.

My top tips for presenting at a TeachMeet event

I should start by clarifying that I am not a professional public speaker. My experiences have led to increased confidence and it has become something I take great pleasure in, but I am still working on improving. Volunteering to speak at educational events, in front of other teachers, should not be a terrifying ordeal; your audience are in the same position and profession as you. Everyone who volunteers to speak at educational events does so because they have ideas, information, experiences or interests that they wish to share with others. No one is judging the speaker, but instead listening with the hope that they can learn something. Below are some of my simple tips and hints, if you are considering presenting in front of your colleagues or at an educational event.

Practice and prepare. Obvious advice but I have seen many presentations where the speaker has openly admitted to not preparing anything in advance and it shows. A lack of preparation and practice can become very obvious, as the individual will stumble or rush through their presentation, forgetting to include key points or lacking clarity in their explanations. There are some fortunate people who can simply wing it in front of a crowd with charm and charisma. It is not easy to do that and I am not one of those people. Invest some time preparing your presentation and practicing, this will also help with any nerves too.

Time yourself. TeachMeet events often have strict timings as there will be a lot of presentations to be delivered. The last thing you want is to be told to stop before you have even introduced your idea or concept. I watched a three-minute presentation, where the presenter spent the three minutes introducing herself and discussing her career. Then the timer buzzed and she was horrified that she could not continue her presentation! If you have three, five, seven or ten minutes then practice several times so you know what you will be able to include and also at a pace that is not too fast. When sharing teaching and learning ideas, think quality over quantity.

Watch yourself back if you get the chance. This can be very embarrassing but it is useful. I presented at an event that was streamed live. My presentation was available to view online after the event. I was shocked to watch it back and realise I was constantly pacing up and down the stage, this was very distracting from the content of my presentation. This then became something I was very aware of and could improve on next time I spoke in public. Also, ask members of the audience for some honest and constructive feedback.

If you are trying to become better at public speaking, then **present at every possible opportunity**. This can be at your school or educational events. Sign up to as many as you can, your experiences will make you a better speaker. As your confidence grows, you will it enjoy it more too.

Include images and visuals in your presentations, rather than heavy information and written content. Use the images as prompts, to remind you what to discuss. This can be applied to the classroom with our presentations. Consider working memory and Cognitive Load Theory. Don't overload working memory by providing too much text when you plan to talk. My presentations now mainly consist of images and this forces me to practice because I don't have any text to rely on.

Use a wireless presenter (clicker), during your presentation. You are not restricted to standing next to or returning to a laptop to move to the next slide. I have my own personal clicker. It was a great purchase, as I use it for presenting and also in the classroom too, it has become my essential classroom piece of equipment. If you are a teacher that uses PowerPoint, Prezi, Keynote or another other form of presentation in your lessons, then you need this tool. No longer are you stuck to your desk clicking your way through your slides – simple but effective.

Finally, smile and use some humour, but keep it clean and appropriate.

Top tips to organise your own TeachMeet event

I lived in an area where there was a lack of educational events and networking opportunities, although this has improved now. After many train journeys and traveling to TeachMeet events across the country I decided, with the support of my headteacher, to host a TeachMeet event myself. Take some initiative and go for it!

My first piece of advice, don't do it alone. I have organised a TeachMeet event completely on my own and I have also organised TeachMeet events with a group of other educators. Trust me on this one! Organising and hosting a TeachMeet can be a lot of hard work in addition to a busy full-time job. It can lead to unnecessary stress, pressure and you will not enjoy the experience as much. It is much better to lead, divide and delegate. There are so many different aspects to consider such as sponsors, promotion, presenters, and refreshments. Hosting a TeachMeet event can be a fun and rewarding experience, but you do not have to do it alone; build a supportive team around you to share the workload as much as possible.

Sponsorship is the task that no one really wants to be responsible for, but it is often important. It is likely you will need money from sponsors either for the venue – although if you can host it at your school, then that will save a considerable amount of money – refreshments, and if you wish to have prizes, which many TeachMeets have become known for. I attended a TeachMeet event that took place at the National Football Museum in Manchester. This was an amazing venue that offered a free bar and meal for all those that attended – lovely! The problem was that sponsors dominated the presentations, more so than teachers, so I didn't gain as much from the event as I had hoped, but I did enjoy the meal and the networking.

I understand that if sponsors donate money or prizes, then they expect time to talk to teachers but often they are selling products that need to be targeted at SLTs or headteachers. Classroom teachers can feedback to SLT about such products, but we often do not have the power or budget to buy these products. It is not the reason teachers attend TeachMeets, so be very mindful of that. A suggestion would be to give sponsors a dedicated area, therefore people have the choice if they want to find out more, but they don't have to. As for prizes, local companies often donate prizes you just have to ask.

Once you have your TeachMeet team and sponsors, you will need to promote the event to encourage people to attend. Pick a date that does not clash with an event on your school calendar. A Friday night can put some teachers off, that is the start of their weekend so if it has been a long week the thought of attending an event full of teachers bursting with enthusiasm might not be that appealing! I have hosted two TeachMeet events on a Saturday and I have attended many events on weekends too. I do limit how many weekends I dedicate to professional development, because we have to have a personal life too and spend time with our loved ones. I would also advise that the event does not run too late, especially on a school night because, again, this can be a negative factor, especially if people are travelling from afar.

After the date is confirmed, begin persuading as many of your colleagues as you can to attend, although no pressure as a TeachMeet is not compulsory CPD; people who attend are all there because they want to be. Email any contacts you have or other nearby schools, this is great for schools within the same area to collaborate and network. Finally, promote the event online. You could use Eventbrite or create a specific website for your event. Again, consider your workload and pick the easiest option. I would certainly recommend using social media too, but don't rely on it as your only form of promotion. Set up a Twitter account, hashtag and/or Facebook page to spread the word online.

The presentations that will be delivered during the TeachMeet are very important. The amount of presenters and how long each presenter will have to present will depend on the timing of your event. Set a limit for how many presenters can speak, then once all slots have been assigned then that's that. I have been to a TeachMeet where every single person who signed up to present was able to, which was great in one sense but also meant the event went on for hours. It lost momentum and people were leaving before the end. It's also wise to aim for a broad range of presenters.

At the event I hosted, #TMNWales presentations varied from primary to secondary, with cross-curricular to subject-specific presentations. At TMHistoryIcons, a subject-specific TeachMeet event, all presentations were by history teachers. We did ensure that there were NQT's presenting in addition to presentations from experienced teachers and leaders. Presenters also included a PGCE mentor, people from across the UK and further afield.

It is difficult to assess the quality of presentations before the event but it is important to be inclusive, which can also mean ensuring a gender balance of presenters. #BAMEed is a movement that have been encouraging event organisers to be aware of Black, Asian and Minority Ethnic educators being represented. Coverage of all fields within education during one event is unlikely, but an attempt to create a diverse line up will be appreciated. An idea is to ask people to submit their presentation prior to the event and the organisers select the presenters, but the quality of a PowerPoint presentation does not always reflect the quality of the presenters themselves. Some events use a name generator to select presenters randomly, which is designed to be a fair method of selecting presenters, but this can be very disappointing for those who have worked hard to prepare their presentation and did not get selected. There is a risk with presenters and it is so important to get this right, because for many people the presentations are the most important part of the event, not the free refreshments or prizes as teachers are looking for high-quality CPD.

I think this is probably the most useful advice I can offer to someone hosting a TeachMeet event – be prepared for those that don't turn up! After hosting three TeachMeet events I realised that not everyone who signed up to attend will show. Firstly, a TeachMeet is a free event, which is ideal for teachers but there is no financial commitment, making it easier for people to drop out. Also, a TeachMeet event takes place after school hours and sometimes life just gets in the way. Some people sign up to the event with all intentions to go, but nearer the time decide they are too busy or just forget, which is why promotion is important. Remember to send out a friendly reminder as the event approaches!

For the first TMHistoryIcons, 115 people signed up, but 80 people attended. This was still a very good turn out but we had paid for 115 dinners using the sponsorship money, so again another risk. When I hosted TMNWales I had a sleepless night the night before thinking no one would turn up (as mentioned in my acknowledgement my sisters attended the TeachMeet, to show me some moral support and for more bums on seats). 80 people signed up and 60 attended, and I was relieved as this was a good audience. Don't be disappointed or disheartened – be prepared.

A #hashtag is great to promote the event, but also the hashtag can be used during and after the event. During the TeachMeet teachers can share online what they have found out and provide feedback using the hashtag. I have followed many TeachMeet events online, that I have been unable to attend (especially now I live abroad) by following the hashtag. Many events are now streamed live, often using Periscope, for people to watch from the comfort of their own homes.

A very important factor to consider is the ICT/ technical support. I will ask presenters to send their presentations in advance, so I can try to avoid any technical errors. There may still be technical errors on the day, so ensure you invite an ICT expert to the event so support will be there if you need it.

Finally, make sure you learn, network and enjoy. I have thoroughly enjoyed every TeachMeet I have ever been to. There is always a warm, friendly and enthusiastic atmosphere when teachers come together to collaborate and network. Prizes, freebies and refreshments add to the enjoyment of the event and are very much appreciated. Those things aren't a priority, don't lose sight of that, but people haven't signed up for an additional department meeting. Make it pleasant and informal. To create a relaxed atmosphere I suggest playing music, providing delicious refreshments and time dedicated to networking. Have fun, share, learn and network!

15-minute forums

In my previous school, we had a morning briefing every day. Each day of the week was designated to different agendas. A typical week would usually include starting Monday with notices for the week ahead. Tuesday would consist of numeracy and/or literacy support. Wednesday would be focused on data analysis, support and tracking. Thursday morning was all about teaching and learning. Finally, Friday briefing involved sharing strategies that supported individuals with additional or special educational needs. These were often led by the leaders in that field but were open to all staff to present; the senior leadership team did encourage this. I found the use of 20 minutes briefing time in the morning very useful. The sessions were a daily dose of CPD, built into our timetable. This was directed time; so all staff members were in attendance. Not all schools do this, but I found it very helpful and believed it was a good strategy. Daily morning briefings are different to 15-minute forums.

Shaun Allison describes 15-minute forums as the most effective CPD strategy that can be set up in a school.[214] At my current school every fortnight, on a Tuesday morning there is a 15-minute forum. Some schools deliver this weekly and it can be at the end of a day, whatever staff prefer or find convenient. The 15 minute forum provides an opportunity for teachers to talk about anything they wish to share with colleagues that they believe will educate, support, interest or inspire others – in 15 minutes.

Although 15 or 20 minutes is only a limited amount of time it can still be used effectively. During a 15-minute forum I showed my colleagues the video Austin's Butterfly with Ron Berger, as mentioned in Chapter 4. The forum can be used as a way of introducing something new to colleagues. The next 15-minute forum I plan to deliver will introduce and explore Cognitive Load Theory (CLT). I won't have enough time to discuss this theory in detail but I will provide an overview of the theory and how this applies to the classroom. There may be colleagues that aren't familiar with CLT, so they will hopefully be intrigued to find out more. I will then provide materials and links for further reading; so even if a forum is used to begin a discussion that's great. Allison teaches at Durrington High School and, along with some of his colleagues, manages the superb blog https://classteaching.wordpress.com. On this blog there are summaries of various 15-minute forums, that have been delivered at his school by different staff members, examples include: 10 simple things to support work-life balance; tips for new teachers; and how to get the best from your TA.[215]

Teaching and learning newsletter

I am very enthusiastic about discussing education and sharing teaching and learning ideas, in case you hadn't noticed! Another method of regularly sharing my teaching practice and educational research with staff is through a monthly teaching and learning newsletter. I like the idea of teachers being able to easily find out what their colleagues are doing in their classrooms in a very simple and accessible way – through a newsletter. There are many schools that have their own newsletters or interactive CPD display and noticeboards. If you do this already in your school, great! If you don't, perhaps suggest it to SLT or take the initiative to create your own as I did.

214. Allison, S. (2014) *Perfect Teacher-led CPD*. Carmarthen, Wales: Independent Thinking Press.
215. No author. (No date) 'Category Archives: 15 Minute Forums'. (Class Teaching) Available at: www.classteaching.wordpress.com/category/15-minute-forums/

What do I include in the newsletter?

Every month, the newsletter will have a similar format. This means that teachers know what to expect from each newsletter and where to look for specific sections that may appeal more to some teachers than others. The content is focused on pedagogy rather than subject-specific content as it is a whole school newsletter. I am aware of departments in schools having their own subject-specific departmental newsletter. What I include in my newsletter are only suggestions, as every school is different. The newsletter can reflect the values, ethos and teaching of the school.

App of the month. At my school we have access to iPads, therefore I only suggest iOS apps as this is relevant to my colleagues. I provide a brief overview of the app, how it works and examples of how the app has been used as either part of my planning or within the classroom. I will always suggest an educational website or blog. Based on the feedback I have received, this is the most popular feature of the newsletter. Some teachers have informed me that they go straight to the recommended website section, and then visit the recommended site. My focus is to share websites that provide a range of teaching and learning resources, research or reflections from other educators.

Suggested reading. I have never had any difficultly recommending educational books to my colleagues as I carry out a lot of reading. The books I recommend in the newsletter are books I or another teacher will have read and recommended. The resource of the month is always well received by my colleagues too. The difficulty with this section is trying to cater for all teachers as my school ranges from Foundation Stage to A-Level. Therefore, I try to share cross-curricular resources (as I have done in this book) that can be used across a range of subjects and easily adapted for different year groups, so everyone can benefit.

The newsletter also provides an opportunity to **share and inform colleagues of any educational events or CPD** taking place within the local area. I share any useful hints and tips that can help with planning, behaviour management, ICT, and so on. I also include a 'Coming up...' section, suggesting what will appear in the next edition and provides the reader with something to look forward to. I try to include feedback and quotes from students, with their opinions about what they have found helpful, in addition to sharing what other teachers are doing in their classrooms too.

How do I create the newsletter?

I use the Apple app Pages on my iPad because it is very simple and quick to create a high-quality and sophisticated newsletter on iOS or Mac (I convert to PDF when I send it electronically). Alternatively, you could use Word or Publisher, whatever works best for you or that you are familiar with. I have seen great examples of newsletters created using Adobe Spark Page or Sway.

When and how is it distributed?

I originally wanted to create a weekly or fortnightly newsletter. It was suggested, I create a monthly newsletter so that it didn't become a workload issue. On reflection, I completely agree, this is a much better idea. At the start of the month, I distribute a digital copy to all staff via e-mail. I can also include any digital attachments of resources or website links, that are featured in the newsletter. I provide a small sample of hard copies placed in the various staff and workrooms. I have seen many teachers on their break, sat with a cup of tea having a quick read and gaining some nice takeaway ideas for their lessons. The feedback from my colleagues has been very positive, appreciative and kind.

Blogging

Blogging has become a regular form of reflection and platform for sharing good practice, for many educators around the world. Many educational authors first began writing through a blog (myself included). When I began teaching, I was unaware that there were teachers blogging about education; I was oblivious to this remarkable online world of educational bloggers. I am sad I missed out on this for the first five years of my career, but I am happy to have now discovered so many excellent bloggers. It was through joining Twitter and following individuals that I discovered they were blogging as well as tweeting. Initially, I read blogs from the sidelines, just taking away golden nuggets of advice or ideas to implement in my classroom.

After feeling limited by the previous 140-character restriction on Twitter, I decided to start writing in more depth about the resources I was creating and sharing. Mark Anderson helped me to create my blog using Wordpress and I am very fortunate to know such an experienced expert. You don't need an edtech evangelist to help you though, as WordPress and other blogging platforms are relatively straightforward to set up and come with various tutorials.

I am so impressed with the high-quality blogs about education and I am grateful for how much I have learned from bloggers sharing or reflecting. Here are ten bloggers/blogs that I highly recommend you read (with their Twitter handle included), in no particular order:

Blake Harvard – @effortfuleduktr – https://theeffortfuleducator.com/

Clare Sealy – @ClareSealy – https://primarytimery.com/

Dawn Cox – @missdcox – https://missdcoxblog.wordpress.com/

Adam Boxer – @adamboxer1 – https://achemicalorthodoxy.wordpress.com/

Victoria Hewitt – @MrsHumanities – https://mrshumanities.com/

Debra Kidd – @debrakidd – https://debrakidd.wordpress.com/

Greg Ashman – @greg_ashman – https://gregashman.wordpress.com/

Peter Ford – @EdSacredProfane – https://edsacredprofane.wordpress.com/

Mark Enser – @EnserMark – https://teachreal.wordpress.com

Hannah Wilson – @TheHopefulHT – https://thehopefulheadteacher.blog/

Subject-specific professional development

The problem with a whole school staff training session on a cold January morning is that this does not cater for subject-specific development. We know as educators that having qualifications in the subject/s we teach is not enough. My main subject, history, is incredibly vast in regards to time periods and countries. Historians will often specialise in a field of their interest. History teachers, however, are expected to be experts in a wide range of fields and periods. To have the required depth and understanding of each topic is very challenging. Being knowledgeable about so many fields or periods is both very time-consuming and demanding.

I am not complaining about teaching a variety of topics because I do relish it, but it is not easy. I believe students should have access to a rich and varied curriculum. Where does professional development fit into this? Professional development time can be limited, but it is important for both senior and middle leaders to recognise that time needs to be dedicated to subject-specific development. Department meetings can often be dominated by administrative tasks rather than discussion of subject knowledge or curriculum planning.

If you are a middle leader then it is vital that staff in your department have time to collaborate, whether that is with planning, moderating, discussing topics, explanations or common misconceptions. A teacher could be struggling with one particular topic, but their colleague may be doing so very successfully. There are subject-specific organisations that offer a wealth of materials for teachers such as the Historical Association, National Association for the Teaching of English (NATE), Geographical Association, The Association for Science Education and more, they can be a very good investment of the department CPD budget. I have invested a lot of my own time to professional development linked to subject specialism. Again, I would stress the importance of reading and collaborating with others.

Allison and Tharby suggest that teachers should aim to read five books a year that will enhance and add extra texture to our subject understanding.[216] This suggestion may seem unrealistic or it may seem appropriate to you, depending on your circumstances and commitments. Reading books focused on the content we teach can deepen our subject knowledge, lead to increased confidence in the classroom and positively impact our students learning.

I have recently created a department staff library of subject-specific books as well as curating and sharing various different links to articles, documentaries, podcasts and so on. This, again, is where Twitter can be so powerful, as teachers will regularly ask for recommended reading for a certain topic. There are always plenty of generous teachers, keen to volunteer suggestions and recommendations. Collaborating with other schools and their departments can also be very useful and supportive. The rise in popularity of TeachMeet events has sparked several subject-specific events and, as mentioned, I have co-organised and co-hosted a subject-specific event, TMHistoryIcons that has now led to others like TMGeographyIcons, TMMathsIcons and TMWellbeing.

Working with others in our phase or department can support our own and our colleagues' professional development. Dylan Wiliam has observed that 'novice teachers typically take around four hours to prepare one hour of instruction, while expert teachers plan lessons of higher quality in five minutes or less. In other words, planning a lesson is something an expert does as much as 50 times faster than a novice. The more often we do things, the better and faster we get.'[217] To put into context, Wiliam wasn't claiming that experienced teachers only spend

---

216. Allison, S & Tharby, A. (2015) *Making Every Lesson Count: Six principles to support great teaching and learning*. Carmarthen, Wales: Crown House Publishing, p. 24.
217. Wiliam, D. (2016) *Leadership for Teaching Learning*. West Palm Beach, Florida: Learning Sciences International, p. 157.

five minutes or less on planning lessons but that, in five minutes or so, they can produce better lesson plans than a novice would in four hours. We should reflect on this and consider what can NQTs do differently and what can more experienced teachers do to provide support.

John Hattie has also discussed the importance of teachers working with and learning from others. We should take advantage of the knowledge, experience and expertise within our own schools. Hattie encourages teachers to plan together. As part of his Visible Learning approach he states: 'Planning can be done in many ways, but the most powerful is when teachers work together to develop plans, develop common understandings on what is worth teaching, collaborate on understanding their beliefs of challenge and progress and work together to evaluate the impact of their planning on student outcomes.'[218] There's no need to reinvent the wheel but instead use all the resources, information and support that you have at your disposal.

Professional development is an aspect of teaching that I truly revel in. I love developing knowledge of my subject, pedagogy or research. I have managed to find methods of doing this independently and on a regular on-going basis. Schools have a responsibility to support staff with professional development, delivering this and also providing financial support. Ultimately, in the same way students are responsible for their learning, we are responsible for our learning and development.

---

218. Hattie, J. (2011) *Visible Learning For Teachers*. Abingdon, Oxfordshire: Routledge, p. 41.

Summary

- Taking control and ownership of our professional development is liberating, enjoyable and empowering. Schools have a responsibility to support our professional development, but we are responsible for our continued learning and progression.

- Social media, such as Twitter and LinkedIn are great platforms for learning, sharing and networking.

- Professional development has become more accessible with podcasts and blogs shared by other educators.

- TeachMeet events provide informal professional development opportunities. We can take away practical ideas for the classroom and meet other, like-minded and enthusiastic educators.

- There are various ways schools can create a culture of sharing and regular professional development: 15-minute forums, Green Light Classrooms and newsletters are methods of doing this.

- We must not neglect subject-specific professional development, as individuals and as departments.

Recommended reading

Switch: How To Change Things When Change Is Hard by Chip and Dan Heath (2010)

Perfect Teacher-Led CPD by Shaun Allison (2014)

The Confident Teacher: Developing successful habits of mind, body and pedagogy by Alex Quigley (2016)

The Slightly Awesome Teacher: Edu-Reseacrh meets common sense by Dominic Salles (2016)

The Learning Rainforest: Great Teaching in Real Classrooms by Tom Sherrington (2017)

CHAPTER 8:
RELATIONSHIPS,
RELATIONSHIPS,
RELATIONSHIPS

'The quality of the relationship that a student has with you is likely to be an important factor in that student's wellbeing.'

John Hattie & Gregory Yates

Not all teachers enjoy being a form tutor and they prefer the academic element of teaching. There can be many frustrations, such as extra reports or additional communication requirements, but it is a role that teachers should embrace and try to enjoy. Morrison–McGill has written about the importance of being a form tutor. He believes that 'being a form tutor is about preparing students to become good role models and well-rounded citizens contributing to society'.[219] In addition to this, tutors are often a student's first port of call if they have any worries or problems, which I think emphasises how important tutors are to their tutees.

I do not think I truly realised the impact I had as a form tutor until my tutor group of three years were leaving me at the end of Year 9. I received lots of thank you cards, letters, chocolates, and there were even some tears. Some students were worried that they wouldn't have a strong bond with their new tutor. Others were concerned about whether or not their new tutor would care or support them in the same way. It really made me realise how important I was to them and how much they relied on me. Teachers often underestimate the role and impact they have on the lives of young people, but especially so in our pastoral role. Fergal Roche writes in his profound book *Mining For Gold: Stories of Effective Teachers*

---

219. McGill, R, M. (2015) *Teacher Toolkit: Helping You Survive Your First Five Years.* London, England: Bloomsbury Publishing, p. 79.

about different teachers he has worked with or known throughout his life and described them as 'ordinary people who produced an extraordinary impact'.[220] I think that is very true but we can easily forget about the extraordinary impact we have on the lives of young people that we work with.

It is a cliché, but it is true that a teacher needs a good sense of humour. The ability to have a laugh, not take yourself too seriously, and show humour in the classroom – or in the staffroom with your colleagues – can make each day a little easier. I am not suggesting poking fun at students or using sarcasm, as both of those approaches can go very wrong. We do not need to try to be a comedian, just show the light-hearted side of our personality to those around us. Students respond well to teachers that are firm, fair and funny. Boundaries need to be made explicit too.

If you are a form tutor or a primary school teacher, then during morning registration you might have a chat with your tutees about their weekend or something that you are both interested in; when you are teaching a lesson that sort of small-talk needs to be left outside of the classroom or at least limited. If students want to talk about a football match or the latest film in the cinema that is great but ask them to do so at break or lunchtime, do not let it creep into precious and valuable lesson time.

The tasks and activities in this chapter were designed purely for that purpose, to develop and build relationships. This is a special chapter as it is the only chapter that does not focus on academic learning. Whilst positive relationships cannot guarantee excellent behaviour or deep learning, it is without a doubt at the heart of teaching and every school culture. Throughout this book, despite sharing tasks and resources, the focus should always be on the learning not the activity. The suggested ideas in this chapter are not focused on academic progress (of course they may contribute to that), but instead have another focus, which can be building confidence or relationships. For that reason I have included an explicit explanation of the intended purpose.

Knowing names

Purpose: Establishing positive relationships with students

A good starting point for building the connection and relationships comes from learning students' names and although this might seem very obvious, it can be a challenge for teachers, not just in the first few

---

220. Roche, F. (2017) *Mining For Gold: Stories of Effective Teachers*. Melton, Suffolk: John Catt Educational Ltd.

weeks of term. It is likely that the first set of names you remember are the students that have caught your attention – for good or bad reasons. My advice, during the early stages, in getting to know your students is to ask them to wear sticky labels with their name written in large, bold text.

I have used the name labels many times, including a lesson observation during the interview process. It is important to talk to and refer to students using their names – but during a lesson observation at a different school and during an interview lesson it is impossible to quickly remember all the names in the class, hence the sticky labels. This idea worked really well, it allowed me to use students' names during questioning, providing feedback, praise and even discipline. My former deputy headteacher commented on the use of the sticky labels as a 'nice personal touch'. It illustrated that I was making an effort to get to know the students and constantly refer to them by name in the lesson, instead of repeatedly asking or pointing at different children.

This is something I continue to use every September with my new classes. I mainly use this with Year 7 as further up the school I will often know the names of students, and when exam classes are often much smaller it becomes easier to recall names.

Pronunciation is important. A child deserves to be called by their name. I struggled with pronunciation when I moved to Abu Dhabi and the students would often correct my pronunciation. They were patient and I would often repeat their name with them until I got it right. I would encourage you to use students' names at every opportunity possible from greetings, during lessons, at break times, on duty – whenever you can, make it a habit. Students will know your name, although they will probably only ever call you 'Sir' or 'Miss', so by trying to learn their names as quickly as possible shows you are prepared to make the effort and are keen to get to know your students; a very small gesture that shows you care.

Getting to know the individual

September is the new January... if you're in a school that is! A new academic year is a fresh start for both teachers and students. The start of the school calendar year is crucial for establishing and building positive students, teacher interactions and launching essential classroom routines. Relationships and mutual trust will take time and develop as the year progresses. Positive connections with students can increase student effort, motivation, and participation, and are important for strong behaviour management. Relationships with students should be pleasant and positive, but at all times authoritative and assertive. Students don't expect teachers to be their friends, but that does not mean that we can't be friendly or show an appropriate interest in the students that we teach.

Meeting your students for the first time is a great opportunity to be welcoming and friendly, but also to set out very clear high expectations.

For six years of my career I was a Key Stage 3 tutor, overseeing transition from Year 6 and 7 and supporting those students until they reached Year 9 where they made the transition to GCSE. In my current role I am House Tutor to a vertical tutor group of girls ranging from Year 10 to Year 13, dealing with very different pastoral issues, such as examination pressures and university applications. The majority of the activities in this chapter are more suitable for younger students but can be adapted and used with older students too.

Didau offers important advice to teachers that work with older students, 'don't assume that respectful and sensitive interactions are only important to younger students. Older students still need to feel that their teachers respect their opinions and interests, even when they appear not to care about what teachers say or do.'[221] Mutual respect is very important and needs to be established and emphasised when meeting our students. We should explain that respect is not earned; students should automatically respect everyone in school, including their peers, teachers and support staff. In the same token their teachers will show them the respect they automatically deserve too. The pastoral role allows us to get to know our students outside of the subject/s we teach. We can find out a lot about our students that will help us to understand them. What are they good at? What do they like/dislike? What are their hopes and aspirations for the future?

Nuthall explores and discusses the importance of peer culture in-depth in his book. Knowing the friendship groups within your classes and being aware of any tension between individuals is very important as 'peers are a major factor in student learning, even in the best run classroom'.[222]

We have a lot of data at our disposal and analysing data at the start of the year can prove to be very useful, if not essential. Knowledge of a student's prior attainment, previous attendance and behaviour record

221. Didau, D. (No date) '20 psychological principles for teachers #14 Relationships'. (Learning Spy) Available at: www.learningspy.co.uk/psychology/20-psychological-principles-for-teachers-14-relationships/

222. Nuthall, G. (2007) The Hidden Lives of Learners. Wellington, New Zealand: NZCER Press, p. 104.

can provide a great insight for teachers, in addition to conversations with other teachers who know the students well. Although we can learn a lot about our students from data, there is even more that the data does not tell us. Getting to know our students on a deeper and more personal level happens in the classroom. Students may divulge sensitive information to teachers that they trust so it is important to be aware, prepared and know who the school Child Protection Officer (CPO) is. Also, as teachers we can let our personality shine through, but we do not need to share any of our private information – I believe in personality with professionalism.

Icebreakers

Below is a range of 'get to know you' style activities that are all tried and tested from my classroom over the years with my students. These ideas can be used and adapted for different ages. As well as helping teachers get to know their students, these tasks are also an enjoyable way for students to introduce themselves and learn more about each other, developing and forming friendships. These types of activities can also develop a lot of skills such as: working with others, leadership, social and communication skills. In a pastoral setting there is no exam pressure, so this time is unique – we can be creative when getting to know our students.

An idea that has been created and shared by Amjad Ali on his brilliant website www.trythisteaching.com – a website that I can highly recommend for all educators, as there is something for everyone on there – is to ask students to complete the following sentence:

'I wish my teacher knew...'

This could be an unusual fact about themselves, something they enjoy or even find difficult. It might surprise you what you can learn about your students. Once again, a child may use this activity to divulge sensitive information, so be sure to refer it to your line manager or designated CPO, following your school policy protocol.

Story of my life

As a historian I am naturally drawn to timelines. It helps give me an overview and see the bigger picture. A good activity to introduce students to timelines is to ask them to create a timeline of their life so far, recording key events from their birth to their first day at school, a sibling being born, losing their first tooth and so on, right up until present day. The teacher can find out what key events they include and view as being important in their lives. There is a useful video on the website squaducation.com (a website with 60-second historical videos and teaching resources for both primary and secondary schools) which introduces students to the concept of a timeline and how to create their own.[223]

A letter to myself

Ask students to write a letter to their future self, that they will receive when they are older – this can be at the end of the academic year, or at the end of their school career. In this letter they should set themselves targets they hope to achieve by the time they get to open the letter. This is a good way to set both short and long-term targets – it is also great if you get to see the students read their letters later on.

Bucket list

Students will create a list of things to do or achieve by the end of the school year. This is great to return to at the end of the year to see which targets have been achieved and which haven't been achieved... yet.

Learning line up

Purpose: Introduction to other students & focus on communication.

Expectations and routines are the foundations of strong and solid classroom management that should not be underestimated. Sherrington has blogged about routines, stating that 'in a good lesson, the routines are well-understood, they are followed and fall into the background without too much fuss'.[224] Routines eventually become effortless for all of those involved. Usually most classes have to line up outside the classroom either at the start of the day or before the lesson. The learning line up is a way to engage students in icebreaker activities before they even enter the classroom.

It is very simple: students have to line up in order in different ways based on your instructions. For example, students must line up in boy/girl order or line up next to someone they don't know. Another suggestion would be line up in alphabetical order according to their first or second name. They could line up in order of their age and birthday. Avoid asking students to line up based on things they may be sensitive about, such as tallest to shortest, as this may cause offence. This means that students have to talk to one another, asking questions and working together to

---

223. No author. (No date) 'What is a Timeline?' (Squaducation) Available at: www.squaducation.com/content/what-timeline-0

224. Sherrington, T. (26 October 2016) '10 Teaching Essentials' (teacherhead) Available at: www.teacherhead.com/2016/10/26/10-teaching-essentials/

line up correctly. This has got the students thinking and talking straight away. This is where you will see those natural leaders take charge!

Talking tasks

Purpose: Develop speaking and listening skills. Build relationships.

These activities do not require any resources or preparation – a much appreciated time saver for busy teachers. They are simple and pleasurable.

- 'Pair presentations' – in pairs, students have an allotted amount of time to exchange information. Telling the other person as much as they want to about themselves, then listening to their partner do the same. The students then have to present either in front of the class, or if this sounds too daunting for new students then to another pair, recalling everything they have found out and remember about their partner. So instead of asking students to stand in front of the class and talk about themselves they have to talk about someone else. This is very good for listening and recalling skills – don't let them take any notes, if they have to recall from memory they will listen more carefully. Some students can lack confidence telling a classroom full of their peers what they are good at, but they will find it a lot easier to describe their partner and their interests, skills and talents.

- Another oracy task is the famous 'speed dating', but without the actual dating element! A timer is required (there are plenty of free online timers available, just do a Google search) and for the class chairs to be rearranged. Students will have a set amount of time to talk to each other; this encourages those who have never met or do not know each other well enough to interact. They can introduce themselves to each other, but this can become repetitive. An idea is to have a theme projected onto the board or said by the teacher and the students will have two or three minutes – time can vary according to class size or session timing – to discuss that theme. As the students move to talk to another person, the theme will change so they have something different to talk about. The theme acts as a prompt to start the conversation. The themes can include talking about their favourite food or holidays, hobbies, films, or books – anything that will promote conversation between the two students. The changing of partners adds pace and keeps the activity engaging, as well as learning lots of interesting facts about each other!

■ Selfie challenges

Purpose: Become familiar with the learning environment and getting to know each other.

Who is not familiar with the modern selfie craze? If your students enjoy taking selfies – I am sure they do – then they will love this activity. This is a good task for those students who are new to the school, or perhaps have relocated to another part of the building. The idea behind this is similar to a treasure hunt, as they will be given different locations around the school they have to find, either using a map or perhaps an older reliable student to help guide them.

When they have reached each destination, they take a photo, either individually or as a group at that location, using an iPad or their own devices, depending on your school policy. Students can explore the school site and take funny photos at different locations. On their return, students can swap and share their images – if they want to – that were taken at the Canteen, Library, Assembly Hall, and so on. An extension task could be to get a picture taken with a specific member of staff, house captain or other key school figure, but be sure to ask them in advance for their permission.

Selfie speech bubble! I would recommend using the Balloon Stickies+ app, available on iOS, as it will be much easier and quicker than using a photo in Word or PowerPoint. This app allows the user to take a photo or upload an image from the camera roll and insert speech and thought bubbles with text. Students can take photos then add some information about themselves in the speech bubble like my example below.

Continuing this theme is the WordFoto self-portrait. If you have access to devices then the WordFoto app, as previously mentioned, is a sensational app, available on iOS and Android and is very adaptable for the classroom. The app allows the user to upload an image from the camera and insert words. Wordfoto combines the images and text together. What can you learn about my lovely niece Ella from the WordFoto below?

Students can create a picture collage by drawing or sticking photos and pictures of images that are of them or connected to them. If you do have access to technology, then the Pic Collage app is available on iOS and Android. It is great – very simple and quick to use. A Year 8 student created the example below using Pic Collage to introduce himself and show the class what is important to him. Thank you to Hayden Van Niekerk and his parents for sharing his Pic Collage. What can you find out about Hayden?

Classroom displays

Purpose: Provide a sense of familiarity & personalise classrooms.

If you have your own classroom where your class is based, or in secondary if a classroom is dedicated to your tutor group, then creating displays is a great way to share the icebreaker activities that you have done and make the students feel that the classroom is their base. Pinterest is a great source of inspiration, including classroom display ideas and a plethora of teaching & learning resources.

- Ideas include creating an 'All About Me' wall. Everyone will write something unique about themselves – that they don't mind going on display and is GDPR compliant – and that can be there for the rest of the year or term for others to read, so they feel like they have made their mark in their classroom.

- Create an inspiration station. Ask students to write down who is their inspiration and why. This can be a famous sporting star, historical figure, celebrity or even a family member or friend. The important reason for doing this is to find out what inspires our students, who their role models are and who they aspire to be like and why. This could make for a lovely display to refer back to and having their role models on show can motivate and inspire.

Transition games

Purpose: Build confidence, relationships and trust. Set short and long-term targets.

The start of year can be exciting and daunting. Transition tasks and icebreaker games are a great opportunity to just have some fun in addition to relationship building. This can also help the students feel more relaxed and comfortable at school, which is very important both in a pastoral and academic setting. All of these suggested activities are not designed to aid learning but instead focus on other aspects of school life such as transition and pastoral care.

Willingham has highlighted the importance of relationships in a school environment, 'the emotional bond between student and teacher – for better or worse – accounts for whether students learn.'[225] Therefore, spending time in a pastoral setting to develop relationships will have a positive impact on student learning, in an academic setting too.

---

225. Willingham, D, T. (2010) *Why don't students like school? A Cognitive Scientist Answers Questions About How The Mind Works And What It Means For The Classroom.* San Francisco, CA: Jossey-Bass, p. 65.

- Pick a Stick. When asked to share some information about themselves, some students can struggle to think of a response, or they don't like the pressure of being put on the spot. Pick a Stick is where students have to randomly select a lollypop/popsicle stick with a question written on and they simply answer that question. Everyone answers a random question, so the class can find out more information about each other.

- Walkabout Bingo has already been discussed as a revision strategy, but this task can be easily adapted for different subjects and ages. I created a Walkabout Bingo Icebreaker game, because students are only allowed to ask each person a question once, this encourages them to interact with other students, not in their friendship groups, whilst learning more about each other.

Walk about 'Ice breaker' Bingo!

Q What is your favourite book?	**Q** What is your favourite subject in school?	**Q** Do you enjoy watching sport?
A Harry Potter Name: Brooke	**A** Maths Name: Josh	**A** Yes Name: Dylan
Q What are your top three favourite films?	**Q** Describe your best friend using three adjectives.	**Q** Do you have any pets?
A Hunger game series Name: Aaron	**A** Funny, Cool, Amazing Name: Carys	**A** Yes Name: Alicia
Q What Primary school did you go to?	**Q** Which do you prefer your birthday or Christmas?	**Q** What is your favourite food?
A Drury Name: Chloe	**A** Christmas Name: Jasmine	**A** Strawberries Name: Jess
Q What music do you like?	**Q** If you could visit anywhere in the world where would it be?	**Q** Who is your favourite super hero?
A Pop Name: Abbie	**A** Florida Name: Robyn	**A** Superman Name: Ellie
Q What is the best thing about being at Elfed?	**Q** What TV show do you like?	**Q** Think of your own question to ask!
A Meeting new people Name: Lauren	**A** Flash Name: Kieran	**A** How old are you? Name: Kate

Similar to the Walkabout Bingo is the 'Find Someone…' game. Students will be given a list and they have to find someone who matches each of the criteria, so the list could include the following:

1. Find someone who has a birthday in September.

2. Find someone who has a brother and a sister.

3. Find someone who enjoys tennis.

4. Find someone who likes to eat chocolate.

5. Find someone who has read a Percy Jackson book.

This involves a lot of questioning and communicating whilst still finding out more about each other and working together. This can encourage students to find out if they have any similar interests. It is great for the students to find out about one another and the observant teacher can gain further insight into their students too.

QR Code Treasure Hunt

Purpose: Working with others and becoming familiar with the learning environment.

The QR code treasure hunt is great for students new to the school, similar to the selfie challenge above. The idea is to place QR codes around the school for students to find, this allows the students to travel around the school and become familiar with the building. Each QR code will have a question and students will have a table to fill in with two columns: Answer and Location: students write down the answer and where they found the QR code e.g. Answer: 1066 Location: Library. The treasure hunt can be used with any subject and students can even create their own for their peers to solve.

You can find a QR code treasure hunt generator at: http://www.classtools. net/QR/

Icebreaker Grid

Purpose: Building relationships, self-awareness and trust.

Learning 6x6 grids have been used throughout this book, showing how adaptable this activity is. The icebreaker grid is an enjoyable task, where students can get to know their peers. If a student rolls the dice and the two numbers are 3 and 4, then 3 across and 4 up would mean the student would have to tell their partner a happy memory. My icebreaker grid can be downloaded for free from my TES page.[226]

---

226. K8SUE. (20 August 2017) 'Ice breaker grid challenge'. (TES) Available at: www.tes.com/teaching-resource/ice-breaker-grid-challenge-11697802

Ice breaker grid – Roll the dice twice and tell your partner...

	1	2	3	4	5	6
6	Your favourite book	A funny story	The date of your birthday	A school subject you enjoy & why	A target you have set for yourself...	Your favourite book character
5	A film you enjoy watching	Something you did in the summer holidays	What your dream job would be...	A joke!	A special memory from school	Who inspires you
4	Your favourite item of clothing	About someone who is special to you	A happy memory!	Your favourite film character	What you hope to achieve one day	Your favourite superhero
3	Your favourite food	A team you support	A special place you have been to	What you like to do at the weekend	A hobby you enjoy	A song you like to listen to
2	About someone that has helped you	Your favourite colour	A special skill you have	What relaxes you	A food you dislike!	Your favourite season and why
1	What you enjoy most about school	Your favourite animal	What makes you smile!	Your favourite singer/band	A place you would like to visit one day	About one of your friends

Circle time

'Circle time brings together teacher and children in an enjoyable atmosphere of cooperation. It is a time set aside each week when children and their teacher sit in a circle and take part in games and activities designed to increase self-awareness, awareness of others, self-esteem, cooperation, trust and listening skills. The activity helps everyone to understand what is important to them and their friends.

Children become more able to express their feelings and it encourages greater tolerance between girls and boys. As children learn more about themselves and each other, a warm and supportive group atmosphere is built, along with improved friendships.' Teresa Bliss and Jo Tetley taken from their book *Circle Time: A Resource Book for Primary and Secondary Schools*. The book focuses on ages 5 to 13.

'Circle time' activities were initially introduced in 1990 to primary schools but later extended to secondary schools too. If a primary school makes regular use of circle time and this is continued in Year 7, it can support with transition and reflection activities as well as providing a sense of familiarity in a new setting. Sitting in a circle – it is recommended to use chairs rather than sitting on the floor to provide extra comfort and keep the shape of the circle during activities and games[227] – provides a more informal setting and allows all students to see one another and promote the use of eye contact.

This is ideal for class discussions and games. Circle time can provide opportunities for students to talk positively about their experiences and themselves, their achievements and develop speaking and listening skills. Circle time involves everyone in the class and everyone should have the opportunity to participate, contribute their ideas, answers or views and know that their opinion is valued.

It is very important with circle time to establish regular rules and routines; simple and basic rules such as 'one person speaking at a time' and 'think carefully before you speak, no negative or nasty comments'. Here are some of the circle time games that I have used with my classes that once again require very few, if any, resources.

Copycat game

This game can be hilarious! Everyone will be sat in a circle but one person either has to turn around or wait outside the classroom for a moment whilst the teacher selects one person that the rest of the class have to mimic. The class are instructed that any action or noise that chosen individual makes they have to repeat. The person waiting outside does not know the person everyone else is copying but they have three attempts to guess on their return. The person can clap, stand up, cough and everyone else must do the same.

Once my entire Year 7 class and I all ended up copying someone doing the Gangnam Style dance – dabbing was also very popular! The students do have to concentrate copying the person carefully or trying to solve who everyone else is copying. I have a lot of fond, funny and happy memories playing this game with my previous Year 7 tutor group. Students require a lot of confidence to participate in this game, so I would recommend playing this once the class are more settled and familiar with one another.

227. Tetley, J & Bliss, T. (2006) *Circle Time: A Resource Book for Primary and Secondary Schools.* London, England: Sage Publications, p. 4.

Icebreaker Beach Ball

I purchased a cheap inflatable beach ball that can be written on with a board pen then rubbed off and used again. The beach ball had different 'get to know you' style questions on each section of the ball. Students throw the ball around the circle, when they catch the ball they have to answer the question that faces them. Then the student passes it onto someone else. The beach ball is a safe option with no worries about broken windows or any injuries!

This is another quick and easy activity to involve everyone in the class, and in a similar way are the icebreaker dice. Dice templates can easily be found online and adapted for use in any subject, great for starters and plenaries with questions linked to the learning. On each section of the dice is a question and students simply roll the dice and answer the question it lands on.

Emoji Exit Ticket

Purpose: Students can reflect on how they are feeling and their level of confidence.

Emoji Exit Ticket
Circle the Emoji(s) that reflects how you got on today in the lesson. Explain your reasons why...

I chose this Emoji because...
....
....

This resource has surprisingly become my most downloaded resource with many thousands of downloads. It is also regularly on the most featured pins in the education category on Pinterest. It has been used in the UK, UAE, Australia, Norway, Canada, Germany and USA, in addition to other places around the world. I have even seen the resource translated in Swedish! Despite its popularity with teachers and students, it is also my most controversial resource. There have been some very scathing and surprisingly rude comments about this exit ticket online, but also some valid points were raised that I will address. I am well aware that if people share resources online they should expect to be challenged or critiqued, it is not all about the likes, retweets and downloads. If ever there were a Marmite of educational activities, this would be it. I will use this opportunity to explain why I created this exit ticket and discuss the purpose of this in my classroom.

The task is very self-explanatory, at the end of a lesson students circle an emoji, or range of emojis, that show how they feel about the lesson and underneath they need to write a brief explanation as to why they selected the emoji/s. I use this resource with students from Year 5 to 8; older students could find this patronising. That's it, simple.

Firstly, this is not a learning activity. I am not educating my students through the medium of emoji. This is designed as a very short activity at the end of the lesson, at no other point in the lesson will my students use emojis to communicate and the written explanation is very important to clarify the choice of emotions. Secondly, this can be used to gauge a student's level of understanding, but I am aware this is not the most accurate method.

As discussed throughout this book, retrieval practice and the testing effect can inform the students and teachers on what a learner knows and doesn't know yet. If I relied on the emoji exit ticket, that wouldn't be accurate as a student may select smiley faces because they are generally happy in the lesson, but they may not have fully understood all of the concepts. Alternatively, they may select an unhappy face because they felt challenged in the lesson – but that does not mean the work was too challenging, some students relish challenge, others don't. We have to explain to our students that learning is not always easy and enjoyable. Learning new concepts can be difficult and frustrating, that is part of the learning process.

I do understand why this resource is not the most accurate form of self-assessment, but I do find it very helpful. It provides an opportunity for students to reflect on the lesson and express how they are feeling about their learning. This can lead to many powerful conversations.

I remember a Year 5 student had selected a sad and a happy face, this confused me and wasn't very clear. I asked her to explain more fully and she told me that, whilst she enjoyed the topic and lesson, she circled the sad face because her peers and I kept using a lot of complex words that she didn't understand – the curse of knowledge. I obviously had not realised that I was using language in this way, but then I became aware of this and I was able to support this student in future lessons. That student never mentioned this in the lesson; perhaps she was embarrassed or didn't have the confidence to say she didn't understand the words being used. This exit ticket gave her the opportunity to tell me something that was very valuable and insightful for me.

The majority of the time students select happy faces and comment they are pleased with their progress and that's lovely to read. I can quickly skim read these responses. Teachers have been using smiley faces or red, amber, green as a way to self-assess and reflect for years. I just adapted this with the popular emojis instead, which students are more comfortable using.

Those are the main reasons I find this exit ticket useful, but other educators have contacted me to provide feedback. Teachers have said this simple method can help students who can struggle to articulate or express themselves when reflecting. The exit ticket has also worked very well with EAL students to gauge their level of understanding. This resource has been used across all key stages and can be used for any subject/topic and many primary school teachers have expressed fondness for this plenary.

You can download my Emoji Exit Ticket from the UKEd Resources website.[228] There have been issues with people downloading this resource online for free then selling to others, which goes against the CC terms. Do not pay. You can download it for free.

228. UkEdChat Editorial. (28 November 2016) 'Exit Ticket Emoji by @87history'. (UkEdChat) Available at: www.ukedchat.com/2016/11/28/exit-ticket-emoji-by-87history-ukedresources/

Vocabulary Exit Ticket
Circle the word(s) that reflect how you got on today in the lesson. Explain your reasons why...

Good	Great	Disappointing	Brilliant
Bad	Awesome	Average	Excellent
Exceptional	Awful	Amazing	Terrible

I chose this word because...

Another criticism I have received, which I understand, is how do we develop vocabulary of our learners if we are asking them to reflect using emojis? I have dedicated a chapter in this book to explicit vocabulary instruction, with plenty of examples from my classroom. A five-minute task at the end of a lesson does not mean that I don't value or appreciate the importance of vocabulary development. I have created an alternative Emoji Exit Ticket entitled the Vocabulary Exit Ticket where students select a word or words to represent how they got on in the lesson, again with a brief explanation. This exit ticket can include tier one or two terms, depending on age and suitability, the example above was designed for younger learners. The purpose remains the same, providing learners with the opportunity to reflect and express their emotions.

Finally, the hardest part of being a teacher

Bereavement is a subject that is rarely discussed within education as it is naturally a very distressing topic. We work in an environment with lots of people such as our colleagues and students and the sad reality is that we might have to deal with the death of a child or colleague during our career. It is inevitable that we will work with children and colleagues that will be affected by the death of someone they love. Whilst this aspect of being a teacher is not linked to any educational research or resources, I felt it was important to include in my book. I wanted to write about bereavement as it is has affected me directly, both as a student and as a teacher. I feel there should be more discussion of this amongst teachers. This is an area where teachers aren't experts or have sufficient training, but will either be impacted by the death of someone during their career or work with those that have.

I experienced the loss of someone close to me during my school years; a classmate, James Echlin, died suddenly in a tragic car accident alongside his father. He was 16 years old. Everybody that knew James was, and still remain, completely devastated at the loss of our much-loved friend. The secondary school I attended, Castell Alun High School, was incredibly understanding and provided lots of services and advice for all students affected. There was external support from various charities and organisations that specialised in offering bereavement counselling. The counsellor came to the school and she knew the family and context well; I was very grateful for this help.

On reflection, I can truly appreciate the care and consideration provided at such a challenging time of my life. When you are 16 you don't expect your friend to die. You assume they will get a job, buy a house, get married and live to an old age. It was so difficult to comprehend and accept that I would never see him again. My teachers were kind, caring and compassionate and I will never forget that. I never once considered the impact that the death of James may have had on my teachers.

As a teacher, dealing with the death of a child in Year 7 and a student I taught was extremely difficult and heart breaking. I was a Year 7 form tutor at the time, so I had the duty to tell my tutor group that their friend and peer had died. Many of the students had grown up with her and they had attended primary school together. I had never anticipated that I would have to communicate information of this nature to children, but I had to do so. An experienced and senior colleague, also a good friend, was with me to deliver this difficult news. I hadn't had any training or preparation for anything like this. To date, that was without a doubt the hardest and saddest day of my teaching career. It is very difficult for me to write about these experiences, but as mentioned I do believe it is something teachers should share more openly with one another.

I didn't cry in front of my students, although I cried in the staffroom, but I did express my sadness to my tutor group. Teachers are human first and it is important students realise we have emotions and feelings too. I remember feeling embarrassed for crying in the staffroom in front of my colleagues; I felt weak, inexperienced and unprofessional. My colleagues did not make me feel this way, I simply felt this way because it appeared to me I wasn't handling the situation as well as others. The death of a student or colleague is very upsetting and it is not unprofessional to feel sadness and express that emotion. Throughout this chapter, I have discussed the importance of relationships, bonding with the people we work with and encounter on a daily basis. So, when someone that we have a connection with dies, it will be very tough.

I know teachers that have taught for several years and have been fortunate to never experience bereavement in a school environment. If this does happen to you I would suggest taking advantage of the services your school or local education authority may provide, such as occupational health, counselling or any literature that may help. A very useful website to find out more about supporting children with grief can be found at:

https://www.winstonswish.org/

This website contains advice, resources and lesson materials that tackle the sensitive issue. There is also a freephone national helpline you can ring if you have any questions or simply want to talk to someone about bereavement.

I would also encourage teachers to talk to other colleagues about your emotions, don't suffer in silence or alone. As for supporting the students we teach, this is where compassion, empathy and all of the other qualities that teachers possess are very important. There can be a fear approaching this topic with a child, in case we make them cry or say the 'wrong thing'. There is no script to deal with this type of situation and in a secondary school setting, if every teacher spoke with a student about their ordeal, that could be overwhelming. If we ignore this then it sends out a message that we are not aware of the death or that we don't care, when that simply is not true.

I have said to a student that I am here if they need me. Those words can be enough because we are recognising their loss and letting our students know there is support at school for them. If a child does come to you about this, I would advise listening carefully and passing the information to a pastoral middle or senior leader. Senior leaders can be working with the family and external organisations. We are not trained counsellors or social workers and we are not expected to provide that level of support or service. We can listen, show patience and flexibility, but it is important that we pass on the role of bereavement support to the experts that are trained to deal with that.

I would like to thank the family of James Echlin – Kaye, Louise, Hayley and Tom – for allowing me to write about my experience of grief in this book. I hope this can act as a tribute to a popular, funny and kind young man who was taken from us far too soon. Time helps, but it does not heal.

In order for positive relationships to flourish, do not put your classes and students before your own health and wellbeing. Teachers need to be healthy and happy to deliver lessons day in and day out. On a plane the cabin crew will tell you to put your oxygen mask on first, before you help others – remember this.

A powerful quote that has really stuck with me and transformed my practice, from Alex Quigley is that 'the day you realise you will never do the job perfectly is the day you can start enjoying and flourishing in your teaching life'. I remember reading that and feeling so liberated. The quote is taken from *The Confident Teacher: Developing successful habits of mind, body and pedagogy* and it is my favourite book about education. It certainly won't always feel like the best job in the world, far from it, and we will have bad days, but we must never take it out on the students in our care. On the difficult days we need to remember that this is such a special, fulfilling and rewarding profession and that is why we love to teach.

Summary

- Getting to know our students takes time and is an on-going process throughout our teaching career.

- Establishing clear routines and professional, yet friendly, relationships are crucial. This can support behaviour management and teaching and learning in the classroom. There should be explicit boundaries, we can talk about personal topics and interests in a pastoral setting ensuring that does not continue into lesson time.

- Pastoral time does not have the same examination pressure as academic lessons, so we can be creative and have fun.

- Pastoral time can develop a wide range of important skills including communication, leadership, working with others, plus much more.

- We are teachers not trained counsellors or support workers, there is only so much we can and should do to support our students.

- Don't underestimate your pastoral role and the impact you have on the children you work with.

Recommended reading

Circle time: Second Edition by Teresa Bliss and Jo Tetley (2006)

Of Teaching, Learning and Sherbet Lemons: A Compendium of Careful Advice For Teachers by Nina Jackson (2015)

Mining for Gold: Stories of Effective Teachers by Fergal Roche (2017)

The Little Book of Bereavement for Schools by Ian Gilbert, Olivia Gilbert, Phoebe Gilbert and William Gilbert (2010)

The Truth Pixie by Matt Haig (2018)

RESOURCES

You scan the QR codes below to be instantly directed to websites where you can download resource templates shown in this book, all are free.

 My TES resources homepage

 My educational website and blog

 ICTEvangelist.com – download Retrieval Practice Challenge Grid templates.

 UKEd resources free Emoji Exit ticket download